Strategy, Organization and Performance Management

From Basics to Best Practices

Soeren Dressler

Universal Publishers
Boca Raton, Florida
USA • 2004

Strategy, Organization and Performance Management:
From Basics to Best Practices

Copyright © 2004 Soeren Dressler

Universal Publishers/uPUBLISH.com
Boca Raton, Florida
USA • 2004

ISBN: 1-58112-532-1

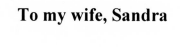

To my wife, Sandra

Strategy, Organization and Performance Management
–From Basics to Best Practices –

Contents – Overview

The Challenge of Organization Management
"Why are some Companies simply better than others?"

Strategic Direction Setting: Organizational Context
"Understanding Strategic Direction and Organizational Capabilities"

Strategic Alignment: Key Design & Delivery Elements
"Why Businesses still need org charts"

Strategic Control: Performance Management and Target Setting
"The new strategic weapon"

Case Studies for Organizational Effectiveness
"Best Practices applied"

Table of Contents

Preface

This book took me almost two years to complete. When I started this project I would never have believed it would be such a tedious and lengthy process. The hectic consulting schedule, work as adjunct professor and family life made it quite challenging to rewrite numerous revisions of my initial idea into a final draft. The organization management discipline is a fast-moving space and requires constant updating. Also, the inclusion of a more comprehensive chapter on Business Process Outsourcing and Offshoring were other reasons that delayed the completion of this project.

This project was made possible only by assistance and guidance from a number of people. I don't want to attempt to mention all of them but I would like to highlight a few and thank for their special input and contribution.

First of all, I thank John Kostolansky and the Department of Management at the Loyola University Chicago Graduate School of Business for giving me the opportunity to teach the course on Strategy and Organization. Working with the students has influenced me and the way I have structured and presented the various aspects of Organizational Effectiveness in this book. Also, I want to thank my colleagues at A.T. Kearney who have been very helpful in offering their expertise on the framework of Organizational Effectiveness. Omer Abdullah, Simon Gilles and Laura Sue D'Annunzio were heavily involved in the early stages of this project. Furthermore, I would also like to thank the many clients over the past decade that have given me the opportunity to gather valuable insights and to apply the organization and performance management toolkit. Shereen Siddiqui from Universal Publishers was a tremendous help to assist me with any administrative issues and Maude Merriman is a talented Graphic Designer who assisted me with the exhibits and layout of the book.

Lastly, but most importantly, I want to thank my wife Sandra. She meticulously reviewed the content and always provided constructive critique. Moreover, she is a constant motivator without whom I would not have been able to finalize this project - and she worked very hard to keep the family life afloat while I too often disappeared into my office to work on the numerous versions of the draft.

I hope this book will be of great use for students generations to come and for interested business practitioners in advanced organization and performance management. The mix of basics, such as organizational designs with innovative approaches, such as Business Process Outsourcing, illustrates the span and complexity of organization management. Hopefully it satisfies the interest of a wide variety of readers – those who want to understand key principles and those who are always curious to learn new and innovative things.

Soeren Dressler

"Why are some companies simply better than others?"

1

The Challenge of Organization Management

Organizational Effectiveness is a phenomenon that can be applied to all different types of groups, teams, and, of course, business organizations. Wherever groups operate in a competitive environment, the question whether they are organized "right" almost automatically comes up. And, subsequently, the question of how to do "better" than others is posed after that. It doesn't matter if people discuss sports, politics, or business: "Why are some better than others?" always occupies their minds. One thing they have in common is the secret of being "better organized," a secret that this book will reveal. Focus of the discussion will exclusively be on the business world. However, sometimes analogies to other areas will be used to make the complex content easier to understand.

Organizations are complex and the result of multiple guiding actions. As Alfred Chandler already pointed out in his ground-breaking work on "Strategy and Structure" in the early 1960s, in most cases the strategy comes first.[1] It is – or at least should be – the overriding designing principle for the organizational structure. However, what has to be summarized under "organizational structure"? Does this mean simply the units in terms of the departmental structure? Does organization structure mean having well-oiled workflows to make sure the organization is the most adaptive player reacting to changing business conditions? Or does organization structure mean having the best skills, teams and individuals available in order to effectively execute a particular strategic goal? Probably all these features characterize the effective organization. Eventually, how well they are interacting and how closely they are aligned with the strategy will determine the Organizational Effectiveness.

1   Organizations, Teams, and Individuals make the Difference

When **Henry Ford** began to produce his T-Car by using an assembly line in 1913, this was certainly a radical innovation in terms of organization management. The scientific foundation of the proactive and innovative car manufacturer was provided by **Frederick W. Taylor**, who invented in 1911 "The Principles of Scientific Management," better known as the "Taylorism."[2] While Ford was focusing on a streamlined production that allowed producing as many cars as possible, Taylor was highlighting the principle of efficient allocation of work by segregating work steps in the smallest units possible and synthesizing them later on. Both men had one goal in common: A more effective organization. By strictly applying Taylorism like Henry Ford did, the concepts of compartmentalization and organizational boundaries were introduced. The workforce was systematically divided according to specific functions and specific skill sets. Although the organization was considered to be more effective in terms of output, some restrictions were soon clearly evident: Communication and new product ideas could not flow around like they did previously when businesses were arranged in houses or workshops.

Innovation and social fulfillment through work were eroding. Allocation of work required reconciliation of activities. Communication had to be re-arranged to fulfill business needs. Thus, scientists like **Henri Fayol** further improved Taylor's work. He, for example, introduced the "Fayol-Bridge" that allowed direct communication between departments without involving the manager level. Back in 1916, this was truly a breakthrough and is, even today, still relevant.[3] This short detour to the history of organization management should be mandatory for all work in this arena. It stresses the basics of what Organizational Effectiveness is all about: Strategic Guidance as pointed out by Chandler; structure, skills and output orientation as discussed by Taylor; and process and communication flow as targeted by Fayol. It is nearly a century since these principles have been seen as a source for competitive advantages – and they are still relevant today.

Successful Organizations

In today's challenging business world, companies have to cope with the overarching basic question: "How do we allocate and *organize* our work?" Implicitly, the organization management has long ago bought in the decades-old "scientific" principles – simply as a necessity to get the work done – nobody would seriously ask today a small group of people to actually design, engineer, build, market, and sell a car all at once. Organizing the work, however, has become quite a complex task since there are multiple organizational design alternatives applicable.

- The **Functional Organization** is normally the first logical structure a company chooses as soon as it hits the start-up phase. That is what Henry Ford did: He clearly separated engineering, procurement, manufacturing, and distribution tasks. So, for a relatively young business, the allocation of work along the various functions appears to be rational, logical, and manageable. Recent experiences with thousands of eBusiness start-ups have brought this principle back in our minds. Most start-ups have automatically chosen the functional logic first. Somebody was assigned to do the product development, somebody took over manufacturing responsibilities, somebody was declared the financial officer, and somebody developed the market. The functional simplistic way of doing business works as long as the business is small enough and transactions are manageable.

- The **Divisional Organization** is the next organizational structure in this evolution. The key principle is allocation of work by *divisions,* business units or product groups. Now, the perspective changes: the organization is seen from a product or product group view. For companies that run more than one product or product group, the demand for allocation of work according to products will further emerge and eventually take over as the guiding organizational principle. The Divisional Organization structure requires some clarification with respect to the chosen terminology. The basic principle of turning from a functional to a product perspective with regard to allocation of work can be done on various levels:

  o Product grouping is basically the first level. Product groups typically incorporate product management functions as well as product innovation and engineering.
  o Business units are the next level. All business activities around a product group that are directly

perceived by the customer take place in the business unit. In addition to the characteristics mentioned under product groups, the order-to-cash process and customer management process are often integrated into the units.

o The next level is basically the full-blown division that operates as an independent business operation. Since product groups and business units still require general "functional" support in terms of finance and accounting, human resource management, and especially operations management, the division takes care of most of them on its own. It acts like an independent company within the broader organization.

The table below summarizes guidelines of how to differentiate the various product-oriented structures:

	Characteristics	Typical Functions
Product Groups	Different products but strong similarities in design, production, and customer base	Product Management
Business Units	Customer perception of single entity Distinct product and market strategies Use of company-wide production and distribution network	Product Management Product Development Order-to-Cash Processes Customer Management
Divisions	Distinct operations, engineering and distribution, Requirements of products	All core functions except typical HQ roles like Investor Relations

Table: Product-oriented Organizational Structures

- The **Matrix Organization** is the next form of organizational design. From a developmental perspective, matrix structures are often found as a result of divisional forms that never performed as expected or have caused even more coordination and reconciliation efforts than the previous functional structure. The matrix idea operates with the basic principle of having at least two reporting lines. It integrates the functional and product-oriented organization and, in variations, the geographic perspective as well. On the one side, allocation of work will be made functionally, and on the other side, divisions or regions will be installed. On a global perspective, matrix organizations have gained significant recognition and are often used due to the tremendous advantage of improved information flow. Additionally, the matrix enables decentralized control. Regional or business-unit leaders make decisions that affect their own areas. On the other hand, bundling of functions supports gaining economies of scale, application of benchmarks, and best practices that lead to high performing service functions. The major drawback of matrix structures is their partly overwhelming need to manage their inherent complexity. Eventually, employees have to cope with the requirement to report to different superiors. They need to balance their tasks sensitively, and have to apply several informal processes to effectively leverage the strength of the matrix. Skills and personal characteristics of employees have to be quite sophisticated to run a successful matrix organization. Hence, concerning the life cycle of companies, the matrix structure basically comes after the company has reached a mature and experienced stage. The following graph illustrates the relation of company life cycle and company size with regard to typical basic organizational structures. As already mentioned, the functional structure usually comes first. With growth and multiple products, the divisional structure emerges. Eventually, matrix organizations will be introduced to leverage functional strength more effectively and to enable operation on a multi-region platform.

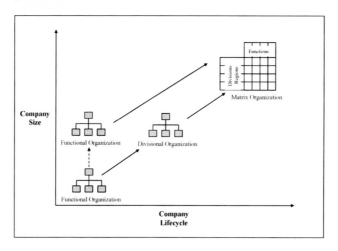

Exhibit I-1: Organizational Structure Development

The timing with regard to company size and its life cycle stage is especially a trigger for redesign. Some companies, in particular those belonging to the previously highly regulated industries such as utilities, telecommunications, or railroads, are still facing strong needs to redesign their current functional structures. They have survived, protected by regulations and subsidization with functional models because they had limited need for customer and product focus. With more and more competition in these industries, customer focus and customized product offerings are required and will ultimately lead to increased use of divisional and matrix structures.

Secrets of Powerful Teams

Besides the plain organizational structure that is the prerequisite to operate successfully, the people working within these structures certainly make the difference. There are a number of characteristics that are typical of powerful teams:

- **Leadership Capabilities**
  The one-great-leader concept has come to an end.[4] In today's business world it is a widely accepted fact that there is little advantage to be achieved through individual performance. Success depends mostly on effective teamwork, although the team in itself is heavily influenced by its leader. Therefore, the team leadership capabilities and the ability of leaders to integrate themselves effectively into their teams are cornerstones for team success.
- **Creativity**
  Responding to new competitive situations with organizational creativity will enable companies to react faster to the market's requirements and fine-tune its operations more effectively. Creativity will be borne by teams, not by single great individuals.[5] Teams often have outstanding forward-thinkers and leaders who, however, will only be part of the team. The real strength of great leaders lies in the ability to connect things and to identify linkages based on knowledge and experience.[6]
- **Overriding Goals**
  There needs to be a clear and overriding goal for the team that is thrilling and challenging but not unreachable at all. Ideally, the defined goal will be

broken down into realistic parts.[7] But still, the goal has to be a real stretch. The desire of the team to reach the goal must be extreme. It is an art to define those types of balanced goals.

- **Clearly Defined Opponent**
  Great teams often identify their competitors as mystified "enemies" whom overcoming is a kind of honor and duty from the company's perspective. When Apple established itself as a competitor to the mighty IBM, the team around founder Steve Jobs often referred to IBM as the "*Great Satan.*" Jobs and his team considered themselves as pirates breaking down the old-fashioned, single-minded, computer-hardware culture for which IBM stood. Having a fearsome enemy obviously creates a strong spirit and encourages successful teams to outperform.
- **Common Social Characteristics**
  Successful teams do not require a demographically homogeneous group of individuals. By contrast, successful teams fuel their potential through diversity and multiple talents. That is one of the reasons why product innovation teams are mostly multi-functionally staffed. Social characteristics of powerful teams are more important but they have to be balanced: Too strong social ties can limit innovative potential, too loose ties can hinder creativity because the team members do not have enough mutual understanding and trust. Common social characteristics are things like a commitment, common language, common behavior, confidential rituals, and sometimes even common clothes.[8] The Manhattan Project team that eventually succeeded in inventing the first atomic bomb developed nicknames for the various scientist groups: physicists were called the "fizzlers" and chemists the "stinkers."

Even the bomb itself got the name "gadget." Through common language, behaviors, and rituals, teams express their strong mutual understanding and respect for each other. A strong team can develop an entirely unique value framework for the period of the teamwork. The team's values are the beliefs and principles that guide the team's behavior.[9] They glue the team together, building team confidence and trust.[10] These are essential requirements for powerful teams.[11]

There are further important characteristics always found in good teamwork. The term **"team spirit"** summarizes the emotions and moods that exist, but nobody can really point them out or describe them in detail. People obviously respect and have fun working with each other. As an analogy to sports illustrates, there is a certain atmosphere in the locker room that indicates that a team "clicks." People trust each other, are absolutely convinced of their potential, believe in all the individual talent around, and are confident of their ability to outplay competitors. In these situations even the head coach doesn't need to motivate the team.

Eventually team spirit is heavily influenced by its members. Being part of a group can be tremendous fun for each individual. Sharing work with outstanding individuals who all have a common goal, a threatening enemy, and certain social characteristics in common can be the most fulfilling and enriching time in the professional life of each member.

The tool to monitor and assess the current potential of teams is the Team Characteristic Potential Analysis. This tool basically integrates the criteria discussed above and enables a systematic evaluation. The exhibit below illustrates how it works:

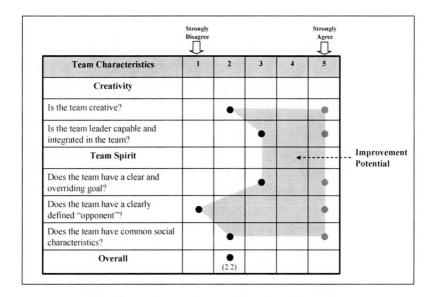

Exhibit I-2: Team Characteristic Potential Analysis

The tool allows both the assessment of today's condition and identification of potential improvements. The assessment to the left indicates the current performance of the team. The assessment to the right describes the desired highest performance levels. A simple Web-based, anonymous survey among a representative group of employees currently involved in team efforts can surface tremendous valuable insights and help to improve the overall team performance.

High-Performing Employees

From an outside perspective, Employee Performance is often evaluated by indicators such as employee turnover and absenteeism.[12] These metrics are important; however, they don't allow any insights about how effectively an individual employee takes care of assigned work and tasks.

Absenteeism is a first indicator that employees do not like being at work. They use minor excuses not to show up and trade pay against free time. Employee turnover provides some additional insights regarding how comfortable employees are with their current work environment. Besides the tangible issues of talent loss and soaring recruiting costs, turnover denotes that something is wrong inside the company. There are hard facts such as pay, benefits, location, or commute that cause employees to change jobs. There are also soft facts such as management style, colleagues, or lack of team spirit.

There are a number of characteristics that provide insights into the individual performance:

- *Commitment*
  Employees need to be fully committed to their work and the company. Some studies describe this phenomenon as the "good soldier" syndrome or organization citizenship behavior.[13] The good soldier is in essence an employee who serves to advance the company's purpose.
- *Balanced Social and Work Life*
  Each individual needs a balanced social and work life. If employees have a misbalanced personal life due to a heavy workload, if they are not able to maintain social relationships, lifestyle, and personal interests, then work must compensate for all the unfulfilled necessities of life. In the short-term, the company can profit from these people; they appear to be fully committed and strong performers. In the long-term, the once-strong commitment can turn completely around, especially when compensation and career goals have not been realized. Those employees often become cynical and negative towards the company and often poison the office or

workshop atmosphere. Or, probably, they will resume their neglected social life and, in the same way they overly invested in their work life in the past, they start to highly prioritize their private life.

- *Appreciation and Career Development*
  Individuals are satisfied and motivated if their contribution is highly valued and appreciated by their superiors and the company. Employees should have confidence that their individual contribution is extremely important to the business. Therefore, tasks assigned to employees have to be meaningful. Superiors have to follow up and provide feedback on everything an employee was asked to work on. Also, employees would like to understand development opportunities. Career perspectives can be a strong driver of individual performance.

A similar tool to that which has been discussed to evaluate team performance works to assess the current state of individual performance:

Individual Characteristics	1	2	3	4	5	
Is the employee fully committed to his work?			●		●	
Does the employee have a balanced work and private life?		●		◄	●	Improvement Potential
Does the employee receive sufficient appreciation?		●			●	
Overall		● (2.4)				

Strongly Disagree ⇩   *Strongly Agree* ⇩

Exhibit I-3: Individual Characteristic Potential Analysis

The two potential analyses (Team and Individual) provide flash snapshots about how well the company is utilizing its inherent hidden potentials. The Team/Individual Effectiveness Portfolio brings the results into context.

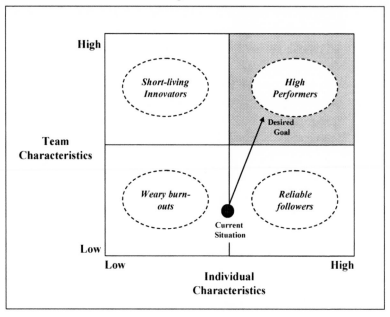

Exhibit I-4: Team/Individual Effectiveness Portfolio

The portfolio clearly displays where a company stands. Strong team characteristics but relatively weak individual characteristics indicate a strong innovative project culture. It tends to be short-living because members are often overstressed, and the project atmosphere gets rocky because individuals' lives are not balanced any more. They are called the *Short-living Innovators.* Another group can be described as the exact opposite: the *Reliable Followers.* Although individuals are pretty happy with their professional lives, these companies are lacking the capability to set up effective teamwork. It's not necessarily a threat, but if the fate of the company relies on innovation and product breakthroughs it represents a serious issue. A real threat arises if the assessment indicates the *Weary Burn-outs* group. Employees have positively no fun working for the company, and team efforts regularly fail. No doubt, immediate action is required. Happy are those companies with *High Performers*. People appreciate their work, seek the extra-mile, and volunteer for team efforts.

2   Optimizing Value Chains

Invented in the late 1980s, *Business Process Reengineering* (BPR) has become one of the most important buzzwords around organizational sciences and practices ever since.[14] The value chain as first introduced by **Michael Porter** illustrates the flow of goods, services, and information through the various functional stages of an organization, as illustrated in the slightly modified version below.[15]

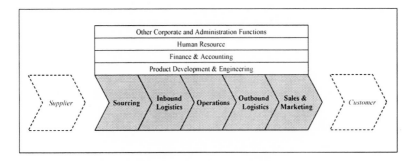

Exhibit I-5: Value Chain

The basic principle of the value chain is quite simple and very relevant today. Supply chain management and optimizing distribution networks is top-ranked on CEO agendas. Value chain management has two perspectives: Internal Value Chains and Vertical Networks.

Internal Value Chain Management

Initially, the concept of value chains was developed to analyze competitive cost structure, position, and differentiation in achieving comparative advantages. The idea was that managing the value chain at lower cost and similar or better quality than competitors would automatically outperform them.

The key trigger for best-in-class value chain management is an e-enabled integrated information flow. Value creation takes place beginning with the receipt of raw materials and parts until the finished product is delivered. Which part actually is the major value driver depends on the type of company. Consumer goods companies, for example, usually have the core value generated in Sales and Marketing, whereas for oil and gas companies, Sourcing, Logistics and Operations are relatively more important. Value in this respect is simply the margin the customer is willing to pay. The core processes of the internal value chain are:

- *Sourcing:* interface to the supplier. Sourcing needs to maintain harmonious supplier databases, connect suppliers with the company via integrated IT systems, and pre-select preferred suppliers.
- *Inbound Logistics:* receiving and storing raw materials and inbound parts. The sourced materials and parts will be stored in the respective stock and routed into the production flow as requested. In some cases, "just-in-time" approaches have been implemented and materials and parts are delivered as requested by the operations process.
- *Operations:* production of goods and services. In production processes materials and parts will run through several production stages. Several times they

are stocked either in production-related "work-in-progress" (WIP) or in buffer stocks that will be built on the shop floor to avoid short-term bottlenecks through part shortages at distinct production steps. Downtime of equipment, deficiencies in quality, or unplanned scrap are causes to operate with buffer stocks. Raw material and part information should be electronically linked with WIP stock and buffer stock levels.

- *Outbound Logistics:* distribution to delivery outlets. As soon as the finished products are in stock they will be transitioned into the distribution network. This network allocates the products to the various distribution warehouses from which they will be shipped to the point of sale (POS). Stock levels of these particular stocks have to be closely linked as well. Shortages in product provision are the biggest fear of each sales organization. Overstocked warehouses are the biggest threat for each inventory manager. Reliable forecasts and integrated information flow from inbound logistics over operations to distribution is key to running a successful value chain.

- *Sales and Marketing:* selling products to end-customers. Sales and Marketing basically takes place in parallel to all the aforementioned activities. In this respect, the description of a value chain sequence is not entirely correct. Sales information actually triggers the whole value chain process and provides important information to each element of the value chain. Sales forecasts are the single most important variable to decide on purchase volumes (for raw materials and parts), production capacity and inventory levels as the exhibit below illustrates:

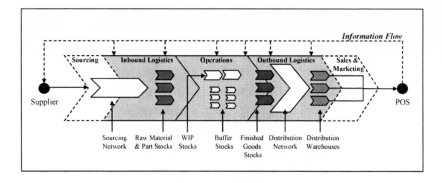

Exhibit I-6: Value Chain Information Flow

Effective information flow is the major differentiator for successful value chain management.

Vertical Networks

Vertical networks are not new, especially in the manufacturing industry. Since the 1980s, industries such as automotive, pharmaceuticals and chemicals in particular have improved their industry value chains by linking suppliers and customers closer to their internal processes.[16] The business partnering principle has widely replaced the isolated value-optimization thinking. The efficiency of an integrated cross-company value chain has been identified as an important source to generate competitive advantages.

Today, using the Internet to speed up data exchange and provide multiple communication interactions further reduces transaction costs along value chains.[17] While Internet-based operations are becoming routine business for the industry's Original Equipment Manufacturers (OEM) and their tiers of suppliers, other industries like banking, insurance, and travel have awakened to realize these advantages, and started creating vertical networks, too. Overall optimization is a common objective for all participants in vertical networks – aiming to reduce costs, increase revenue, and improve agility. But to function and benefit as a whole, the participating companies need to be convinced that the value inherent in the integrated cooperation is greater than the individual parts. Therefore, the positioning and development of each company within a vertical network is decisive for both the company's and the network's strategic course and benefits.[18]

Initially, each company needs to understand and communicate its required contribution and its expected payback. And they must continuously monitor its effectiveness and profitability. Moreover, complexity is increased by the fact that certain supplier companies participate in various networks. Proactive, carefully planned product and service agreements are important, and a well-defined governance model is a necessity. Usually, the network partner with the strongest bargaining power takes the lead and defines the governance model. However, just applying one company's structure to a vertical network partnership won't work. Each partner is still independent and won't automatically subordinate its activities. Human guidance and co-operation are critical to maintain an effective vertical network and realize its promised benefits. There is a need to develop a mutual partnership model, which has to be executed, managed, and coordinated extremely insightfully and sensitively.

A vertical network can be compared with all other types of strategic alliance or partnership. However, its purpose is unique: a vertical network attempts to integrate the most important steps along the industry-specific value chain. Thus, it does not cooperate with another company to optimize utilization of manufacturing capacities or to share a distribution network. It is comparable to a single company with its various value-chain elements. An entire industry does have value-chain elements, too. In certain industries, like aerospace and defense or automotive, products are produced via a chain of an OEM and up to four tiers of major suppliers. The OEM eventually just assembles modules. Typical of a vertical partnership is that each player maintains its unique value-chain proportion. The network works in a way that the OEM, its key suppliers, and, if separated from the OEM, the distribution organization are linked together in a partnership. The purpose is to maximize the overall margin and value creation of the network by assigning responsibilities and contributions within the network according to strategic capabilities and respective strength.

In a functioning vertical network it occurs that entire manufacturing steps, R and D, or engineering tasks, for example, are moved entirely from OEM to suppliers and vice versa. Eventually, based on its resources and capabilities, each member of the vertical network should be enabled to perform in the best way possible. The network requires thoughtful allocation of core functions and a governance model that regulates the rules of the game:

- Price ranges between retailers – OEM – suppliers;
- Mitigating risks of declining and unexpectedly increasing demand;
- Margin allocation based on strategic capabilities and core functions;
- Responsibility to monitor and manage the network margin (mostly assumed by the OEMs);
- Arrangements for information flow, coordination process, and decision-making for the day-to-day business.

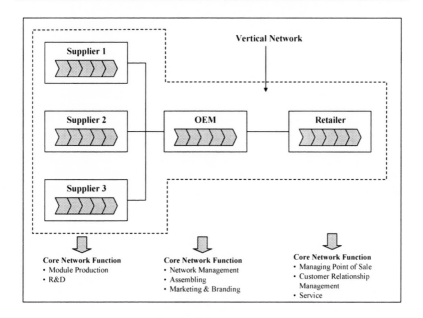

Exhibit I-7: Vertical Network

Managing vertical networks is a significant challenge because of multiple risks.[19] Most of the risk is related to information sharing. Company-specific, confidential data will be shared among the various network partners who are still in supplier–customer relationships. This issue has been present in practical and theoretical discussions about strategic partnerships. It is referred to as the "prisoner dilemma."[20] The dilemma can be summarized as risk assessment of how likely a network partner will leave a network and use confidential information for its own benefit in the marketplace. However, Organizational Effectiveness can be significantly improved through Vertical Networks due to avoidance of continuous and lengthy negotiation processes. Once a stable network has been established most of the transaction costs are eliminated. Especially industries with year-long and trustful supplier-customer relations can overcome the prisoner dilemma and leverage all advantages.

3   Economic Downturns and their Implications

As the world and U.S. economy have to cope with the economic downturn started in late 2000, companies have to downsize and cutback their operations. Some immediate actions to mitigate economic pressure are violating basic principles of organizational management and will, in turn, reinforce the troubles of many companies. But as a simple necessity to survive, those actions are nevertheless taken. To a certain extent the stock market has perverted the way business is currently done. It has become an overriding mantra which all senior executives grudgingly obey. Wall Street and its relentless analyst community set increasing pressure on companies to meet shareholder expectations, which has partly led to awkward decision-making with regard to internal organizational issues. And, as the result of economic downturns, lots of companies have downsized and laid off employees as quickly and massively as possible without considering the consequences for Organizational Effectiveness.

Shareholder Expectations

Doing business within today's publicly listed companies, especially Corporate America has always focused strongly on the shareholder. Stock price and earnings per share are dominating the business news. Sometimes it's even hard to find out what a company is actually developing, producing, or selling. Finding their stock performance is much easier. Based on forward thinkers such as **Alfred Rappaport** and **Thomas Copeland** the value paradigm has taken over and rules over today's business activities for all publicly listed companies. Both were the first to apply capital market models and finance theories to management principles.[21]

Consulting firms like Stern Stewart, Holt, and Marakon have picked up the subject and developed tools around shareholder management. The shareholders are considered to be the center of the business-universe and every single management action has to ensure that their "value" in terms of total returns will be maximized.

Shareholder value can be plainly described with the principle of returning profits on invested capital. The shareholders have, in fact, invested capital by buying the stock and are expecting an appropriate return. Additionally, the stock price may soar and offer them the opportunity to sell stock and yield a trading profit. There are many different concepts to measure the return on investment. However, the basic principle is almost always the same.

- The concept of **Economic Value Added** (EVA) focuses on the value created for shareholders by comparing adjusted accounting profits after tax with capital charges.[22] The following exhibit illustrates the principle:

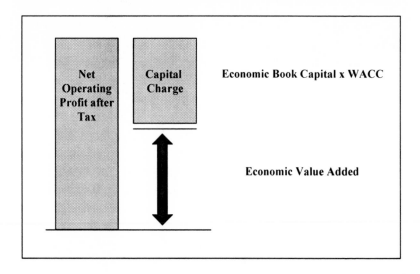

Exhibit I-8: Economic Value Added (EVA)

The capital charge will be calculated as the Economic Capital (book capital plus operating leases and other adjustment) multiplied by the Weighted Average Cost of Capital (WACC).[23] This capital cost is the result of the current debt/equity ratio of the firm and its specific risk profile. Adjustments to the accounting profits are mostly the addition of leasing charges (because they are now capitalized and counted as part of the capital), and capitalizing of R and D and advertisement expenses. The latter two items have to be converted to an economic life instead of an accounting life. There are numerous other adjustments to align accounting and economic perspective (overall there are more than 150 adjustments required).

• The concept of **Market Value Added** is based on a different principle: instead of adjusted accounting profits, it operates with the current market value.

Profitability considerations are not part of this approach. The current market value has to be reduced by the economic capital to calculate the MVA.[24] Thus, as the following exhibit illustrates, there are some similarities in the concepts of EVA and MVA with regard to the economic book capital. However, EVA focuses on profits whereas MVA works with market value to identify if value has been created from a shareholder's perspective:

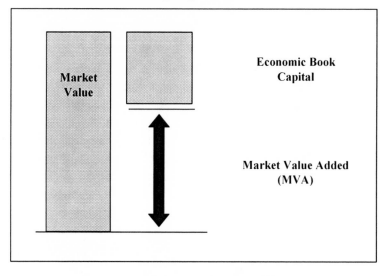

Exhibit I-9: Market Value Added (MVA)

The MVA concept emphasizes primarily the market evaluation perspective. That means the value creation depends heavily on the current stock price and neglects the profitability aspect. In theory, however, the EVA is considered to be the fuel for the MVA.[25] In practice, this idea has not really been applied. In essence, rigorous application of the MVA approach does not rely on the earnings as long as the shareholder community values the particular stock highly enough. The experiences with the burst of the Internet bubble in 2000, the plunging high-tech stocks, and the depressed stock market have shown that the MVA idea is not very helpful to monitor shareholder value though.

- The concept of **Total Shareholder Return (TSR)** is a variation of the Market Value Added approach. In contrast to the MVA method, the TSR does not include the economic book capital in the shareholder value creation calculation. The TSR concept focuses entirely on the value created within a period of one year. To do so, it monitors the change in a firm's market capitalization over the one-year period and adds the dividends paid out to the shareholders.[26] The created shareholder value is eventually expressed as a percentage of the market capitalization plus dividends as a percentage to the initial value. The TSR approach puts a strong emphasis on the market valuation of the stock. However, compared to the MVA method it has the slight advantage of including the dividends as a kind of profitability index. Thus, shareholders are often particularly interested in the TSR because it reveals the hard facts of what a shareholder has earned within a one-year period. However, within the one-year period stock price evaluations can overplay weak profitability.

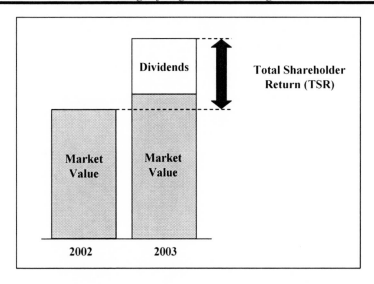

Exhibit I-10: Total Shareholder Return (TSR)

- The concept of **Cash Value Added (CVA)** turns back to the return on investment philosophy. However, it works with a different perspective on earnings than EVA. Instead of adjusted accounting profits, cash flows are used to indicate if a company is able to cover its capital costs. By introducing the metric Cash Flow Return on Investment (CFROI) this approach compares cash flows with the capital base initially invested in the business.[27] The CFROI officiates as an internal rate of return that indicates the cash-oriented return on the invested capital.[28] This rate is compared to the capital charge using the WACC as internal rate of return, as shown in the EVA approach. In contrast to the EVA method, the CVA uses the acquisition values instead of the economic book values. Eventually, the difference between CFROI and WACC-based capital charge indicates the CVA as shown on the following exhibit:[29]

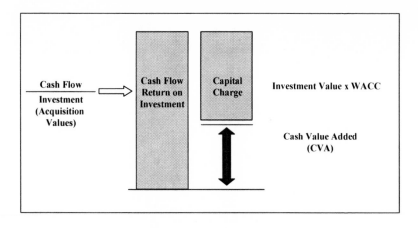

Exhibit I-11: Cash Value Added (CVA)

As a result, the general guideline to define shareholder value is that it is mostly the profitability measured either in adjusted accounting profits or cash flows and, to a smaller extent, the actual value of the stock. The pure market-driven perspective to measure shareholder value is more or less an exceptional case and not mainstream.

Value Orientation

The value orientation, especially in the U.S., was strongly driven by big institutional investors like CalPERS and TIAA-CREF.[30] These retirement funds have a strong focus on continuous and sustainable value growth of their investment. TIAA-CREF was managing an asset volume overall of $280 billion in 2000[31]. And although reduced by 7.2%, the overall investment volume of CalPERS in 2001 still counted for $156 billion.[32] It is understandable that these major investors urgently request better transparency, clear corporate governance principles, and stronger shareholder value orientation. The SEC has basically responded to those requests by enforcing disclosure regulations that allow detailed insights into the financials of publicly listed companies on a quarterly and yearly basis. SEC 10K and 8K filings provide detailed breakdowns of financial figures. It has become a quite common and regular ritual in Corporate America to announce and comment on quarterly earnings through presentations and conference calls in which the CEO and CFO and the entire executive team are regularly "grilled" by a challenging analyst community. Over-achievement of expectations will be acclaimed and usually rewarded by a "buy" recommendation (as long as all other indicators are positive); even minor failures are punished with a "hold" or even "sell" assessment. CEOs and, in particular, CFOs spend a lot of their time in managing shareholders' expectations. Outlooks for upcoming quarters are questioned and challenged over and over again before being communicated to Wall Street. Businesses that were never used to preparing detailed quarterly earning forecasts have today a serious requirement to think in quarterly dimensions. Thus, senior executives of the Fortune 1,000 companies have developed a "quarter-by-quarter" management behavior and mentality. To obey the stock market has good reasons, though.

- The risk of a **hostile takeover** soars if the stock has dropped to a dangerous low.
- **Revenue growth** is limited because low stock prices lead to limited capital funds which will result in lowered earnings. Low earnings will result in further dropping of the stock price.

Organization management is an important source of profitability. Organizational structure and processes, teams, and individuals are valuable contributors to a strong bottom line. The value requirements from a shareholder and stock market perspective single out profitability as the key for success. There is, in fact, a psychological effect of stock markets. The hype on the stock markets in the late '90s was extraordinary and it appears, in retrospect, that everybody lost sanity.[33] However, for those who are in search of true and long-term value creation the psychological effects have limited significance. Organizational Effectiveness is one of the key drivers of profitability and far more important.[34]

Cost Cutting and Downsizing

In the last 20 years almost every company that belongs to the Fortune 500 has undergone restructuring.[35] The reason why companies run through phases of growth and downsizing can be explained through economic cyclicity. It is heavily dependent on the worldwide economic situation and on its regional and industry-specific trends. The fact that industries have to reduce size is not new and it is not a bad thing either. Like **Joseph Schumpeter** pointed out in his work published prior to World War II, business cycles are repetitive and are always stimulated by demand-pull and corresponding supply-push behavior.[36] Markets, therefore, are continuously moving around the equilibrium; sometimes with too short a supply and not enough competitors, sometimes with exactly the opposite. Hence, both downsizing and growth are necessities of business life. Another important trigger for downsizing can be seen in the strong Merger and Acquisition (M&A) trend since the late '90s.[37] It's fairly obvious that, besides synergy effects and new market access, most mergers are driven by cost-reduction potentials. Redundant functions can be eliminated, economies of scale and scope can be utilized, and company-wide supply-chain and distribution networks can be leveraged more effectively.

The magnitude of cutback decisions since the economic downturn is significant, as the examples of two industries demonstrate:

- Since the year 2000 some players in semiconductors have downsized their workforce markedly, by up to one-third.

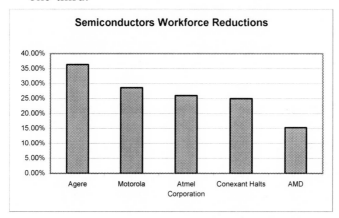

Exhibit I-12: Semiconductors Workforce Reductions 2000 - 2002

- The retail industry has trimmed down resources substantially, too. On average, the apparel retailers in the US have cut back employees by 9% since 2000 and have reduced the number of stores significantly, too.

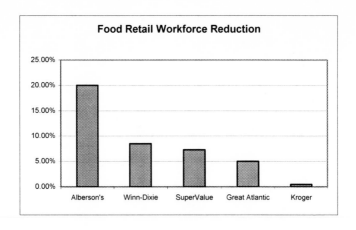

Exhibit I-13: Food Retailer Workforce Reduction 2000 - 2002

There is a close link between downsizing and crisis management.[38] Companies that are downsizing are considered to be in a "crisis," meaning their existence is immediately threatened. In reality, a more balanced perspective might be more appropriate, as the discussion surrounding shareholder expectation and value orientation has highlighted. Today, downsizing decisions are driven mainly by the objective to keep profitability and stock price up. The business world reacts more quickly on indication of downturns than theoretically assumed. Nobody is waiting until the last line of defense is reached.[39] There is certainly a tendency that companies are pulling the trigger of cost cutting too quickly and too often. The effects on Organizational Effectiveness are immense:

- On the positive side, economic challenges put pressure on organizations to test new, creative models to arrange the workload with fewer employees. There are several examples where innovative organizational solutions have been realized through the necessity of downsizing. Self-guided teams or assigning two different functions to one employee are examples of this.[40]

- On the negative side, headcount reduction very often doesn't lead to immediate results. Massive layoffs need to be very well analyzed, prepared and executed. HR and legal issues have to be resolved and the program needs to be managed effectively. Big mistakes while executing a massive layoff can lead to disaster: redundancy and severance costs are major financial burdens, class action lawsuits can lead to rehiring and compensation fees. Last but not least, public opinion about companies is under increased scrutiny when layoffs occur.

- Also on the negative side, people don't like to live and work in uncertain environments;[41] feeling unprotected is certainly not the foundation of high performance. It hinders capabilities as discussed under successful team and individual characteristics and creates an atmosphere of mistrust.[42] Eventually, the entire value framework that is so important for employees to outperform can be diminished and fall apart. Studies of employee behavior in downsizing situations, the so-called "survivor behavior," have found that quantity of work is still the same or even better but quality of work will decrease significantly.[43] Anxiety, stress, and depression are typical characteristics of people in such situations. Downsizing is sociologically perceived as failure.

Downsizing is a necessity to survive in business cycles. Rebuilding Organizational Effectiveness should, therefore, have absolute priority. Even if employees have survived a downsizing period, the company is still at great risk to lose employees and essential talent because people are in search of safe havens and loyalty has been damaged.[44] In particular, companies that often go through downsizing and rehiring phases should seriously reconsider their actions. Besides the fact that rehiring is expensive and partly offsets savings through job cuts, the inherent strength of the organization gets weaker and weaker over time. Companies that are considered socially responsible and good corporate citizens use downsizing as truly the last possible means to stay in business. These companies tend to be more successful. As some long-term studies reveal, on average, they are larger in size and stronger in financial performance. [45]

[1] Alfred D. Chandler, *Strategy and Structure: Chapters in the History of the Industrial Enterprise* (Cambridge: M. I. T. Press, 1962).

[2] Frederick W. Taylor, *The Principles of Scientific Management* (Mineola, NY: Dover Publications, 1997; originally published: New York: Harper & Bros., 1911).

[3] Henri Fayol, *Industrial and General Administration*, Geneva, 1930 (trans. by John Adair Coubrough).

[4] Charles C. Manz and Henry P. Sims, Jr., *Business Without Bosses: How Self Managing Teams are Building High-Performing Companies* (New York: John Wiley & Sons, 1993), pp. 1-3.

[5] Dennis A. Romig, "Structured Teamwork to achieve organizational breakthroughs," *Breakthrough Teamwork: Outstanding Results Using Structured Teamwork* (Chicago, IL: Irwin Professional Publishing, 1996), pp. 1-10.

[6] Lynda C. McDermott, Nolan Brawley and William W. Waite, *World Class Teams: Working Across Borders* (New York: John Wiley & Sons, 1998), pp. 138-147.

[7] Harvey Robbins and Michael Finley, *Why Teams Don't Work: What Went Wrong and How to Make it Right* (Princeton, NJ: Peterson's Pacesetters Books, 1995), p. 34.

[8] Susan A. Wheelan, *Creating Effective Teams: A Guide for Members and Leaders* (Thousand Oaks, CA: SAGE Publications, 1999), p. 3.

[9] Lynda C. McDermott, Nolan Brawley and William W. Waite, *World Class Teams: Working Across Borders* (New York: John Wiley & Sons, 1998), pp. 79-85.

[10] Jon R. Katzenbach and Douglas K. Smith, *The Wisdom of Teams: Creating the High-Performance Organization* (Boston: Harvard Business School Press, 1993), p. 65, 92: Importance of Commitment to each other.

[11] Teresa M. Amabile, Constance N. Hadley and Steven J. Kramer, "Creativity under the Gun," *Harvard Business Review*, August 2002, pp. 52-54. The Time-Pressure/Creativity Matrix (p. 56) provides a sounding framework why the Manhattan Project eventually succeeded.

[12] Allen I. Kraut, *Organizational Surveys: Tools for Assessment and Change* (San Francisco, CA, Jossey-Bass Inc., 1996), p. 101.

[13] David L. Turnipseed, "Are good soldiers good? Exploring the link between organization citizenship behavior and personal ethics," *Journal of Business Research*, Vol. 55, No. 1, January 2002, p. 1.

[14] Michael Hammer and James Champy, *Reengineering the Corporation: A Manifesto for Business Revolution* (New York: HarperBusiness, 1994).

[15] Michael E. Porter, *Competitive Advantage: Creating and Sustaining Superior Performance* (New York: Free Press, 1998).

[16] John Sheridan, "Now It's a Job for the CEO," *Industry Week* (Cleveland, OH, 2000), Vol. 249, No. 6, pp. 22-26.

[17] Segil Larraine, *Intelligent Business Alliances: How to Profit Using Today's Most Important Strategic Tool* (New York: Times Business, 1996), p. 12; Jay R. Galbraith, *Designing Organizations, An Executive Briefing on Strategy, Structure, and Process* (San Francisco, CA: Joessy-Bass Publishers, 1995), pp. 119-120.

[18] S. Dressler and K.-H. Mueller, "Competitive Advantage for Integrated Value Chains," *Cost Management*, 2003, Vol. 17, No. 5; pp. 5-13.

[19] Ron Ashkenas and others, *The Boundaryless Organization: Breaking the Chains of Organizational Structure* (San Francisco, CA: Jossery-Bass, 1995), pp. 204-213.

[20] John Child and David Faulkner, *Strategies of Cooperation: Managing Alliances, Networks, and Joint Ventures* (New York: Oxford University Press, 1998), pp. 26-31. Jerry Spector, Strategic Marketing and the Prisoner's Dilemma, *Direct Marketing*, 1997; Vol 59, No. 10, pp. 44-45.

[21] Alfred Rappaport, *Creating Shareholder Value: the New Standard for Business Performance* (New York: Free Press; London: Collier Macmillan, 1986); Thomas Copeland, Tim Koller, and Jack Murrin, *Valuation: Measuring and Managing the Value of Companies* (New York: Wiley, 1990).

[22] G. Bennett Stewart, *The Quest for Value: A Guide for Senior Managers* (New York, NY: HarperBusiness, 1991).

[23] Alan D. Gasiorek, *Merger & Acquisition: Valuation and Structuring* (Norcross, GA: Corporate Development Institute, 1997), pp. 57-86.

[24] G. Bennett Stewart III, *The Quest for Value: A Guide for Senior Managers* (New York, NY: HarperBusiness, 1991), pp. 153-154.

[25] G. Bennett Stewart III, *The Quest for Value: A Guide for Senior Managers* (New York, NY: HarperBusiness, 1991), p. 153.

[26] Anonymous, "A Star to Sail by?" *The Economist*, pp. 53-55, August 2, 1997.

[27] Dirk Hachmeister, "Zeitschrift fuer betriebswirtschaftliche Forschung," Duesseldorf, Germany: *Verlagsgruppe Handelsblatt*, Vol. 17, No. 6, 1997, pp. 556-579.

[28] Aswath Damodaran, *The Dark Side of Valuation: Valuing Old Tech, New Tech, and New Economy Companies* (Upper Saddle River, NJ: Prentice Hall, 2001), pp. 442-444.

[29] Karl-Ludwig Kley, "Das neue Wertsteigerungskonzept der Lufthansa," *Zeitschrift fuer Controlling*, Dortmund, Controlling, No. 6, 2000, pp. 289-294.

[30] California Public Employees' Retirement System (CalPERS); Teachers Insurance and Annuity Association College Retirement Equities Fund (TIAA-CREF).

[31] TIAA-CREF Annual Report 2000, p. 1.

[32] CalPERS Annual Report 2001 (period ended June 30, 2001), p. 1.

[33] Gregory v. Milano, in Joel M. Stern and John S. Shiley, *The EVA Challenge: Implementing Value-Added Change in an Organization* (New York: John Wiley & Sons, 2001), pp. 209-232.

[34] Joel M. Stern and John S. Shiley, *The EVA Challenge: Implementing Value-Added Change in an Organization* (New York: John Wiley & Sons, 2001), pp. 27-50.

[35] Zeinab A. Karake-Shalhoub, *Organizational Downsizing, Discrimination, and Corporate Social Responsibility* (Westport, CT: Quorum Books, 1999), p. 53.

[36] Joseph A. Schumpeter, *Business Cycles* (2 Volumes) (New York: 1939).

[37] Robert Johansen and Rob Swigart, *Upsizing the Individual in the Downsized Organization: Managing in the Wake of Reengineering, Globalization, and Overwhelming Technological Change* (Reading, MA: Addison-Wesley, 1994), p. 3; and Hema A. Krishnan and Daewoo Park, "The Impact of Workforce Reduction on Subsequent Performance in Major Mergers and Acquisitions. An Exploratory Study," *Journal of Business Research*, Vol. 55, No. 4, April 2002, p. 285.

[38] Zeinab A. Karake-Shalhoub, *Organizational Downsizing, Discrimination, and Corporate Social Responsibility* (Westport, CT: Quorum Books, 1999), p. 56.

[39] This is confirmed by a study conducted by Hema A. Krishnan and Daewoo Park, "The Impact of Workforce Reduction on Subsequent Performance in Major Mergers and Acquisitions. An Exploratory Study," *Journal of Business Research*, Vol. 55, No. 4, April 2002, pp. 290-291.

[40] Robert Johansen and Rob Swigart, *Upsizing the Individual in the Downsized Organization: Managing in the Wake of Reengineering, Globalization, and Overwhelming Technological Change* (Reading, MA: Addison-Wesley, 1994), pp. 46-51.

[41] Zeinab A. Karake-Shalhoub, *Organizational Downsizing, Discrimination, and Corporate Social Responsibility* (Westport, CT: Quorum Books, 1999), p. 53/

[42] Alan T. Belasen, *Leading the Learning Organization: Communication and Competencies for Managing Change* (New York: State University Press, 2000), pp. 214-215.

[43] Zeinab A. Karake-Shalhoub, *Organizational Downsizing, Discrimination, and Corporate Social Responsibility* (Westport, CT: Quorum Books, 1999), p. 63.

[44] Zeinab A. Karake-Shalhoub, *Organizational Downsizing, Discrimination, and Corporate Social Responsibility* (Westport, CT: Quorum Books, 1999), p. 62.

[45] Moses L. Pava and Joshua Krausz, *Corporate Responsibility and Financial Performance* (Westpoint, CT.: Quorum Books, 1995), pp. 42-56; Kim S. Cameron, Sarah J. Freeman and Aneil K. Mishra, "Downsizing and Redesigning Organizations," as cited in George P. Huber and William H. Glick, *Organizational Change and Redesign: Ideas and Insights for Improving Performance* (New York: Oxford University Press, 1993), pp. 44-46.

*"Understanding Strategic Direction and
Organizational Capabilities"*

Strategic Direction Setting:
Organizational Context

Organizational Effectiveness has been the focus of a wide variety of research efforts in the past. Disciplines like sociology, psychology, and business sciences like human resource management and organization management have developed various perspectives on Organizational Effectiveness from different angles. As a result, hundreds of studies have been published between the mid-1960s and the mid-1980s dealing with Organizational Effectiveness from different perspectives. **Barton Cunningham** provides a useful overview by comparing different approaches on Organizational Effectiveness in selected situations.[1] Basically, he comes to the conclusion that there is no single best approach, only best approaches by situation. The following table displays the results.

Organizational Effectiveness Model	Evaluation Situation
Rational Model	Organizational structures
Systems Resources	Organizational structures
Managerial Process	Human resources
Organizational Development	Human resources
Bargaining	Decision impact
Structural Functional	Structure and performance
Functional	Organizational activities impact

Table: Organizational Effectiveness Models & Application

Kim Cameron, who has published a book on multiple models of Organizational Effectiveness, summarized precisely the dilemma that organization science was facing back in 1983:

> *"Unfortunately, the plethora of writing and research has failed to produce a meaningful definition of organizational effectiveness, let alone a theory of effectiveness. The writing has been fragmented, noncumulative, and frequently downright confusing."*[2]

4   The Framework of Organizational Effectiveness

It appears to be impossible to develop one common framework or concept that describes organizations as objective phenomena. Organizations are *constructs* and not *concepts*. That means they cannot be described as clearly as tangible concepts and, therefore, are a kind of mental abstraction that needs interpretation.[3] Along with other constructs such as leadership, motivation, and knowledge management, there is no absolute right or wrong, true or false, or dos and don'ts in organization management. However, Organizational Effectiveness has driven companies to top performance, but there is no *concept* to determine the state of effectiveness upfront.[4] It relies on the capacity to connect achieved performance with existing organizational patterns and to predict how these patterns will work for a company and its specific challenges in the future. This gap will be closed by a holistic and integrating approach to Organizational Effectiveness. Business today has radically changed its face compared to the mid-1980s . There are numerous trends that require a more proactive management of organizations:[5]

- Plurality of management paradigms – There is no one single, successful management paradigm unilaterally applied across the business world.
- Globalization – Literally most industries and their major players are operating on a global basis.
- Digitization – Business interactions today are vastly supported by modern, digitized technologies.
- Flexibility – Organizations' paradigms have to enable flexibility in a business world that is far more uncertain than decades ago.
- Shorter Planning Horizons – Product life cycles are getting shorter and business models are mostly built on radically reduced break-even periods.
- Stakeholder – The shareholder has emerged as a dominating stakeholder group; companies today are scrutinized with regard to their corporate citizenship role and attractiveness as employers.

Since social and business sciences have not provided a comprehensive definition of Organizational Effectiveness, as of today there is a need to outline a comprehensive, integrated, and holistic approach. The framework of Organizational Effectiveness here is built around five categories:

- ***Organizational Context***
- ***Corporate and Business Unit Structure***
- ***Organizational Infrastructure***
- ***Team and Individual Capabilities***
- ***Performance Measurement and Target Setting***

Each category covers a certain perspective of organization management and they are all interrelated.[6] The Organizational Context describes the backbone of the business activities. It describes how the purpose of a business has been translated into mission and goals, how values and strategic capabilities have evolved, and how the company fits into its environment.

- *Purpose* - The main purpose of the business and the entrepreneurial spirit are the key drivers for a company's mission, vision, and strategy.
- *Structure* - Corporate and Business Structures are focusing on the task of how to effectively and efficiently allocate the work.
- *Processes* - Organizational Infrastructure defines the processes and how decisions are made.
- *Capabilities* - Team and Individual Capabilities subsequently challenging the skill base that is required to run the organization as its mission and goals have been outlined.
- *Control* - Target Setting and Performance Management deal with the control mechanism to ensure strategic goals are pursued as intended.

This approach to organization management basically explains how organizations work today and enables effective execution of strategic goals.

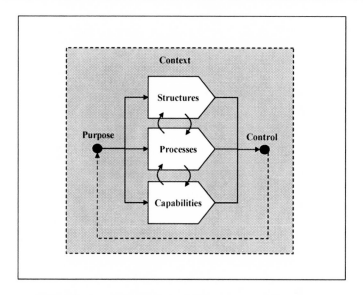

Exhibit II-1: Organizational Effectiveness Framework

A definition in this regard that serves both the business practioner and the organizational science researcher is:

"Organizational Effectiveness is the result of effective interplay of a company's vision and strategic goals with the chosen structural design, processes, assigned responsibilities, available skills, knowledge and capabilities, and reliable performance measurement."

Each category of the definition fits to a particular stage of the strategic management process:

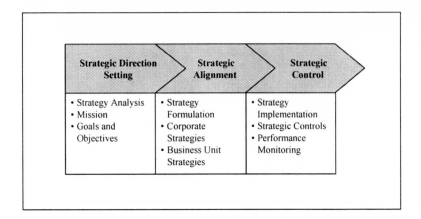

Exhibit II-2: Strategic Management Process

Eventually, by combining the strategic perspective and the core categories of Organizational Effectiveness, a robust, simple and plausible framework can be created.

*   Organizational Context covers the requirements highlighted under Strategic Direction Setting. Determining purpose, deriving mission and strategic goals, understanding the environment from a competitive perspective and from a stakeholder perspective all clearly overlap. Thus, strategic direction-setting is the first common goal of strategic and organization management.

*   Strategic alignment summarizes various activities to define and execute strategies on corporate and business-unit levels. In particular, the execution part requires design activities. By creating appropriate structures, processes, and capabilities, the organization has to respond to the strategic guidelines to ensure appropriate delivery.

- Strategic Control needs a counterpart in organization management as well. Performance Management and Target Setting provides this linkage.

By combining process steps of the strategic management process and core categories of Organizational Effectiveness, a framework has been created that is strategically driven, holistic and comprehensive in application to all organizational management activities, and applicable to today's business requirements:

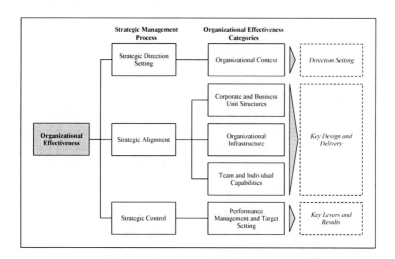

Exhibit II-3: Organizational Effectiveness Framework

This framework will serve as a guide through the following chapters.

Core Elements of Strategic Direction Setting

The systematic view of Organizational Context starts with the purpose of a company. Long before a business hits the market, it has been created with a clear entrepreneurial sense. The initial business idea born by ideation, necessity, incident, or simply to earn money lays the ground for Organizational Context. Purpose and its subsequent mission lead to a value framework and, as a next step, the interplay of implicit and explicit values creates a culture. Purpose, values, and culture are the foundations for building capabilities. Strategic Capabilities, which are often considered to be a "given" to a firm, are mostly the result of decades-long efforts to develop them. The incredible marketing capabilities of Procter & Gamble or the outstanding quality of Mercedes Benz are more the expression of values and cultures that have formed those skills over years than the result of short-term campaigns. Another aspect stemming from culture and value background is how a company interacts with its environment. Organizational Fairness describes how fair a company deals with its key stakeholders such as communities, environment, shareholders, and employees. Stakeholders like unions, suppliers, and customers are important, too, to understand the company's reputation of "fairness." In summary, the key aspects of Organizational Context are the following attributes:

- *Purpose, Mission and Values*
- *Organizational Culture, Capabilities and Fairness*

Business runs in heavy cycles since general economic conditions, competition and other conditions are constantly changing. Hence, a company needs the ability to be adaptable to organizational change. Industries like construction, professional services, or luxury consumer goods are typically faced with the most severe effects of up- or down-swing cycles. If business has to cope with excessive demands and market growth rates, like the software industry in the mid-1990s or e-business in the late-1990s, the need for creativity emerges. There is simply no time to apply controlled and coordinated organizational changes. People need to find creative solutions to keep the business running and growing. Last, if business operates either in very mature markets or in extremely innovative segments it is essential to nurture entrepreneurial spirit. In both cases entrepreneurship provides the remedy to outdated product offerings. In summary, all these elements can be combined in the Organizational Context.

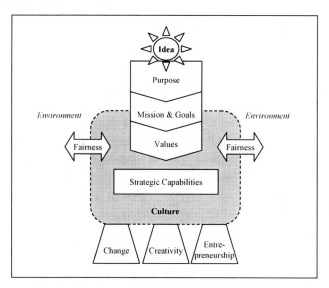

Exhibit II-4: Organizational Context

5   Purpose, Mission, Goals and Values

Every single company has been established with a fairly clear purpose, a good reason for a company's existence and the basis for value creation. In most cases the major purpose can be clearly identified and categorized. However, lots of corporations have either changed their initial purpose significantly over the years or have deliberately added multiple other types of business that hinder clear categorization. Whereas for some companies business conditions lead to a conversion of purpose, other companies are forced to find a new purpose due to changes in laws, health concerns, consumer behavior, or ethical shifts in society. The tobacco industry, for example, is heavily impacted by the shift to a healthier lifestyle and the governmental attempts to restrict smoking due to surging health costs associated with the consumption of nicotine. Players in this industry have proactively taken steps to change their course away from the initial purpose of being cigarette companies. Besides the companies that have transformed or evolved to multifaceted purposes, there is the group of companies that have attached different kinds of business activities to their core business. Each company that has integrated others along its industry supply chain has automatically added another activity. Airlines today, for example, are operating as travel agencies, too. And the automotive-industry players run their own banking and leasing operations. Although the business scope has enlarged, the purpose is still being car manufacturers. Purpose should not be confused with the mission and Strategic Capabilities. The purpose is the basis of each company; mission statements and Strategic Capabilities are results and should be aligned with it.

Mission statements summarize purpose and values and serve as a guideline for future activities. They express clearly the purpose and idea of a company, the way to achieve strategic goals and the value concept.

The mission statement outlines the simple reason for existence, as the following example illustrates:

> "*A mission statement is an enduring statement of purpose for an organization that identifies the scope of its operations in product and market terms, and reflects its values and priorities.*"[7]

Writing a mission statement has evolved to an art. Since everybody has one and investors, customers, and potential new employees are attracted through smart and convincing statements, some key principles have to be taken into account:

- Unique and specific
- Quick to grasp, easy to understand - not too long
- Clear and crisp message - no flat notes
- Accessible to all recipients
- Ideally, in a pretty nice format or even framed
- Contain keywords

A recent study has shown that certain words are very often mentioned in mission statements: [8]

- Customer (appears in 70% of all statements)
- Service (68%)
- Quality (56%)
- Employees (52%)

Companies have also identified the mission statement as a useful vehicle to market themselves on the investment and employment markets or to differentiate themselves from competition. Hence, mission statements often are overloaded with state-of-the-art keywords and presented or posted on the Web in a splendid format. But if statements are too flashy, their honesty and trustworthiness will be questioned because they have degenerated to marketing vehicles and are pursuing different objectives. Employees should be able to identify themselves with the articulated mission. If this is the case, they will feel stimulated and energized to pursue the corporate mission because it is simply aligned with their own values, goals, and objectives.

Value management or business ethics has evolved to its own management discipline. It is taught at business schools and universities. There is a wide range of journals and websites dedicated to this subject, and even specific associations and institutes around this topic have emerged.[9] There were certainly major breakthroughs that have brought the meaning of ethics to the field of business and management. Just a century ago, children under age ten had to work six days a week and workers were disabled through their risky jobs – without any insurance coverage. Some industries have been controlled by corrupted trusts leaving no space for small- and medium-sized businesses to survive. Today, unions and laws control wages and labor conditions, weekly work hours are limited, and employees are insured against disability. All these are society's achievements. There are some indications that business ethics are getting worse again, as seen in the accounting scandals of the early 2000s and increasing "white-collar" criminality indicate.[10]

Values and ethics are very important for the effective organization and they should be exactly aligned with the mission. The value concept of a firm is often called the "credo." It generally describes the value framework to which the company aspires to operate.[11] The credo defines the company-wide dos and don'ts that are implicitly considered in each decision-making process. A credo or code of ethics can be found today in each different type of organization. In most cases the code of ethics is, like the mission statement, written down and appropriately published either in brochures, framed presentations, or on the website. Despite all of the positive intent, there is a good portion of skepticism about codes of ethics.[12] Some employees consider the content of these codes as platitudes and nonsense. The ethics would be somewhat disconnected from business realities.[13] If this is the case, the code of ethics is useless.

Being a good corporate citizen pays back, as the report on the one hundred best corporate citizens has just recently pinpointed. In this study it is shown that the leading corporate citizens perform more than ten percentile points higher than the average in terms of sales growth, profit growth, and return on equity.[14] The selection of the top hundred is made based on a stakeholder analysis incorporating shareholders, employees, community, environment, minorities and women, and customers.

6 Organizational Culture, Strategic Capabilities and Fairness

Missions, goals, and codes of ethics ideally are found in brochures, presentations, booklets and/or on websites. That is different from the Organizational Culture, as the latter hardly can be summarized or described in a presentation or a statement. The Organizational Culture is always there, even if an attempt is made to avoid having a certain culture. The culture can be seen as good or bad, and it might be hard to understand how to effectively change it.[15] Like the character of an individual, the Organizational Culture is the personality of the organization. It is the sum of values, codes of ethics, assumptions, behavior and decision-making practices.[16] Additionally, it is expressed through tangible signs, the so-called artifacts:[17]

- Architecture and décor of the buildings and offices
- Clothing people wear
- Rituals, symbols, and celebrations
- Commonly used language or jargon
- Written and published mission statements or credos
- Status symbols such as company cars, office style and furnishing, window offices, paintings and other art
- Structural organizational design (very rigid and multileveled functional hierarchical designs reveal a different culture than a flat network-based structure with multiple communication cross-bridges)

It is a challenging task for an outsider to interpret a distinct culture by analyzing structures and processes. Very often, only insiders are able to create the implicit link between artifacts and Organizational Culture by being part of the culture day after day. On the other hand, insiders very often do not sense symbols as expressions of a specific culture any longer and only with the help of outsiders (new hires, consultants, customers or suppliers) is an articulation of the culture possible.

With regard to Organizational Effectiveness, the foremost interest lies on how to shape an Organizational Culture that enables the organization to perform stronger. However, if mission and value are made up for marketing purposes only and do not reflect the true goals and ethics, it will negatively impact the culture. Organizational Effectiveness can vastly profit from the "right" culture.[18] Although culture is truly the result of different intangible characteristics like value, behavior, assumptions, feelings, and rewards, there are some distinct tangible levers that can be designed in a way to promote effectiveness. If mission, goals, structures and processes, and artifacts reflect the true value framework of an organization, the pursued "personality" of the organization should emerge quasi automatically. Additionally, the leader should be a proactive influence on the culture through leadership by example.

Strategic Capabilities

Strategic Capabilities can be described according to certain patterns and by using distinct examples.

- *Alignment:* Strategic Capabilities should be aligned with purpose, mission and values. Although this is a matter of course, some companies sometimes simply disregard their initial purpose and the subsequent Strategic Capabilities built years earlier and do not make use of them. Apple, for example, had basically forgotten about its entrepreneurial roots and was struggling to find its place in the competitive computer hardware market. By turning back to its inventive spirit, it bounced back with innovative product designs.

- *Core Competencies:* Strategic Capabilities should reflect the core competencies that are available within the firm and that can be leveraged across different products and markets.[19] In particular, formerly regulated industries that were not customer-focused, such as utilities, telecommunications, and railroads need to refocus: their initial core competencies were based on streamlined operations, maintaining and managing complex networks, and asset utilization. Now they need customer focus and marketing skills. Whereas previously the markets were regulated and customers had only limited choices, today brand names and images have to be developed and proactively managed.

- *Uniqueness and Sustainability:* It is certainly not enough to just copy the capabilities of key competitors. Strategic Capabilities evolve over a longer term, so copying does not yield significant short-term market success. They should have a long-term effect and should be difficult to copy.

- *Competitive Advantage:* A competitive advantage is the bare minimum a Strategic Capability should provide. Competitive advantages are traditionally categorized in cost leadership, differentiation, and focus.[20] Ideally, a competitive advantage created through specific Strategic Capabilities is the source of entrepreneurial surplus profits and shareholder value.

Strategic Capabilities are often considered to be just a "given" to a company. This is not true, though. Even if a brand name was introduced in the market years ago, in some cases more than a century ago, and has established strong name recognition, it still requires lots of effort and targeted marketing activities to keep it alive and valuable.[21] The appropriate foundation is a prerequisite for a Strategic Capability, and developing and nurturing the capability can take decades to leverage it successfully in the market.

Strategic Capabilities are extremely important in the face of today's competitive markets. They are not easy to acquire and, in most cases, are deeply rooted in a company's history. The management of Strategic Capabilities to foster Organizational Effectiveness is based on two main pillars:

1. *Alignment of* **Company Focus** *with Strategic Capabilities*
   Strategic Capabilities should express the clear focus of a company. Of course, it would be great being the quality leader, a superb marketer, the greatest inventor, and best product designer of the industry. But that's not realistic. The company needs focus; it needs a center of gravity as an overriding principle and guideline.

2. *Alignment of* **Strategic Direction** *with Strategic Capabilities*
   As a result of strategic direction changes, restructuring, and M&A situations, companies sometimes lose the "feeling" for their capabilities. It is one of the foremost tasks of designing effective organizations to ensure that capabilities are considered while changing strategic direction. If certain capabilities are simply not available as soon as a new strategy gets executed, the likelihood of success is very low. Change of strategic direction should also be scrutinized in detail to ensure that important capabilities won't erode over time.

Organizational Fairness

The stakeholder group of a company can be described as a group that has a legitimate interest in the company's activities. Typical *external* stakeholders are:

- Customers
- Suppliers
- Unions
- Communities

- Charitable organizations
- Tax authorities
- Governmental authorities
- Environment

Typical internal stakeholders groups are:
- Shareholders
- Employees

All these constituents are influenced by the company's activity; they profit from them, they suffer from them, or they are a real threat to them. The stakeholders are particularly interested in how "fair" a company treats them. Honesty and fairness are a part of the business ethics and Organizational Culture. Especially in difficult economic conditions, fairness does not always prevail, as major restructurings and massive layoffs indicate.[22]

The elements of Organizational Fairness can be clustered in several aspects:[23]

- Fair payment and treatment of employees
- Stronger shareholder dividends growth than employee compensation
- Company's contribution to community affairs
- Payment of fair share of taxes (versus use of offshore havens)
- Fair treatment of customers
- Fair treatment of suppliers
- No questionable business dealings
- No convictions or lawsuits regarding environmental violations
- Executive compensation growth in line with non-executive employee compensation growth

- Executive compensation in line with shareholder earnings.

These aspects reveal how fairly a company behaves. And Organizational Fairness is important because it can be spotted easily and influence the public opinion of a company domestically and internationally. Besides the fact that "bad" corporate citizens perform statistically slower than best-in-class firms, negative image will threaten the immediate relationships with customers, suppliers, and strategic partners.[24] Effective organizations tend to be fair partners to all their constituents. Mostly, fairness emerges as a consequence of having established clear missions and values. However, in order to make sure that negative impacts through questionable behavior towards stakeholders are avoided, regular screening of the aspects mentioned above is advised.

7   Organizational Flexibility

Organizational Culture and Strategic Capabilities are important for the strategic direction-setting process. Once a strategy has been determined and carried out, it is important for a company to react within the strategy's boundaries with utmost flexibility. Organizational Flexibility contains three major elements:

- Organizational Creativity
- Organizational Adaptability
- Entrepreneurship and Intrapreneurship

Organizational Creativity

Initially, creativity is defined as an individual skill. It is essential in all moments of life. It determines how appropriately, crisply, and clearly people communicate; it influences the way they think; it is a guide for actions and reactions; and it influences behavior. Everybody has creativity. It is not unique to selected individuals.[25] Creativity can be applied to organizations as well. Especially in unexpected situations (positive and negative), an organization, as a group of individuals, needs to be creative too. The term corporate creativity deals with this phenomenon on a company level.[26]

Companies almost never reach a balanced and sustainable state. Business involves fluctuation around healthy growth and profitability figures, but somehow it appears to be impossible to uphold a certain amount of revenue growth and profitability over a long period of time As a consequence, change will always be part of a company's business. Sixty years ago economist **Joseph Schumpeter** created a phrase that highlights the positive aspect of change: *creative destruction.*[27] This means a redesign effort for a company is beneficial as long as the result is a more creative solution than before. The threat of changing business conditions can also be a useful moment in the lifetime of a company to regain strength and rebuild eroding capabilities. Organizational Creativity is decisive for such moments in which appropriate reaction is required. The ability to improvise is an expression of creativity. In some companies, the tendency to improvise is very present, based on the need to find temporary solutions to bridge long and complex decision processes to agree on a long-term remedy. Often these improvisations automatically become the final solution over time.

The management for corporate creativity is characterized by distinct elements:[28]

- Creativity is aligned with the mission and the value framework of the firm
- Self-initiated activity by employees is encouraged and appropriately rewarded
- The company does not punish or prohibit unofficial activities. For the sake of a creative environment, it is often useful to violate some policies and procedures. The guideline, "Don't ask for permission, ask for forgiveness" illustrates a creative approach.
- Corporate creativity is pushed through rewards and diverse stimuli
- Seamless cross-company communication is good ground for creativity
- Product development is viewed as a company-wide task and not dedicated to a specialist group only that operates in a silo
- Executive sponsorship for distinct and product-focused group efforts. The term "skunkworks" has gained popularity since a separated product development team of Lockheed succeeded in the 1940s to develop the first turbine-driven warplane.[29] The team operated confidentially, in a secret mission. Skunkwork efforts are strictly product-focused

Effective organizations deserve appropriate room for creative thinking. They try to create a culture in which creativity is fostered, rewarded, and tolerated, even if it stands in opposition to certain policies.

Organizational Adaptability

Change is a necessity with respect to the company's existence, but mostly it is viewed negatively. Companies and employees are always anxious about change: change is characterized as a monster illustrating all the complex and sometimes scary human emotions and social dynamics that emerge as soon as a change situation has to be mastered.[30] However, the need for change is a reality and will increase in light of major structural changes impacting the business world.[31]

- Information as a key production factor has been made much more readily available and it can be leveraged more effectively.
- Information technology has changed entire business landscapes and the effects of e-business are revolutionary in terms of how business is done and interaction with business partners takes place.
- Communication has gotten a different meaning since information flow is much quicker, more transparent, and efficient.
- Further geographic expansion of industrialization will massively change the business landscape.
- Manual work and, increasingly, administrative functions, too, will be outsourced to low wage countries.
- Intellectual work like software development or accounting will take place in countries such as India, China, etc. where skill is available at much lower cost than in Europe or North America. Business Process Outsourcing has become a key trend.
- Population growth in highly industrialized and developed countries will slow further, whereas

growth rates are expected to rise for most developing countries. While the population in the developed countries will be aging within the next two decades, developing countries will have stronger growth potential due to a younger work force.

- The meaning of work and our attitude towards work have changed. Work is no longer considered to be a necessary evil to make a living. People are treating work as a means to fulfill their personal missions and to gain overall satisfaction. On the other hand, people have a stronger focus on living a balanced life, meaning work has to be in harmony with time for families and friends, hobbies, and other social activities.

Organizational Adaptability is eventually the capability to master the traditional change process effectively and efficiently. The process itself basically contains four different phases:[32]

1. Stagnation - the phase where internal or external reasons indicate a misfit of an organization with its competitive and stakeholder environment;
2. Preparation - the phase when decision and direction on change has been made;
3. Determination - the phase that contains the essential implementation of change;
4. Fruition - the phase when change is over and expected results are achieved.

This is just one typical framework of change. Entire theories on change management have been developed, which should not be part of an in-depth discussion at this point.[33]

Organizational Adaptability, thus, is a necessary capability that should apply to all different types and magnitudes of change.[34] As indicated, the necessity for change is based on a multitude of reasons. And change itself can take place in multiple scopes, as well. Organizational Effectiveness will profit from strong adaptability to a change situation. The quicker and quieter a company copes with it, the stronger the performance of the organization. Those companies that are able to incorporate restructuring as part of the day-to-day business do not have to deal with major downtimes or interceptions of business or a paralyzed workforce. People need to understand that change is part of business; it is a good thing and it is a necessity.

Entrepreneurship and Intrapreneurship

Entrepreneurship summarizes the business-founding spirit. It includes characteristics like risk taking and wealth creation. Each corporation is based on an inventive business idea, the acquisition or franchise of a business, and the aim to set up an independent organization. The whole theory of the firm is based on entrepreneurship. An intrapreneur has comparable characteristics. The only difference is the intrapreneur acts as an entrepreneur within large organizations.[35] The existence of intrapreneurs is important for successful organizations since these individuals introduce entrepreneurial spirit into the company and foster Organizational Creativity, openness towards change, and innovativeness. It is even possible that, through entrepreneurial spirit, an advantageous Organizational Culture evolves.[36] Intrapreneurs can be employees who search constantly for new business ideas with the objective to set up an independent business. Those types of people volunteer for new business ventures or leverage industry knowledge and work experience for their own business. They act as innovators, enablers, leaders, change agents, animators, and adventurers.[37] The latter type describes the willingness to reach out to unknown terrain, meaning entirely new types of business or organizational practices. Ideally, intrapreneurs are present across the entire company, bringing in their unique strength on all levels, functions, and processes.[38]

¹ J. Barton Cunningham, "Approaches to the Evaluation of Organizational Effectiveness," *Academy of Management Review*, Vol. 2, July 1977, pp. 465-474; Daniel R. Denison, *Corporate Culture and Organizational Effectiveness* (New York: John Wiley & Sons, 1990), pp. 36-37: Summary of Conceptual Frameworks on Organizational Effectiveness.

² Kim S. Cameron and David A. Whetten, "Organizational Effectiveness: One Model or Several?" *Organizational Effectiveness, A Comparison of Multiple Models* (New York,: Academic Press Inc., 1983), p. 1.

³ Kim S. Cameron and David A. Whetten, "Organizational Effectiveness: One Model or Several?" *Organizational Effectiveness, A Comparison of Multiple Models* (New York,: Academic Press Inc., 1983), p. 7.

⁴ Daniel R. Denison, *Corporate Culture and Organizational Effectiveness* (New York: John Wiley & Sons, 1990), pp. 4-6.

⁵ Stewart Clegg, Thomas Clarke and Eduardo Ibarra, "Millennium Management, Changing Paradigms and Organizations Studies," *Human Relations* (Thousand Oaks, CA: SAGE Publications, Vol. 54, No. 1), pp. 31-36.

⁶ Geary A. Rummler and Alan P. Brache, *Improving Performance: How to Manage the White Space on the Organization Chart* (San Francisco: Jossey-Bass Publishers, 1990), pp. 15-18 introduce an "organization," "process," and "job/performer" structure.

⁷ Jeffrey Abrahams, *The Mission Statement Book, 301 Corporate Mission Statements from America's Top Companies* (Berkeley, CA: Ten Speed Press, 1999), p. 14; Richard L. Daft, *Organization Theory and Design*, 6th ed. (South-Western College Publishing, Cincinnati, OH: 1998), p. 48.

⁸ Jeffrey Abrahams, *The Mission Statement Book, 301 Corporate Mission Statements from America's Top Companies* (Berkeley, CA: Ten Speed Press, 1999), pp. 25-26.

⁹ Richard T. George, *Business Ethics*, 4ᵗʰ edition (Englewood Cliffs, NJ: Prentice Hall, 1995), p. v.

¹⁰ Verne E. Henderson, *What's Ethical in Business* (New York: McGraw-Hill, 1992), pp. 15-23.

¹¹ Patrick M. Lencioni, "Make Your Values Mean Something," *Harvard Business Review*, July 2002, pp. 113-114. Reveals an illustrative example of failed value management; John Dalla Costa, *Ethical Imperative: Why Moral Leadership is Good for Business* (Reading, MA: Addison-Wesley, 1998), pp. 203-204.

[12] David Drennan, *Transforming Company Culture: Getting Your Company From Where You Are Now to Where You Want to Be* (London, UK: McGraw-Hill, 1992), pp. 47-48.

[13] David Drennan, *Transforming Company Culture: Getting Your Company From Where You Are Now to Where You Want to Be* (London, UK: McGraw-Hill, 1992), p. 48 and William Roth, "Business Ethics – Grounded in System Thinking," *Journal of Organizational Excellence*, Vol. 21, No. 3, Summer 2001, p. 4 explains why companies fail to improve ethics.

[14] Business Ethics, Corporate Social Responsibility Report, 100 Best Corporate Citizens 2002.

[15] Rob Goffee and Gareth Jones, *The Character of the Corporation: How Your Company's Culture Can Make or Break Your Business* (New York : HarperBusiness, 1998), p. 59.

[16] Daniel R. Denison, *Corporate Culture and Organizational Effectiveness* (New York: John Wiley & Sons, 1990), p. 2

[17] Jeffrey R. Cornwall and Baron Perlman, *Organizational Entrepreneurship* (Homewood, IL: Irwin, 1989), p. 67.

[18] Daniel R. Denison, *Corporate Culture and Organizational Effectiveness* (New York: John Wiley & Sons, 1990), p. 8: The Consistency Hypothesis.

[19] Danny Miller, Russell Eisenstat and Nathaniel Foote, "Strategy from the Inside-Out: Building Capability-Creating Organizations," *California Management Review*, Vol. 44, No. 3, Spring 2002, p. 41.

[20] Michael E. Porter, *Competitive Strategy: Techniques for Analyzing Industries and Competitors* (New York: The Free Press, 1998), pp. 60-78.

[21] Gerry Khermouch, Stanley Holmes and Moon Ihlwan, Cover Story, *Business Week*, August 6, 2001.

[22] John Dalla Costa, *Ethical Imperative: Why Moral Leadership is Good for Business* (Reading, MA: Addison-Wesley, 1998), p. 161.

[23] Leslie Bendaly, *Organization 2005: Four Steps Organizations Must Take to Succeed in the New Economy* (Indianapolis, IN: Park Ave. Productions, 2000), p. 30.

[24] John Dalla Costa, *Ethical Imperative: Why Moral Leadership is Good for Business* (Reading, MA: Addison-Wesley, 1998), p. 161.

[25] Robert Lowe, *Improvisation, Inc.: Harnessing Spontaneity to Engage People and Groups* (San Francisco, CA: Jossey-Bass/Pfeiffer, 2000), p. 1.

[26] Alan G. Robinson and Sam Stern, *Corporate Creativity: How Innovation and Improvement Actually Happen* (San Francisco, CA: Berrett-Koehler Publishers, 1997), pp. 5-6.

[27] Paul Taffinder, *Big Change: A Route-Map for Corporate Transformation* (New York: John Wiley & Sons, 1998), p. 266.

[28] Alan G. Robinson and Sam Stern, *Corporate Creativity: How Innovation and Improvement Actually Happen* (San Francisco, CA: Berrett-Koehler Publishers, 1997), p. 12.

[29] Warren Bennis and Patricia Ward Biedermann, *Organizing Genius: the Secret of Creative Collaboration* (Reading, MA: Addison-Wesley, 1997); Gregory G. Dess and G.T. Lumpkin, *Strategic Management: Creating Competitive Advantages* (New York: McGraw-Hill, 2001), p. 398.

[30] Jeanie Daniel Duck, *The Change Monster: The Human Forces that Fuel or Foil Corporate Transformation and Change* (New York: Crown Business, 2001), preface.

[31] Leon Martel, *Mastering Change: The Key to Business Success* (New York, NY: Simon & Schuster, 1986), p. 45-178

[32] Jeanie Daniel Duck, *The Change Monster: The Human Forces that Fuel or Foil Corporate Transformation and Change* (New York: Crown Business, 2001), pp. 19-35.

[33] Soeren Dressler, *Reorganisation und Krise* (Stuttgart, Germany: Schaeffer-Poeschel, 1995), pp. 225-227.

[34] Paul Taffinder, *Big Change: A Route-Map for Corporate Transformation* (New York, NY: John Wiley & Sons, 1998), pp. 36-38.

[35] Jeffrey R. Cornwall and Baron Perlman, *Organizational Entrepreneurship* (Homewood, IL: Irwin, 1989), p. 7.

[36] Jeffrey R. Cornwall and Baron Perlman, *Organizational Entrepreneurship* (Homewood, IL: Irwin, 1989), pp. 68-69.

[37] Ronnie Lessem, *Intrapreneurship: How to Be an Enterprising Individual in a Successful Business* (Hampshire, UK: Wildwood House, 1988), p. 3.

[38] Ronnie Lessem, *Intrapreneurship: How to Be an Enterprising Individual in a Successful Business* (Hampshire, UK: Wildwood House, 1988), p. 7.

"Why businesses still need org charts"

Strategic Alignment: Key Design & Delivery Elements

The previous chapter discussed in depth the meaning and importance of the Organizational Context for Organizational Effectiveness. The context has to be managed proactively and each opportunity to do so should be used accordingly. The potential of a well-aligned Organizational Context is tremendous and, as pointed out, there are multiple occasions to form, shape, influence, and manage it. However, managing the context is a much more indirect activity compared to designing an organizational structure or defining a process flow. The techniques to be used require ongoing fine-tuning and show their effects mostly in a mid- or long-term perspective. The change of an Organizational Culture cannot be executed overnight. If done right, it can take years. By contrast, the change of an organizational structure or a process design can be done relatively quickly. That's the terrain on which most CEOs focus because they can expect immediate results. Mistakenly, that is often the reason why the Key Design and Delivery Elements are perceived by most senior executives as the entire framework of Organizational Effectiveness. But only if the context is aligned with the overall business strategy is a fruitful organizational design management possible. Even the smartest and leanest design, the most powerful and streamlined processes, and world-class recruiting and training programs won't heal a severely unhealthy Organizational Culture where people mistrust each other, fiefdoms are maintained, creativity is parched, and the mass of employees silently opposes every change effort going on. It's not possible to stress it strongly enough: Organizational structures and processes and even talented people are useless if the Organizational Context is not effectively aligned with the strategy.

A useful term to paraphrase Key Design and Delivery Elements is "Organizational Architecture." This term evolved in the early 1990s as an attempt to enlarge the focus of organization management from the purely structural perspective, i.e., what is in the boxes and how to connect them, to a broader design perspective of complex organization.[1] Besides the formal structures, it includes processes, technologies, people selection and development, and social aspects.[2] An architect takes care of the basic *structure* of a building and materials, use of natural daylight, air conditioning and heat, connection of sectors and different floors, emergency exits, water provision, waste disposal, and so on. The organization manager has to work on much more than on the organizational *structure,* as well. In particular, information technology has had a major influence on organizational architecture. Since, in the history of organization management, information flow was closely related to the hierarchical structure of an organization and power within corporations was based on information monopoly, the use of modern information technology (IT) has changed this principle radically. While organizations before the use of IT were mostly designed to allow efficient information allocation and reporting, process coordination today can be executed much more flexibly and creatively. Eventually, IT opened the door to a new set of innovative and effective organizational designs and processes unavailable before. Corporations in the new millennium will look significantly different from the templates used by Ford and Taylor. Although their principles are still relevant today, there are some significant advancements and key trends to be taken into account.

- *Digitization*
  The last decade has seen rapid growth for the use of digitized data techniques.[3] Most major corporations today are using some kind of Enterprise Resource Planning system (ERP) that provides an integrated information technology and data landscape of the entire business. Through ERP systems, operations, supply chain, customer management, and financial information are interlinked and consistent. Integrated dataflow concerning each business transaction is possible. Other elements are technologies such as barcode scanning and navigation systems. Scanning techniques are used, for example, to make complex distribution networks transparent. Firms such as UPS, Federal Express, and Amazon.com offer their customers the ability to track their delivery status online. Even industries such as railroads are using these techniques. They provide power plants with information on coal deliveries by tracking the status of their various coal trains. Credit cards, mobile phones, pagers, airline and hotel customer programs, and Internet purchases – there are multiple entry points for digitized data. Thus, by using digitized data points, a company is able to manage end-to-end processes effectively and can reduce functional allocation of work. Digitization reduces the frequency of organizational silos.
- *Globalization*
  Globalization has been a buzzword for almost two decades.[4] Expansion of markets and access to low-cost suppliers and a low-wage workforce were

traditionally the core motives to expand business operations on a global level. Due to customer requirements some companies were basically forced to get on the global stage.[5] The increase of the Foreign Direct Investment volume to more than 600% after 1985 is a clear indication of this.[6] The Internet and eBusiness have further strengthened the trend to do business abroad. Before becoming a global company, each company has to do its homework, defining which market segments to target, which sales channels to utilize, how to design the supply chain, and how to ensure quality levels. From an organization management perspective the need to build international activities has to be managed carefully. Going global often means adding a new dimension to the existing structure. Thus, the matrix organization is often the chosen structure for global companies with a geographic and functional /divisional dimension.[7] Furthermore, leveraging of Strategic Capabilities has to be made possible within global organizations, which requires knowledge transfer, expatriate programs, and global branding, just to mention a few examples.

- *Business Process Outsourcing (BPO)*
  As companies in the new millennium struggle to keep administrative costs as low as possible to cope with the recent economic downturn, BPO has become an emerging organizational solution. Whereas companies in the 1980s and even more so in the 1990s started to outsource in particular IT- related tasks and software development, BPO has a much broader perspective: In order to realize best-in-class performance and to manage back office functions with the highest-quality service possible, entire HR, Finance and Accounting, Customer Management, and Procurement processes, for example, are being

outsourced and managed by specialized service providers. And instead of shifting only distinct process pieces to external service providers, such as payroll, entire business processes are targeted, such as the entire HR function including benefits administration, employee services, training and development, and compensation. BPO providers have proven to be reliable partners, and more and more companies trust them to deliver back-office processes. Due to the direct impact of BPO on Organizational Architecture, it will be discussed as Emerging Structures later in this chapter.

- *Merger and Acquisitions*
  Comparable to the globalization trend, merger and acquisition activities significantly soared in the 1990s and, as a result of the "merger mania" in some industries, only a few big players are left. Examples are the cigarette industry, defense industry, soft drinks, and shipbuilding. Merger endgames indicate how concentrated a particular industry is and which consolidation aspects can be further expected.[8] There is obviously a continuous trend that leads to merger activities according to the competitive structure of particular industries. M&As will continuously challenge traditional organizational designs since each merger situation is unique. Different structures, processes and technologies, and last but very importantly, different cultures have to be integrated.

- *Alliances and Networks*
  Companies are not only using M&A strategies to pursue their goals of market entry, technology access, and value-chain optimization. The more collaborative trend to achieve these goals is alliance and network building. Horizontal partnerships enable competitors to share resources like distribution networks or manufacturing facilities more effectively. Vertical networks focus on enhanced customer-supplier relationships to optimize entire industry value chains. In both cases, the organizational architecture will require a seamless and effective integration of the partnership activities, as well. This will lead to specific organizational units, processes, and governing principles.

- *Business Ventures*
  Companies today are intensively searching for opportunities to promote and leverage innovation. The Internet wave has provided good opportunities to establish new business ventures dedicated to the new Internet sales channel or dedicated to further improve the corporation's e-business capabilities. Furthermore, corporations are trying to cope with the recent economic downturn by refocusing on their core competencies. Non-core activities are outsourced or bundled in new business ventures. Another alternative is to establish shared service units that focus on support processes in a more efficient way than the corporation has done previously. This trend leads to various organization management challenges. Fine differentiations between core and non-core activities are required, new business ventures have to be established as independently as possible, but they have to be connected to the corporation as effectively as possible. Shared services have to be integrated into

the business processes, service pricing and service levels need to be determined.

- *Self-regulating organizations*
  Conditions will continuously change and companies will be faced more intensively than before with unforeseeable circumstances that need flexible and creative responses. Organizational Creativity and Organizational Change Adaptability stand for self-regulating mechanisms that will play a significant role in the future of organization management. Hence, teams and individuals will be required to work and operate in improvised environments and to find customer-oriented and efficient organizational solutions without corporate guidance.

- *Fuzzy boundaries*
  The new trends will blur the boundaries of today's organizations. The company's activities in mergers, partnerships, networks, business ventures, and shared services will lead to tomorrow's corporations with overlapping legal and organizational units, partnership engagements, and network activities. To define the "company" as one element will hardly be possible.

- *Project Teams*
  Teamwork is of course not a "new" trend. It is a paradigm that has been taught over decades. The importance with regard to Organizational Effectiveness has been discussed in Chapter I. However, new trends in project work will have some impact on organizational architecture, as well. As project teams have gained substantial popularity and are utilized to work on multiple companies' issues with a cross-functional perspective, the project organization of a company becomes a success factor. Project team members become stronger than today, employees

with more than one job and more than one reporting line.

- *Talent Management*
  The war for talent has become a phrase during the time of the Internet boom that has reawakened the importance of managing leadership potential and talent. Today, corporations maintain talent recruiting, selection, and retaining programs and are conducting systematical leadership development and succession planning. Providing the required team and individual capabilities will be dependent on how effective future leaders have been developed, which international experiences they gathered through expatriate assignments, and how well they are prepared for their leadership tasks.

All these trends will change substantially the organizational architecture of the business world of tomorrow. Therefore, the Key Design and Delivery Elements have to respond appropriately to all of them. Additionally, they have to make sure that the senior management can use design and delivery activities to execute the chosen strategic direction. The discussion around Key Design and Delivery Elements occurs in two major parts:

- **Part 1:** Corporate, Business Unit, and Emerging Structure
- **Part 2:** Organizational Infrastructure

Part 1:   Corporate Structures, Business Structures, and Emerging Structures

The following table illustrates how the discussion of the first part is organized.

Business Unit Structures		Corporate Structures		Emerging Structures
Basic Structures	Complex Structures	International Structures	Corporate Structures and Partnerships	Shared Services/ Business Process Outsourcing
• Functional Organization • Divisional Organization • Geographic Organization	• Matrix Organization • Hybrid Organization • Tensor-Cube Organization • Horizontal Organization	• Global Organization • Multinational Organization • International Organization	• Vertical Network Organization o Alliances o Joint Ventures • Modular Organization	• Shared Services • In-Sourcing • Business Process Management • Shared Utilities

Table: Business Unit, Corporate, and Emerging Structures

The differentiation of Corporate and Business Unit structures is mainly driven by distinct strategy focus and the subsequent organizational implications, as the following table highlights:

	Corporate	Business Unit
Strategies	**Corporate strategy** defines the scope of the company in terms of the industries and markets in which its various business units compete	**Business unit strategy** defines how the company competes within a particular industry or market **Functional strategy** defines the detailed deployment of resources at the operational level
Organizational Design Implications	• Provide support processes to Business Units, e.g., shared services • Execute and integrate M&A • Integrate international business • Integrate horizontal and network partnerships • Design of the corporation and corporate center	• Design market-facing activities • Define competitive design • Coordinate business unit, product, and functional activities

Table: Corporate and Business Unit Strategy

Emerging Structures are discussed separately from Corporate and Business Unit Structure because they can combine both. Shared Services and Business Process

Outsourcing are often driven from a corporate perspective because processes for Shared Services or BPO often impact the entire company. However, it is also possible that single business units drive certain outsourcing decisions, for example, outsourced call centers serve exclusively for certain units or even product groups. Hence, BPO can occur on both levels – corporate and business units.

8   Basic Organizational Structures

In general, four different types of Basic Organizational Structures can be distinguished:

- Functional Organizations
- Divisional Organizations
- Geographical Organizations
- Matrix Organizations.

Functional Organizations

The Functional Organization allocates the work strictly according to different functions from top to bottom. That means functional tasks like procurement, operations, marketing, sales, customer service, logistics, R and D, finance, HR, and other administrative functions are bundled in separate organizational units. The functional organization is a mono-level structural design; employees normally have only one direct reporting line to their respective functional superior. Due to the nature of each task, it is possible to differentiate up to ten different functions on the first level below the CEO. In this structure the CEO has to manage a broader span of control. Coordination between certain tasks is very important because some activities are closely related like, for example, marketing and sales or operations and procurement.

Exhibit III-1: Functional Organization

The more common application of the Functional Organization is to cluster several functions on the second organizational level below the CEO and then break down various functions in detail on the third level below the CEO. This option allows setting up a smaller Management Team that focuses closer on the strategic tasks of the corporation.

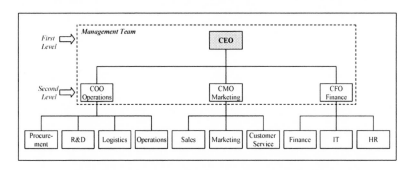

Exhibit III-2: Cascaded Functional Organization

The Functional Organization gained popularity in the early 1900s because it allowed companies to efficiently mass-produce relative homogenous products and, thus, to satisfy growing market demands. And still, for companies with a single major product line or similar product lines, the Functional Organization fits best and allows leveraging economies of scale. Additionally, Functional Organizations are often found in environments with moderate growth rates, relatively low technology, and stable business conditions. Hence, it is not surprising that functional structures still is applied in industries that formerly operated in regulated markets. Certain industries still have some players working primarily with Functional Organizations today, such as

- Railroads
- Utilities
- Airlines
- Telecommunication.

Other characteristics are specialization and volume bundling. By strictly focusing on functional capabilities, these organizations can develop in-depth knowledge and skills to best fulfill their functional tasks.[9] Mainly, sophisticated operations, sales, and finance knowledge and skills allow efficiency advantages. Bundling can increase efficiency. The company-wide concentration of procurement volume is the basis for selecting preferred suppliers, achieving low purchasing cost and excellent supply quality. Bundling of other functional activities, such as operations, finance, HR, R and D, and logistics, allows application of benchmarks and best practices and guides the way towards a leading edge financial organization, for example. In contrast to other organization forms in which functions are spread over various business units and/or regions, concentration of functions will improve the respective functional activity significantly. All these advantages work out as long as the company aims to bring only one or few very comparable product lines to market. Due to their product focus, functionally structured companies have a tendency to vertically integrate suppliers and customers to expand their business and get better control for up- and downstream value chain proportions. Accordingly, it's often the case that the aforementioned industries own parts of their supplier network. Risks of Functional Organizations are closely related to the nature of this organizational type. Lower flexibility is often the result of activity concentration and bundling. If certain capabilities and decision authorities need to be decentralized in various business units or regions, it will certainly be a disadvantage to have them centralized elsewhere in a functional silo.[10] If the sales force always has to reach out to finance to check back payment terms, it will delay and hinder the selling process. Also, if R and D pursues product development strategies that are far off customer requirements and realistic price ranges, the inflexibility of the structure is obvious. This highlights a second challenge of Functional Organizations: communication flow and decision-making practices are hierarchically organized. It will take much too long to inform operations about quality issues that are reported to the customer management desk. Vice versa, information regarding potential logistical problems causing delays in deliveries will be transmitted to sales and customer management too slowly to inform the customer before the delay occurs. Furthermore, the functional structure creates bottlenecks on the top. Since information flows vertically, decisions can pile up at the management level and not be made timely enough. The communication issue of functional structures has been addressed often and basically opened the door for all types of multidimensional organizations. Since information flow is so cumbersome in this structure, innovation and creativity is hampered too. Useful feedback from customers gets processed and transmitted too slowly to R and D and operations, and new technological breakthroughs, product features, and materials will not be communicated to sales quickly enough to promote the unique selling proposition of certain products.

Despite the disadvantages and risks of the Functional Organization, it is still important and relevant. It is the "mother" of all organizational designs and illustrates the basic principle of allocating work. Regardless of how many business units or geographies will be incorporated in the organizational structure and how many dimensions will be added, there will always be a functional split of work. An organization like Nestlé, who maintains 9 divisions, 18 business units and more than 120 brands units in more than 150 countries, will still have certain dedicated manufacturing operations, marketing activities, sales force, and customer management tasks for one single product line. Thus, they still have a functional root in their structure despite dominance of other organizational types.

As already indicated, functional structures are the first organizational principle to be applied in the company's start-up phase. From a strategic perspective, Functional Organizations work best if cost leadership is the predominant goal. The effects of focus and bundling can drive cost out of functional processes. Furthermore, through use of benchmarks, cost-saving data can be defined as targets. The functional perspective is often preferred in environments in which the operations function is considered the single most important source for success. Thus, an automotive firm like Ford, for example, operated until the late 1990s with a Functional Organization. Although Ford maintains multiple different product lines and operates across the globe, on the second level below the CEO a differentiation in administration, operations, finance, and financial services was made. Disregarding financial services for the moment – it can be characterized more as a division than as a function – the functional allocation of work can be identified as the guiding organizational principle. On the third level the functional principle is cascaded further down. Even marketing and sales is categorized under the roof of operations. This mirrors the immense predominance of operations within Ford. The assignment of regional responsibilities in addition to the functional breakdown indicates further improvements of the pure functional model.

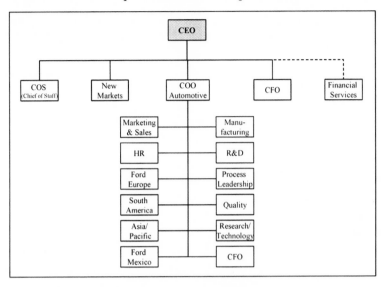

Exhibit III-3: Ford's Functional Organization until 1998[11]

Predominance of the operations function can often be found in network-based businesses, also. Railroad companies, for example, have to operate large and complex rail networks. The ability to manage the network efficiently means train schedules have to be interlinked, connection times have to be short but cars should be able to make their connection, yard operations have to ensure that the right cars are attached in a timely manner to the right trains, and slow orders due to track maintenance or bad track conditions should be as few as possible. Market conditions for railroads are relatively stable and new products are not often introduced in this industry so that Functional Organizations fit this industry very well.

Another application of Functional Organization is in restructuring situations. Corporations that have differentiated in too many units or gained a large number of units through a merger situation often temporarily choose the functional structure to consolidate and realize saving potentials. However, in these cases, the functional structure will be replaced very soon by more advanced organizational models.

Divisional Organization

The Divisional Organization describes all types of organizational structures in which a "unit" and not a function is the guiding organizational principle. The divisional structure allows a corporation to be organized according to products and services, product groups, major products group, product programs, business units, divisions, profit centers, or legal entities.

The basic idea of a Divisional Organization is to produce several independent units that operate like "miniature businesses." Comparability of products and product groups, similar market and customer conditions, and strategic conformity are distinguishing factors that lead to the creation of divisions. Within single divisions we often find a replication of Functional Organizations. An example that very clearly illustrates divisions is Sara Lee, with food and beverage, intimates and underwear, and household products divisions.

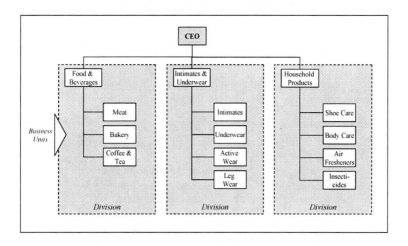

Exhibit III-4: Sara Lee's Divisional Organization

Within the distinct divisions and business units, the further breakdown according to product groups depends on the uniqueness of production, R and D, marketing, and sales activities. In the Sara Lee example, the meat business unit obviously has significantly different functional requirements than the other business units (bakery and coffee and tea). Thus, it is required to maintain specific production facilities, manage a unique supply chain, and partly use a specific distribution network. On the level below the business units, the functional structure with some overlapping activities can be found again.

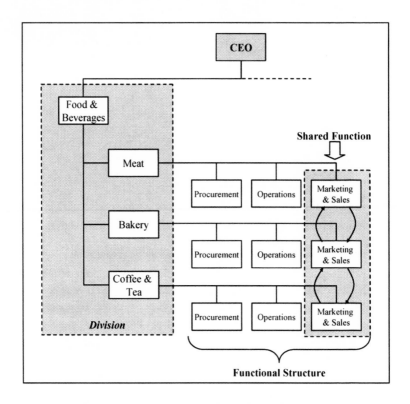

Exhibit III-5: Sara Lee's Functional Breakdown

The Divisional Organization fits best to situations in which companies maintain a wide variety of product groups and differences between product groups are significant. Through bundling of all functional activities in smaller units, coordination and communication between departments can be accelerated and improved. Product-specific market inputs can be quickly transmitted to operations, R and D, and procurement and vice versa. Hence, the divisional structure is much more flexible than the functional model in reacting to customer requirements, market changes, competitive moves, and general changes in the environment. In particular, if industries are heavily dependent on new technologies, the divisional structure enables development and implementation of market- and supply-driven new technologies and products much more effectively than the functional structure would. By delegating decision rights to the divisional level this organization can furthermore act and react more quickly in the marketplace. The division is basically a stand-alone business venture and, if it is defined as a profit center, advantages are even greater since it has to manage its own profit and loss statement.

Although adapting to unstable business conditions is a core strength, there is a potential risk that the better market and competitive knowledge of the division will be used to misinform the corporate level about true performance. For a division manager it can be beneficial to hide certain business issues and to use its stronger business knowledge to explain actual weak performances. In the same way as Functional Organizations create functional silos, divisional structures can develop a strong divisional fiefdom culture, too. Division managers interpret their role as almost entirely independent and are often unwilling to follow corporate strategies and policies. Any kind of corporate service and control will be neglected, and yielding advantages through shared services is strongly hampered. Sometimes strategic actions taken by divisions can even violate the overall corporate strategy. Further risks are the elimination of economies of scale. Particularly, in cases in which product lines have only a few overlaps and basically all functional activities have to be designed specifically for the division, it can become a "boutique" that has less competitive potential than competitors with much bigger shares of the market. Also, corporations with divisional structures are generally pretty open to further diversification. The firm can easily lose its focus and initial Strategic Capabilities and wind up in a complex and non-consistent product portfolio.

Maintaining a clear strategy is the toughest challenge for corporations with multiple divisions and business units. As indicated, fiefdoms and unclear strategic focus can weaken a corporation's position and can have negative impacts on the corporate brand. The Divisional Organization is usually chosen to execute a differentiation strategy. The limited potential to use economies of scale indicates the restriction of cost-leadership strategies. Multi-brand companies like Nestlé, Procter & Gamble, Unilever, and Johnson & Johnson are, for the most part, using the divisional philosophy. But other industries, like pharmaceuticals, chemicals, office equipment, or electronic appliances, will find a good use for divisional structures, as well. Companies like Hewlett Packard that had too many different business units have streamlined their unit structure to comprehensive divisions that can ensure compatibility of products and reduce complexity. As a result, HP has consolidated its more than eighty business units into three divisions: computing systems, imaging and printing, and IT services.

Geographic Organizations

The Geographic Organization is relatively closely related to the divisional structure. In contrast to creating divisions, geographies are the guiding organizational principle. Basically, the mono-level Geographic Organization consolidates all business activities including sourcing, operations, marketing, and sales within one particular regional unit. The Geographic Organization should not be mistaken with the legal entity structure that corporations establish as soon as they start international business activities. Among the first steps to do business in foreign countries is to set up legal entities. From a business perspective, divisional or functional principles often overlay the legal structure, as the example of a European construction supplier illustrates:

Guiding Organizational Principle	Divisions	Legal Entities					
		Company France	Company Spain	Company Germany	Company Italy	Company Austria	Company Poland
	Division I Concrete	Production facility Sales facility	Production facility		Production facility Sales facility		
	Division II Bond Concrete		Production facility Sales facility	Production facility Sales facility	Sales facility	Sales facility	
	Division III Bricks	Sales facility			Production facility Sales facility	Production facility	Production facility Sales facility
	Division IV Brick Components	Production facility Sales facility		Production facility Sales facility		Production facility Sales facility	Production facility Sales facility

Exhibit III-6: Divisional Organization with Regional Legal Entities[12]

The Geographic Organization can be found when a company decides to organize its business around geographies independent from existing legal entities. Geographies are the predominant structure to allocate decision rights and authority.

The basic idea of Geographic Organizations is somewhat comparable to the divisional structure. The corporation defines "smaller" units that operate basically as a replica of the entire firm with the only difference being region-specific. In most cases this organization form is driven by specific customer needs, products, supply chain, and manufacturing requirements that are unique to a particular region. The Geographic Organization can be cascaded essentially two ways: either a breakdown by function or a breakdown by divisions. The following example illustrates:

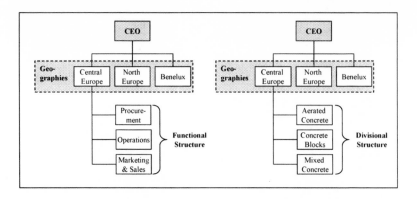

Exhibit III-7: Geographic Organizations with Different Breakdowns

In particular, in situations where operations and customer management are more effectively done in certain regions, the geographic approach should be considered. Requirements from an operations perspective are access to raw materials and parts, a simple and direct supply chain, relatively low manufacturing cost, and a simple production technology. By this, manufacturing facilities can be set up quickly and easily, operations know-how won't be a bottleneck, and transportation cost for raw materials or unfinished input products can be kept as low as possible. Marketing and sales will be favorable for geographies if customer requirements are heavily dependent on the regional conditions. This is the case if there are regional differences in products, tastes, and needs. These criteria can very often be found in the food processing industry. Service industries, like insurance, banking, consulting, and auditing, often operate with a regional approach because customers demand close proximity to their service supplier. They would like to have immediate access to their consulting, audit, or tax experts if required, and are skeptical about a cultural fit between service supplier employees and company employees.

Risks of the Geographic Organization are to some extent identical with the risks of the Divisional Organization. Since the definition of regions can lead to relatively small organizational units, Geographic Organizations can lack critical mass and eliminate economies of scale. Information can be a further bottleneck, as well. Also, regional managers are very likely to obtain the best market insights (from a supplier and customer perspective). They often define a region as their "kingdom" and act too independently, not coordinated with corporate goals as initially intended. Examples are price strategies, global brands, and the product portfolio. Additionally, regional management often tends to create its own back office for functions such as procurement, legal support, finance and accounting, HR, and marketing. Eventually, the corporation cannot leverage its size and the independent geographic units operate on a sub-efficient level. Furthermore, knowledge transfer between regions is often very difficult due to lack of coordination.

From a strategic perspective, the Geographic Organization works best in the commodity business. If the product portfolio is standardized and not too complex, the regional approach can be used to make the most of decentralized market knowledge and gain competitive advantages. The regional management generally has a better understanding for specific regional account strategies and regional sponsorship.

9 Complex Organizational Structures

Complex Organizational Structures attempt to address the major issues of the basic structures. The goals are:

- higher flexibility;
- faster reaction;
- quicker decision-making.

The following organizational design types will be discussed in detail:

- Matrix Organizations
- Hybrid Organizations
- Tensor-Cube Organizations
- Horizontal Organizations
- Network Organizations
- Modular Organizations

Matrix Organizations

While Functional Organizations, Divisional Organizations, and Geographic Organizations can be characterized as mono-level structural designs, the Matrix Organization operates with a multi-level design. Basically, matrix organizations are the result of the interplay of functional, divisional, and/or geographic activities as described previously. The matrix tries to address and to eliminate the illustrated weaknesses of these organizational designs by combining them as equal organizational guiding principles. Matrix Organizations can be composed of different dimensions: functions and divisions, functions and regions, regions and divisions. It is also possible to link one of these categories with a project structure in a matrix. Which combination to choose depends on the type of business, the product portfolio, and the current strategy. For a matrix it is important that one dimension does not overrule the other. The decisive factor is the equal allocation of decision authority to both sides of the matrix.

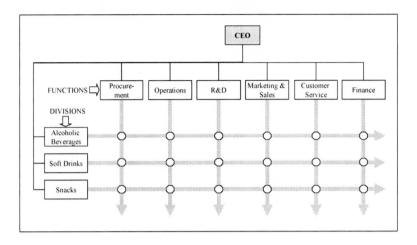

Exhibit III-8: Matrix Organization

As the example of a consumer goods company indicates, there are many points in the organization where employees have to serve for a function and a division at the same time. Employees at this crossroads are neither part of the finance organization, for example, nor part of the alcoholic beverages division. However, the head of accounts payable for alcoholic beverages has to report to the CFO and to the division head of alcoholic beverages. Furthermore, they have to coordinate accounts payable activities with the respective colleagues managing accounts payable for the soft drinks and snacks divisions to ensure consistent supplier management. Suppliers are likely to provide different divisions with services and would be confused if, for example, payment terms vary. To understand the real challenge of the matrix from an employee perspective, one has to envision that salary decisions, for example, are made mutually by the division head <u>and</u> the functional manager.

The Matrix Organization is well known for the term "constructive conflict", sometimes also called inherent conflict. From an organizational theory and psychology perspective, there is the assumption that employees are able to balance functional and divisional conflicts and provide services on a reasonable level. Despite putting employees in this stressful situation, there is also the assumption that their performance will increase and their motivation will be stimulated. Fundamental organizational conflicts are cascaded to the individual level hoping that knowledge and rationale on this level will help find the appropriate balance of different business interests.

Pure Matrix Organizations are not very common due to the challenges mentioned above and the risks associated with this organizational form. However, there are explicit strengths of this structure. The issue of Divisional Organizations to create divisions or units that are too small to gain scale advantages can be reduced. The use of shared resources, better utilization of operations facilities, leveraging of distribution and supply-chain network capacities are enabled through an effective matrix. In today's business environment it can be a necessity to be cost-efficient and customer-focused at the same time. Particularly if key employees are able to balance the conflict of interest in a reasonable way, companies with matrix structures are able to pursue different strategic routes at the same time.

Overstraining employee capabilities is probably the biggest threat to Matrix Organizations. They need sophisticated skills and strong personalities to deal with the "constructive conflict" on a day-to-day basis. If they feel they can't cope with the challenge, their motivation will run low, and they will be anxious about their job, feeling paralyzed and unhappy. The balancing effect is mostly gone and employees decide internally to go with one side of the matrix. Informally, the organization re-evolves to a Functional or Divisional Organization. Another disadvantage of Matrix Organization is the relatively high effort to coordinate activities within the matrix. To ensure coordination of routine business, multiple meetings, conference calls, e-Mail traffic, or phone calls are required to inform each participant in a matrix and to reach consensus on critical decisions.

Although the Matrix Organization marks a sophisticated development stage that eliminates major weaknesses of the functional and divisional structures, it will only persist in specific industries or as temporary solutions. Typical industries are various types of non-profit organizations, agencies and institutes, R and D firms, or educational institutions. These companies have a need to balance product and service offerings with functional expertise. R and D and high-tech companies often face an unstable environment. For them, the matrix can provide maximum flexibility and adaptability. Furthermore, through focus on the service quality, there is an inherent need to incorporate divisional requirements and functional knowledge. Since cost leadership or pricing in non-profit organizations has a lower priority, the matrix is able to balance this. The same logic applies to public agencies and authorities. Strategically, the Matrix Organization should be chosen if multiple, relatively small business units are maintained. Critical mass of functional capacities as provided through a matrix can fuel further growth. If cost leadership is a serious criterion for a company, the matrix structure is not likely to fit very well. Eventually, before introducing a matrix, the individual capabilities of employees have to be coordinated and conflict-resolution skills have to be instilled in this organization form.

Hybrid Organizations

The Hybrid Organization also operates with the dual-reporting line philosophy. In contrast to the matrix structure that uses two equitable reporting levels on each side of the matrix, the hybrid structure operates with a prioritized reporting line, the so-called "solid line," and the second reporting line, the "dotted line." The solid line presents usually a similar logic as discussed in the previous chapter, which means it displays a functional, divisional, or geographic structure. Employees have to report primarily to their solid-line superior, and to a certain extent, to a dotted-line superior as well. Although this principle looks very much like the Matrix Organization, it is different because one dominating principle (solid line) is simultaneously applied with an inferior organizational principle (dotted line). The hybrid structure is one of the most widely chosen organizational principles today because it reduces the disadvantages of mono-level structures without adding the complexities of a pure matrix structure.

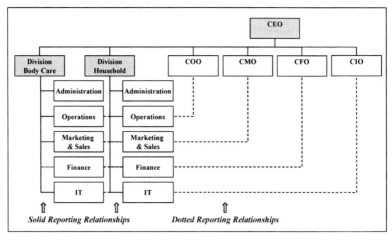

Exhibit III-9: Hybrid Organization

The biggest strength of the hybrid structure is the balance between functional interests and divisional needs. Divisions can operate as flexibly and independently as required by market conditions. On the other hand, they can profit from the functional expertise and the corporate-wide capacity for coordination provided by the functions. Additionally, the employees are not overstretched like in a matrix model because their reporting relationships are clearly differentiated. Another advantage is the close strategic control through the corporate organization. The functional management can provide strategic guidance that is in line with corporate goals and strategic missions. The divisions can blend in divisional/business unit-specific strategic directions. Therefore, the issue of strategic disconnects that can occur in particular in Geographic Organizations can be mitigated.

A major weakness of the Hybrid Organization is the administrative overhead. Since functional management and divisional management have to maintain overlapping structures, it tends to increase overhead. Additionally, there is more corporate staff required to oversee, support, and coordinate divisions.

From a strategic perspective, industries that operate multiple divisions in different regions are in favor of the hybrid structure due to its potential to provide both divisional/geographic uniqueness and functional expertise. Essentially, if the need for flexible product differentiation has to be combined with competitive cost structures, the Hybrid Organization provides a powerful solution.

Tensor Cube Organization

The hybrid structure typically combines two dimensions: either functions and divisions or functions and geographies. However, sometimes there is a need to combine more than two dimensions. A company that, for example, operates with a divisional/functional matrix structure wants to include multi-geographic business activities in its structure, as well. In these cases, in addition to the existing matrix, a third regional dimension is added that operates like the inferior dimension in the Hybrid Organization.

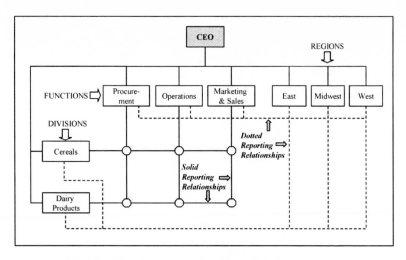

Exhibit III-10: Tensor Organization Complexity

The consumer food company illustrated above is structured primarily according to two divisions: cereal and dairy products. The employees within the divisions have one additional reporting requirement towards a functional head and one reporting requirement towards a regional head. Their dominating superior, however, remains the division head.

In organizational design research, the Tensor-Cube Organization is a design type that is not very widespread. This is related to its theoretically high level of complexity and the fact that it has not been really established as a textbook solution. In practice, however, many companies operate with tensor-cube structures – mostly without being aware of it. Most major corporations implicitly apply a Tensor Organization simply due to the fact that they operate unique divisions on a global basis and are in need for functional best practices and expertise. The reason why a tensor structure can hardly be detected from outside (or, often, is not even perceived by employees) is the dominance of the chosen guiding principle. Employees belong clearly to a division and have their univocal reporting relationships.

Their second reporting obligation along the dotted line to a functional superior gives them the impression of operating in a hybrid structure. The third reporting requirement along a dotted line to a geographic superior is not perceived as a subordinate function. But the third dimension is important. The company leverages regional knowledge and marketing power, coordinates cross-geographically to utilize capacities, and behaves optimally adapted to the regional conditions – without having an explicit regional structure. It simply manages this dimension from the background.

The core strength of a Tensor-Cube Organization is the combination of product focus through divisions, functional knowledge through functions, and close supplier and customer management through regions. The multi-level structure enables ideal adaptation, flexibility with regard to market needs and business conditions, and economies of scale. If played right, the Tensor-Cube structure can be extremely powerful for global players with wide product portfolios and the need for functional service excellence. Innovativeness can be another advantage since, in the Tensor structure, inventions can be funneled through a dedicated R and D organization that develops new product services according to product requirements and regional-specific customer needs.

A major drawback of the Tensor organization is the relatively high level of complexity. Especially if companies try to enforce a matrix structure and explicitly add a third dimension, people are often overstrained. As it can happen in a matrix, employees simply treat one dimension as dominating and the second and third dimensions in the Tensor structure will be neglected. As a side effect of the high complexity, the Tensor-Cube Organization creates significant overhead costs compared to mono-level structures. Maintaining multiple reporting lines and reconciling direct and indirect reporting relationships cause additional administrative efforts.

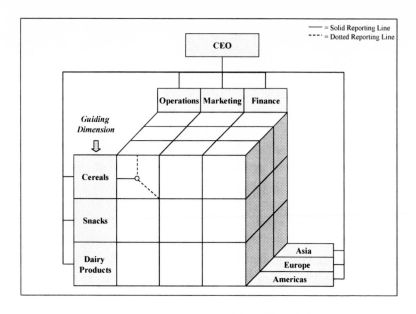

Exhibit III-11: Tensor-Cube Organization

International professional service firms often maintain Tensor Cube Organizations due to the necessity to provide functional and industry-related expertise in different regions. Thus, the structure is often primarily regional, for example, Americas, Europe, Asia. According to the expertise of its consultants, they are aligned into service practices, such as operations consulting, IT consulting, and industry practices, such as automotive, financial service, and telecommunication. The company's internal administrative functionsm such as finance, HR, and marketing, are primarily serving the regions. Strategically, the Tensor Cube is chosen whenever there is a high need for functional expertise on a regional and divisional level at the same time. This is often the case for differentiation leaders or niche players with global reach.

Horizontal Organizations

A distinct process perspective primarily characterizes the Horizontal Organization. The entire structure is built around processes and workflows rather than functions. The guiding organizational principle is focused on the core processes, whereas functions obtain the roles of secondary, or dotted, reporting lines. The customers, their needs, desires, and demands, are leading the process build up. The basic idea of the horizontal structure enables as many employees as possible to get direct or at least close access to the customer. Through better understanding of customer needs, employees will be quicker and more closely incorporated with products and services. The same applies to the suppliers. Here, as well, employees should get in direct contact with suppliers to better understand their needs, requirements, and limitations. The process structure has led to the name "Horizontal Organization." While vertical structures are seen as steep hierarchical patterns of responsibility split according to functions, the horizontal model goes across several functions. By operating in processes, employees are in close contact with a wide variety of people through the entire company. Since the functional department walls are either permeable or exist only as dotted reporting lines, the Horizontal Organization can quickly adapt to changing requirements of the business processes, the customers, suppliers, or the competitive environment. The horizontal model is, therefore, sometimes called the "Integrated Enterprise".[13]

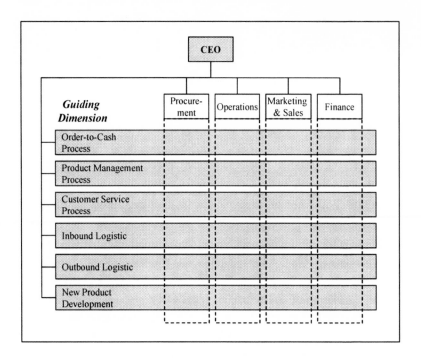

Exhibit III-12: The Horizontal Organization

Examples from the telecommunication industry highlight the benefits of horizontal structures. Historically, the industry was very technically driven because everything to offer a customer depended on technological capabilities. Since the telecommunication business was deregulated, new technological breakthroughs like data and cell phone services have boosted customer demand. The market today is strongly customer driven. Thus, close cooperation between various traditional functions is required.

- New products have to be developed based on the customer demands.
- Marketing and sales have to specify product features and reasonable price ranges.

- Technological feasibility has to be ensured early in the process through operations.
- Finance has to provide insightful business cases and breakeven analysis.
- Procurement has to be involved to assess opportunities to purchase services or parts of services instead of producing them at likely a greater cost.
- Each new product idea has to be assessed throughout the entire organization.

This example indicates the significant strength of the Horizontal Organization: the ultimate customer focus. Since almost every process involves the customer, each employee gets a first-hand understanding about market requirements. Generally, people will develop stronger customer management behavior. Additionally, horizontal processes allow participation and improved communication flow. This empowerment of people will positively influence motivation and enthusiasm for the business purpose and strategic goals. Besides motivating people, adaptability to market requirements is another plus. This is beneficial, in particular in the current environment with rapidly changing market conditions, increased global competitions, and the importance of new technologies to gain competitive advantages.[14]

Risks associated with the horizontal model are the immense complexity and the required coordination efforts. Since basically all decisions regarding processes require a team-based approach, close coordination, multiple meetings, conference calls and e-mails are needed. Another issue related to the horizontal structure is the functional expertise. Since functions are clearly subordinated in this model there is a risk that expertise will fade out and eventually impact process quality.[15] Finance functions, for example, often struggle in horizontal organizations to enforce policies and rules and are faced with decreasing quality in the widespread process teams. In one telecommunication case, multiple versions of breakeven analyses were performed by different product management teams. None of them was compliant to the standard calculation instructed by the CFO. Another challenge is the "new thinking" that is associated with the Horizontal Organization. People need to get used to a new perspective and they have to learn how to interact in a process organization.[16]

From a strategic perspective the horizontal structure works best for multi-product companies that operate in local markets. Process coordination for global players is difficult because of the requirement for close coordination of the process team. Additionally, the horizontal design is useful due to the creative and entrepreneurial culture it creates. Therefore, niche players in technological market segments will find it useful. In markets requiring cost leadership the Horizontal Organization won't be the most effective design: process structures tend to generate higher administrative burden and cost control is difficult due to the segregated process landscape.

10   International Structures

The ways in which companies approach international business are manifold.[17] Three main structures can be distinguished:

1. Entering new markets without setting up distinct facilities. This structure is chosen if products should simply be sold in new international markets and maintaining a small sales force abroad is sufficient (the same applies if materials or parts are purchased internationally).

2. Setting up distinct facilities for assembling and distributing but retaining strong focus on selling products provided by the corporation. Often in this stage a country-specific organization and legal entity is created.

3. Full-blown independent country organization that produces, distributes, and sells its product for the most part independently from the corporation.

The reasons for international business activities are manifold as well. They can be categorized as follows:

- Companies that need to source raw materials or parts outside their domestic region have by their nature international relationships.
- Companies that approach international markets to optimize asset utilization by creating additional demand.
- The continuous pressure to grow triggers international business activities. Growth is still seen, and in fact is, a major driver for shareholder value.[18] A.T. Kearney has found in a long-term study that shareholder value creation is very closely correlated with continuous revenue growth. Hence, international expansion is a valid strategy to push shareholder value.
- Global brand recognition, image, and attractiveness as an employer.

There are three different organizational types for international business activities:

- International Organizations
- Multinational Organizations
- Global Organizations.

These organization forms are often seen as sequential development steps.[19] But companies approaching the international marketplace do not necessarily have to go through each distinctive stage. From a perspective of Organizational Effectiveness they can instead be seen as general types to incorporate international business activities.

International Organizations

International Organizations mean more than just selling or purchasing in outside markets. Instead of handling the international business through an export department only, the corporation sets up a division for international business activities. The core business is still domestic and is represented in domestic divisions, in distinct domestic geographies, or in functions. In most cases the international division focuses on marketing and sales activities in foreign countries only. Manufacturing, procurement, and supply chain services are provided by the domestic business functions. The same applies to the support functions: R and D, finance, HR, and other administrative activities are still part of the domestic operations. However, some activities have to be transitioned to the international marketplace, like supply-chain activities outside of the domestic market, distribution of products in the target market, and some procurement activities for the international business. Country-specific packaging, labeling, or product instruction manuals often have to be sourced specifically for the international business. European breweries, for example, exporting to the U.S. have to use specific labels stating nutritional details, alcoholic content, and health risks to comply with U.S. government regulation. Developing and sourcing of these labels is typically a task assigned to the international division.

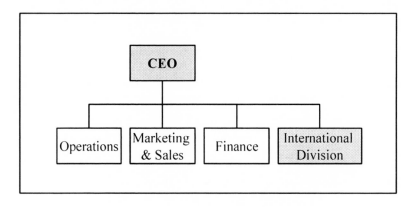

**Exhibit III-13: International Organization
with International Division**

Although it is not useful to set up redundant activities in the international division, some activities, in particular marketing and supply-chain activities, will be replicated but with a different scope. However, the combination of the functional and the divisional model to incorporate international activities is normally just a temporary solution to push international sales. The more common model to incorporate international business is a pure divisional structure or a hybrid model including at least one distinct international division. The next step is to further evolve the structure to a Hybrid Organization including one international division.

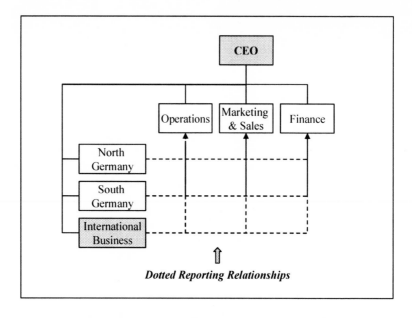

Exhibit III-14: Hybrid International Organization

In addition to the international division it is useful to set up international subsidiaries in parallel in the target markets to get better control and efficiency for marketing, distribution, and sales activities. The role of the subsidiary is strongly focused on leveraging core capabilities of the parent company like brand name, brand image, product quality, or product innovations.[20]

The strength of an International Organization is its high level of flexibility. It allows a company to test the international field as a potential market and source for further growth. A domestically well-proven market position can be tested on foreign markets with limited risks. The International Organization has the advantage over the domestic company operating with an export department to install fully dedicated operations, supply chain, marketing, distribution, and sales expertise for the international market needs. Specifics in distribution channels, taste and flavor of the customers, pricing, product features and brand management, and labeling and packaging can be handled by the dedicated international team. At the same time, the risk of market failure is limited. Since the international business is still organized in a distinct unit, the corporation can very easily decide to terminate its international activities without causing major disturbances and restructuring. Additionally, the international division and the activities in the international market place provide a unique learning experience for the entire organization. Even parts of the domestic business that are focused on the home country will get involved in the out-of-country requirements and the corporation can slowly evolve to an international player.

On the negative side, the International Organization is threatened by a certain organizational imbalance. Because only one distinct part of the corporation deals full time with the international business, it will be disconnected from the rest of the business. Often it is specifically required to hire an entirely new type of employee to respond to the international business needs, which can be costly and can hamper the integration of the new business. There is a risk that international activities are treated as a "strange animal" and hardly get accepted by the rest of the company. The cultural integration of the international group is a challenge that requires special attention.

From a strategic perspective, the International Organization – like all international structures – will fit best in the case of growth strategies. Companies in search of new markets and new sources for revenues often have to go abroad to keep up with the targeted growth pace. The desire to build a global brand is another strategic trigger to go international. Global brand presence also provides a push to local business. Although it does not matter if a company approaches international markets with a cost-leader or differentiation strategy, it is required to differentiate the product and service offering due to local requirements. Typically, the International Organization is chosen if a company is not ready yet to align the entire business according to the international markets. Thus, it builds on its strong domestic heritage and pilots certain foreign market segments, preparing the company for the international challenge. In this regard, a niche strategy is often the appropriate strategic direction on the international platform.

Multinational Organizations

Generally, the Multinational Organization is a response to the differences in local markets.[21] The best possible adaptation to the local markets can be achieved through independent country organizations. Very often product designs and features are specifically dedicated to local demands. Hence, the width of the product portfolio tends to increase in multinational companies. The quantitative differentiation between an International and Multinational Organization has been suggested as soon as more than one-third of the total revenues are contributed through international business activities. However, the use of quantitative figures to differentiate both types is arguable[22]. The most common organizational structure to operate a multinational business is the Geographic Organization model or the hybrid model, combining divisions with geographies.

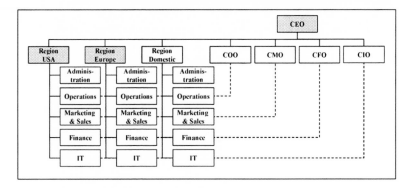

Exhibit III-15: Hybrid Multinational Organization

When the corporation reaches out to certain target markets abroad, the respective countries are set up as geographical units. If various different countries are targeted, they may be combined in an organizational unit like "Region Europe."

Ideally, the parent company establishes fully independent, decentralized subsidiaries that actually perform most activities along their particular value chain. This includes the core value-chain activities and support activities. Regional competence centers can act across country boundaries and, by this, easily reach a critical mass to operate extremely efficiently. In some cases it is impractical to set up all support activities in all distinct foreign countries. In these cases regional support centers are often a solution to combine both cost effectiveness and high quality of back-office services on international markets. A support center in Germany, for example, can serve for Austria and Switzerland, as well, or a center in Belgium can cover back-office needs for operations in the Netherlands, France and Belgium.

The particular strength of this model is its enormous potential to adapt to the local market needs. Since the local subsidiaries operate to a vast extent independently, they can react faster and more directly to the customer needs than the parent company from its remote location. By staffing the subsidiaries with primarily local employees, the cultural connection to the supplier and customer base is much closer, too. Furthermore, local presence and business operations create trust and a certain level of regional identity.

The challenges for the Multinational Organization are dominated by the lack of control over local subsidiaries. One of the core weaknesses of the Geographic Organization model is the tendency of local managers to create insular fiefdoms. To a certain extent, these fiefdoms are a necessity because an organization's success depends on powerful interaction with external actors to access crucial resources.[23] A subsidiary abroad has to integrate itself in the country-specific environment to be accepted and supported by local stakeholders. But execution of corporate strategic objectives, maintaining a balanced product portfolio, and, of course, operating a homogenous pricing strategy are challenged by the local interest of the decentralized subsidiary management. Often, local management is more strongly dedicated to the local market than to corporate guidelines. Managers try to negotiate favorable transfer prices and to reduce royalty payments or patent fees charged by the parent company to maintain low price levels for "their" customers. In particular, if the corporate strategy is to build global brands that can be associated globally with certain features, service levels, and pricing, local violations of this strategy can cause massive damage to a brand or even hinder the global spread. Furthermore, there is a risk of inefficiencies and redundancies. To gain better control over business operations and to act as independently as possible, local subsidiaries often establish their own support activities, such as finance and accounting, which leads to "shadow" activities: redundant back-office operations.

The Multinational Organization is mainly chosen as the next logical step to further evolve an international company towards a global market. Through the distinct operations in foreign countries it is best suited to the differentiation strategy. Although product portfolio management is a real challenge, this approach leads to a widely diversified and locally adjusted portfolio structure. A cost-leader position will face some issues in the multinational structure. Only if costly operation activities can be directed to low-cost and low-wage countries can cost advantages be achieved. But in this case the main characteristic and strength of the Multinational Organization – to produce or operate in the target country – would not be leveraged.

Global Organizations

While the Multinational Organization still has a domestic parent company, the Global Organization evolves to a center- or stateless corporation. It's a new approach to reduce the traditional corporate control mechanism by a network of relatively independent business units, divisions, and strategic alliances managed by a group of executives.[24] It can be characterized as a non-linear model that uses different structures for different product groups, business units, or geographies. The basic idea is that firms using the centerless approach are able to arrange quickly best practices and knowledge as required by the market conditions without control from the corporate headquarters. Literally, headquarters do not exist any more; an extended leadership team will replace it. The traditional corporate center will be replaced by the global core, which consists basically of the CEO, his or her team, and some limited services that can add value to the corporation as a whole. The business units and divisions either carry out all support functions such as finance, HR, or IT, or they use independent Shared Services support centers that either act as corporate-owned captive operations or are outsourced to specialized providers. The Global Organization considers the entire world as one integrated, global marketplace. Hence, the entire self-conception of this company type is global. The organizational model can often be characterized as divisional structure that will be combined with a geographic structure in a matrix that will be coordinated through a corporate leadership team. Nestlé is an example of a company that maintains a remarkable global presence. Its distinct product groups operate across geographical zones, which provide a second organizational layer on an equal footing. The corporate leadership team is supplemented through functional experts providing R and D support, corporate finance and legal services, and strategy and marketing expertise.

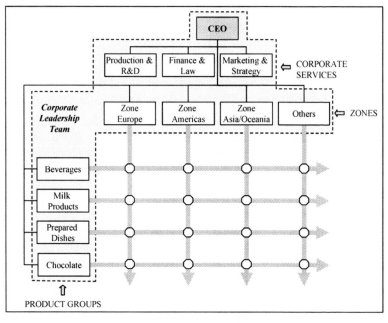

Exhibit III-16: Global Matrix

An often-chosen variation to the global matrix is the hybrid model with dominating divisions and dotted-line reporting relationships to the respective regions and/or functions. Functions in Global Organizations are generally subordinated organizational layers. They provide knowledge and best practices as true support units and are mostly concentrated around the small corporate core or provided by distinct Shared Services. Thus, the corporate headquarters remains effective and extremely flexible.

On the positive side, the Global Organization has great capabilities to manage global brands. Since no specific country is associated with the products they are, in fact, global products. Another advantage of this structure is the close adaptation to market needs. Since countries do not exist in this approach, the continental or global operating division has the opportunity to segment product and market segments across country boundaries. Hence, profitable segments can be identified with a more holistic perspective and customer needs can be satisfied with appropriate product and service offerings.

The weaknesses of this organizational structure are the challenges to coordinate and control globally allocated organizational entities. Realizing synergy effects is limited, due to the often-chosen matrix or hybrid structures and the significant physical distances between organizational units. Divisions often operate as entirely independent companies. Additionally, knowledge and best practices won't easily find the places where there is a need for them. The principle of free-floating information, communication, and coordination is, in reality, less applicable. Thus, lots of redundancies and inefficiencies are created.

Companies pursuing global strategies are very likely to push towards a Global Organization. Another strategic characteristic is a strong and distinct focus on certain business groups. Since the customer-focus is a strong driver of globalization efforts, this organizational type is well-suited for each type of differentiation strategy.

11   Corporate Structures and Partnerships

In contrast to the organizational alternatives discussed under Business Unit Structures, Corporate Structures and Partnerships present ways of cooperating, designing corporate functions, and leveraging core competencies.

Vertical Network Organizations

Lots of companies today cover multiple steps of their respective industry value chain through vertical integration. To execute the vertical integrations, two basic options are possible:

- acquisition of upstream suppliers and downstream customers;
- partnerships with upstream suppliers and downstream customers.

Whereas the acquisition strategy would very likely lead to a divisional structure in the sense that newly acquired value chain partners will act as full profit and loss accountable divisions, the partnership strategy takes place as a joint venture or alliance. The focus here is on the partnership model only.

Each value-chain step within the vertical partnership model has to be defined as independently as possible, for example, autonomous legal status, joint ventures or independent organizational unit. Based on historic product and service costs and the respective forecast data, an appropriate transfer pricing range considering appropriate profit margins will be negotiated. Subsequently, asset charges have to be agreed. They are calculated based on the planned volume. If the actual purchased volume is lower, the charge will nevertheless be applied because the supplier has aligned its capacity according to the planned figures. The network customer should get the opportunity to cover part of his demand by purchasing from other suppliers as well. Hence, prices will stay competitive and additional capacity on the supplier side is not required if volume forecasts are fluctuating. By this, capacities are optimally utilized and prices are always kept on competitive levels.

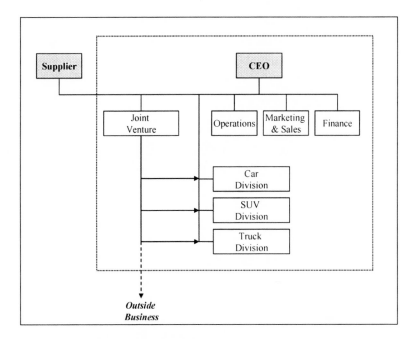

Exhibit III-17: Simplified Network Organization

Elimination of redundancies is one of the key strengths of Network Organizations. As indicated in the exhibit above, the automotive firm can outsource all its transmission operations to the joint venture with one supplier instead of producing transmissions internally. By bundling all its related activities, the joint venture can optimize asset utilization by covering the needs of all network division and the outside market.

The drawback of this organization is its tremendous complexity. To determine fair price ranges and services, it requires high level of sophistication. Furthermore, although suppliers are integrated in the network, they still need to maintain marketing and sales to serve the outside market. The same applies to the buying divisions if they have to reach out to the external supplier market because demands cannot be satisfied through the integrated partner only. Creating a new organizational unit under multiple ownership creates additional administrative costs. Also, the need to negotiate and determine transfer price ranges, asset charges and volumes leads to complexities.

Strategically, the network organization is recommended for industries that have long and complex supply chains. Automotive, aerospace and defense, electronic equipment, computer hardware for example can leverage advantages by applying a network structure. In other examples like the restaurant chain business, construction supply, or apparel, it is useful to integrate vertically to ensure certain quality levels.

Types of partnership solutions are usually arranged in two different basic models: Alliances and Joint Ventures.

- The **Alliance** is more or less a loose cooperation that has been established between the partners and is mostly legally based on a contract package.[25] The contract package typically contains the following:

  o Detailed descriptions of the cooperation and interaction
  o Service agreements
  o Transfer pricing ranges
  o Ootential penalties

The contracts are an extremely important tool enabling Alliances to work. They provide the legal foundation for the partnership. Otherwise, partners could easily drop out of an informal agreement, significantly hurt the competitive position of their partner by using insider information, and use the knowledge gained through the alliances to improve their own competitive position. As a recent study found, Alliances tend to fail if the governance structure is misaligned with the features of the transaction.[26] Additionally, if Alliance leaders undergo major strategy shifts, the partnership needs to be reassessed and repositioned. Thus, Alliances between horizontal competitors always tend to be fragile and instable. CEOs are often very cautious before joining a partnership. The risk of sharing valuable information should not be underestimated. The "prisoner-dilemma" applies in particular to horizontal partnership models. Each partner leaving the network could easily use the insights gained for its advantage. The creation of a stable and "bulletproof" legal frame requires significant experience and costs.[27] But if the rules of the game are fair and defined clearly, if infringements against written agreements will be penalized to the full extent possible, and if partners develop the required amount of mutual trust and understanding, Alliances can be very powerful. Partnerships can, of course, contain more than just two partners. Comparable to a Vertical Network they can consist of multiple partners. The manageability and the strategic objective of the group determine the number of players involved.

- The more formal concept to pursue partnership advantages is the **Joint Venture.** Joint Ventures can be found in both Vertical Networks and Horizontal

Partnerships. In the Joint Venture the management of both partners decides to establish basically an entirely new company that operates as a subsidiary of both companies. Ideally, the ownership is split fifty-fifty but, depending on the type and strategy of the partnership, one partner might dominate. Both sides normally take joint care for the new operation and install a management team representing both partners. The Joint Venture should act independently of its parent companies and pursue its own defined strategic direction. The lifetime of a Joint Venture depends on type and strategy of the partnership. For R and D efforts the purpose of the Joint Venture might be over as soon as the new technology or product has been invented. Other partnerships for operations and distribution, for example, can last for decades. The enormous advantage of a Joint Venture compared to an Alliance is the much more stable legal frame and, with it, the visibly high commitment of both companies to the partnership. However, an under-performing Joint Venture creates additional assets, capacities, staff, and managers. To close it down is far more complicated and costly than to drop an Alliance.

Modular Organizations

Modular Organizations are a further development of network structures. Whereas the Network Organization is characterized as a corporation-internal structure to cover multiple steps along the industry value chain, the Modular Organization does leave the boundaries of the corporation. Within a modular organization, the corporation defines itself as a broker who basically does not own any production, marketing, or sales facilities. It purchases all services and owns only a few key activities such as strategic planning, product development and design, corporate finance, and investor relations.[28] Sport footwear companies such as Nike and Reebok are often named as examples of focusing on design and marketing only. All manufacturing, distribution, and sales activities are outsourced.

The modular structure uses "virtual" products or projects to serve the market. For the limited timeframe of a product range or a distinct project, all organizational modules are lined up as requested. The corporation merely provides the entrepreneurial impulse and orchestrates the network of suppliers. Partners in Modular Organizations do often have longstanding relationships. Therefore, mutual trust and reliability are normally given. As soon as a product range will be taken off the market or a project is completed, the Modular Organization will be dismantled.

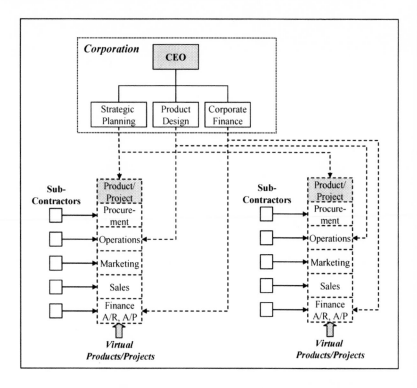

Exhibit III-18: Modular Organization with Virtual Products

The key advantage of this model is flexibility. The corporation is not forced to set up a specialized asset base and skill base. Withdrawing unsuccessful products from the market is easier, as long as the legal framework does not lead to severe penalties. The assets required for the product range or project are extremely specific and will be written off over the length of the engagement. Through engaging multiple network partners, the risk of underutilizing assets can be allocated to multiple network partners. Another advantage is associated with the high level of functional expertise that can be acquired through a Modular Organization. By utilizing specialized knowledge the functions perform on a high level allowing high quality products and strong market penetration.[29]

The biggest obstacle of a Modular Organization is instability. Subcontractors can leave the network by accepting a contract penalty or they can be forced to leave due to quality, service, or delivery issues. Finding replacement contractors can become a major threat to the entire network and can lead to substantial loss of profitability for the corporation. The efforts to initiate, coordinate, and orchestrate the Modular Organization are another disadvantage. The search for suitable partners can be time consuming and difficult. Additionally, orchestrating the supply chain and delivery network without being part of it is another challenge. The simple-minded belief that electronic communication will enable and guide these activities is deceptive: as soon as serious obstacles occur, coordination in person is required. The corporation takes on the role of a firefighter; project managers will travel hectically to subcontractors' locations, and lengthy coordination meetings are needed to regain network stability. The focus will be primarily internal instead customer-oriented. Eventually, the corporation that operates with modular structures tends to weaken its Strategic Capabilities. The purpose of the organization degenerates to a coordinator role and real value is added through subcontractors. Combined with the fragility of Modular Organization, this can lead to the loss of a competitive advantage if value-contributing contractors decide to leave the network and cooperate with a competitor.

Industries that operate with relatively short-living product ranges will find the strongest strategic fit with Modular Organizations. Apparel and fashion are good examples because their product lifecycle lasts often less than a year. For the most part, all types of project businesses often operate with a kind of modular structure. Movies are basically produced in a couple of months and most value-chain steps, from preparing locations, to catering for the film crews, to the sound work will be provided by subcontractors. The same applies to the construction industry that has been used to operating with subcontractors in modular networks over decades. As soon as a project is completed and the aftermath is done, this particular Modular Organization will cease to exist.

12   Emerging Structures: Shared Services, Offshoring and Business Process Outsourcing

How to support the core business has become a topic of particular interest in the late 1990s due to increased cost pressure and the need to improve competitiveness through streamlined enterprise services. But the role of the headquarters and its relationship to the divisions has been part of the discussion since 1920 when **Alfred Sloan** started as CEO of General Motors. Within his tenure he introduced the principle to separate day-to-day operations from strategic headquarters activities.[30] Other companies besides GM often had their headquarters attached to one of the dominating operations or commercial facilities and were partly merged with the business activities.

Today, there are basically two extremes of how companies with divisional structures (business units, geographies) support the core business:

1. The headquarter organization takes care of all administrative tasks. All major back-office functions such as finance and HR reside within the headquarters and support the businesses (divisions, geographies) from there.
2. All back-office functions are performed within the distinct divisions. Each division subsequently has its own finance, HR, etc. operations. The headquarter is only in

charge of consolidation of financial reports, for example, and focuses on core strategic tasks of the company.

Both extremes are quite unrealistic. In most cases companies have decided to arrange support functions through a combination of both. Certain activities reside within the divisions, others are performed by the headquarters. From an organizational perspective, the allocation of work can be organized in two fundamentally different reporting governance models. Both models are Hybrid Organizations:

1. Back-office functions are part of the headquarter and the functions "deploy" resources to support the dedicated divisions. The back-office employees have solid reporting lines to the functional leaders in the corporate headquarter. They have dotted reporting relationships to the division management to ensure that support is as business-oriented as possible. The physical location is not relevant. People can be either located physically within the divisions or remain in the headquarter.

2. The back-office functions report with a solid line to the division. Through dotted reporting relationships the headquarter ensures compliance to strategic goals and corporate requirements. However, the back office function is primarily focused on business requirements as they perceive themselves as part of the businesses.

Which model to choose depends on the strategic direction of a company and the philosophy as expressed in the personal flavor and style of the leadership. During the decentralization trend of the late 1980s and early 1990s, most companies took the path of the second model but compliance issues and cost pressure in the late 1990s and the new millennium have reversed this trend. Redundancies and hindered knowledge transfer as well as underutilized scale effects make the second model less attractive from an efficiency perspective.

Shared Services

A key enabler to improve efficiency of support functions is Shared Services. Spearheaded by a bold move of the Ford Motor Corporation in 1981, the concept got strong momentum and today over eighty percent of the Global Fortune 500 companies are using a Shared Services model.[31] What are Shared Services? They take over primarily transactional activities that support both the headquarter operations or distinct divisions and business units. The following exhibit illustrates how transactional activities can be differentiated from decision-support and corporate-strategic activities.

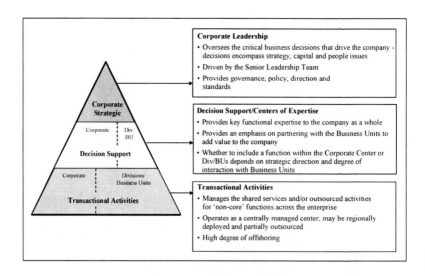

Exhibit III-19: Differentiation of Transactional Activities

The term transactional refers to the kind of work, meaning it is repetitive, to a vast extent manually driven, needs a predetermined skill-base, and requires execution in fixed patterns. The opposite would be managerial and decision-support activities, which are characterized through flexible skill and knowledge requirements, unpredictable action and decision-making, and situational execution. As an example, the various accounting functions are predominantly transactional activities whereas strategic planning is typically a managerial activity.

Both transactional activities and decision-support activities are performed by the corporate organization and the divisions or business units. It depends on the philosophy and strategic direction of a company where exactly the dotted line is drawn. Often the CEO's understanding of the corporate role determines the level of decision-support and transactional activities conducted on a corporate level versus the divisional level. The following exhibit provides an overview on typical functions found in Shared Services:

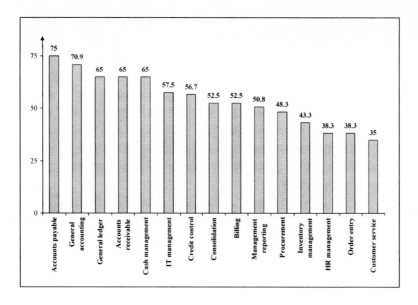

Exhibit III-20: Typical Shared Service Functions (%)[32]

All theses functions have a substantial share of transactional activities. The study above conducted in 1998 revealed that, at the time, already three-quarters of all surveyed companies in Europe had decided to use a form of Shared Services. Almost seventy percent were already utilizing a form of Shared Services. While the majority has used Shared Services primarily for finance, accounting, and IT functions, there is a trend visible that more and more nonfinancial functions, such as HR, move to a Shared Service environment as well or even become outsourced. The following exhibit provides two examples of how the transactional, decision-support, and corporate-strategic activities can be differentiated on a functional level. Finance and accounting and HR have very distinct processes that can be categorized according to this differentiation but identifying a process as "transactional activity" doesn't automatically mean that the entire process can be consolidated in a Shared Service Center. Rather, it means that substantial parts of these processes have transactional characteristics that can be centralized because of the repeatability, standardization and leveragability of technology. Certain parts of even very transactional driven process still have decision-support or even strategic-policy setting characteristics as the following example emphasizes: The accounts payable process consists mainly of repeatable activities such as matching invoices and purchase orders or processing vendor payments. However, smaller proportions of the process, such as determining and updating payment terms or problem resolution, have other characteristics. Thus, probably ninetyfive percent of a typical accounts payable process are transactionally driven and could be performed by a Shared Service Center.

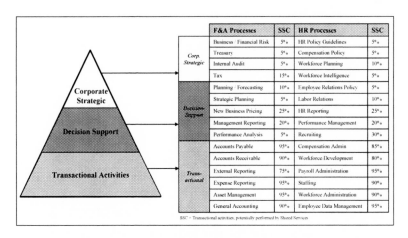

F&A Processes	SSC	HR Processes	SSC
Business / Financial Risk	5%	HR Policy Guidelines	5%
Treasury	5%	Compensation Policy	5%
Internal Audit	5%	Workforce Planning	10%
Tax	15%	Workforce Intelligence	5%
Planning / Forecasting	10%	Employee Relations Policy	5%
Strategic Planning	5%	Labor Relations	10%
New Business Pricing	25%	HR Reporting	25%
Management Reporting	20%	Performance Management	20%
Performance Analysis	5%	Recruiting	30%
Accounts Payable	95%	Compensation Admin	85%
Accounts Receivable	90%	Workforce Development	80%
External Reporting	75%	Payroll Administration	95%
Expense Reporting	95%	Staffing	90%
Asset Management	95%	Workforce Administration	90%
General Accounting	90%	Employee Data Management	95%

SSC = Transactional activities, potentially performed by Shared Services

Exhibit III-21: Finance & Accounting and HR activities - Examples

A Shared Service Center is in most cases a distinct organizational unit that is managed to provide efficient and high-quality back-office/support functions to the firm's core business. They focus on leverage, standardization, simplification, offshoring and outsourcing. The latter aspect

– Business Process Outsourcing – will be the subject of the following chapter. Ideally, service level agreements (SLA) are made to regulate compensation between the center and the receiving divisions and business units. However, in order to keep the organizational relationship to a Shared Service center simple and effective, the center runs on a fixed budget and the units get charged with a fixed rate. Performance metrics based on competitive services are often used to determine the fixed charges and to monitor the efficiency and quality of the center. Continuous orientation on best-in-class benchmarks will ensure the utmost efficient services are provided by the Shared Service Center.

There are basically three different organizational models for Shared Services:

1. *Functional Mode*
   The services are consolidated internally under the appropriate function (e.g. finance and accounting, HR, procurement) and operated by a Shared Service Center. In this model, the center is basically an extension of the functional department with focus on consolidated, decentralized support activities to leverage economies of scope and scale and enforce certain company standards. Thus, the reporting relationship is mostly strictly functional oriented, that is, an accounting Shared Service reports to the CFO and a benefits administration center reports to the senior vice president of HR. The functional Shared Service Center is organizationally a cost center that operates with an expense budget like any other cost center as well. The service-receiving units (corporate, divisions, business units) are being charged for the services, but since the center is a cost center only, it wouldn't be very wise to establish a full-blown and detailed allocation and charge-back method. A fixed charge based on projected service volumes and

standard cost rates is the simplest and most efficient solution for a functional Shared Service model. The center location is flexible: in some cases it resides within the corporate headquarters; in other cases a more cost-efficient onshore solution is chosen. It is also possible to locate a functional Shared Service Center nearshore (a more cost-efficient location in another country on the same continent) or even offshore, but for functional models this would rather seldom be the case.

2. *Independent Multi-functional Center*
   The center is a separate internal organization serving multiple internal clients. The multi-functionality is a key differentiator to the functional model and, as a consequence, the reporting relationship in one function only is – theoretically – not an option any more. However, for practicality reasons some companies link the multi-functional center into the CFO organization, although the center performs HR and procurement tasks, for example, as well. Ideally, the independent multi-functional center reports to the CEO or CAO (Chief Administrative Officer). Another characteristic is the full profit and loss accountability, which means that the center has to manage its expenses and revenues. In this regard, clear rules and compensation models with the receiving units need to be in place, and service level agreements will be used as the key vehicle to determine the relationship. By definition, the independent multi-functional center is in competition to external providers: business units, for example, can decide to contract certain services with external providers if they can demonstrate that the third party provider is less expensive and/or provides better service than the Shared Service Center. The idea of competing internal Shared Services with external

providers has pros and cons: on the positive side, the comparison with the outside world puts the center under constant pressure to provide cost efficient services and to improve quality. On the negative side, it bears the risk of designing subscale Shared Services and inconsistent service levels across the enterprise. There is clearly a gray area on how to control this Shared Service organizational model and, as a result, it is the most ambiguous one that needs lots of governing principles to make it really work. From a location perspective it's not very different than the functional model, but due to the competitive element, it is much more likely that an independent multi-functional center is located outside the corporate headquarters and at a highly cost-efficient place. Nearshore and offshore solutions are more often found for independent Shared Services than for the functional model.

3. *Stand-Alone Center*
   The stand-alone center is a separate subsidiary established to serve internal clients and to leverage resources and skills serving third parties. Stand-alone centers are, in most cases, multi-functional but they can function as a mono-functional oriented unit, as well. Due to their organizational independence, they have no direct reporting relationships to the company. The interfaces are defined by the services provided and can be characterized as customer-vendor type relationships. Thus, the stand-alone center stands in direct competition to every other third party provider but does have the opportunity to generate revenue with other customers than the parent company. In essence, the stand-alone center operates as an independent third party provider on the marketplace and offers its services as Business Process Provider to a wide range of potential

customers, with the parent company being the key customer. A logical customer base is clearly the vertical network of the parent company. Suppliers to the parent and customers of the parent are likely candidates to outsource accounting functions, payroll, benefits administration or other related support activities to their key customer/vendor Shared Service Center. But stand-alone centers can go even one step further and offer their services to other industries as well. Because of the external third-party characteristics, pricing mechanisms applied by the stand-alone center are similar to every other outsourcing provider and can be fixed-price arrangements, gain-share agreements, or service level-based pricing. In the current environment of stronger acceptance of Business Process Outsourcing, major corporations with well-running stand-alone centers are enlarging the external market-facing role of their Shared Services subsidiary as an additional source for significant revenues. Locationwise, stand-alone centers are based in low labor-cost environments, either nearshore or offshore.

The concept of Shared Services has become part of the organizational toolkit to optimize support services over the past two decades. In particular, the term "captive Shared Services" is a key word for efficient Shared Services operated in labor arbitrage environments such as India, Philippines, Eastern Europe or the Caribbean. Major corporations operate centers in these nearshore/offshore locations mostly according to the independent or stand-alone model. The advantages of Shared Services are obvious:

- Higher efficiency through consolidation
- Economies of scope and scale

- Better standardization and harmonization of back office services
- Leverage of technology
- Significant labor cost savings due to nearshore and offshore locations
- Additional revenue generation through stand-alone Shared Services

However, there are some risks to be taken into account when launching a Shared Services initiative:

- High technology and infrastructure investments during implementation phase
- Less contact and understanding of the company's core business
- Risk of insufficient service levels to effectively support the core business
- Less control over Shared Services, in particular if independent or stand-alone model in nearshore/offshore location
- Cumbersome pricing and compensation methods for support services

Overall, the positive aspects are clearly outweighing the negative and, subsequently, Shared Services today are more thriving than ever. From a strategic perspective, companies using a cost-leadership strategy will clearly benefit from a Shared Services concept. They can proactively control and manage support service costs and, by offshoring them, achieve substantial competitive cost advantages. Even differentiation strategy followers can apply the concept for their benefit. By consolidating all nonvalue and back-office activities in a cost-effective Shared Service Center, they can free up resources to focus on key customer needs and customized service solutions.

Business Process Outsourcing (BPO)

The economic downturn of 2000-2001 has shown how vulnerable most businesses still are, even though the menace of stronger competition and the urgent need for competitiveness has been addressed over and over again in the 1980s and '90s. Further globalization of most industries, unfavorable political factors, accelerating new product development cycles, and more and more demanding customers will determine the business landscape in the new millennium. Last but not least, most players in global markets have successfully applied various organizational design options, gained valuable experience, and have further refined and optimized existing models. As discussed in the previous chapter, far more than three-quarters of the major global players have already made the progressive move to create a form of Shared Services. Gaining advantages through smart organizational design needs a lot of creativity, courage, and cleverness. The challenging business conditions lead to competition for the most effective organizational design and, currently, the most prominent emerging structure is Business Process Outsourcing (BPO).

As defined by the Accenture Institute, BPO can be described as contracting with an external organization to take primary responsibility for providing a business process or function.[33] It differs from traditional outsourcing in significant ways because it can be viewed as an extended organizational design. More detail is provided by the definition of the analyst group IDC. It explains BPO as a transfer of business activities, process or functional area to an external service provider to gain efficiencies and improve performance.[34] Transfer of assets and personnel to an external service provider can be part of a BPO engagement, which usually is based on a long-term contract that can run up to ten years. Today's organizations have to extend themselves to stay competitive. As a result they have to depend on specialized service providers, irrespective of their location around the globe, to support processes and deliver services.[35] Early frontrunners such as BP had already decided ten years ago to step on– at the time – the relatively untapped field of BPO by outsourcing operations to Accenture. They have broken ground for BPO, which has no become a serious alternative to Shared Service organizations which was the favorite choice over the course of the 1990[36].

Finance and accounting, HR, payment services, procurement, supply chain management, sales support, customer care and logistic services are very likely the business processes to be strongly outsourced in the near future. Optimistic outlooks by research firms such as the Gartner Group estimate a market growth from $119 billion in 2000 to $234 billion in 2005 for BPO.[37] This would represent a growth rate of 14.4%. As a result, BPO has evolved to much more than an interesting concept of contracting out discreet processes. It is an integrated model of shifting entire functions in the hands of specialized service providers.

Generally, two frameworks of BPO can be distinguished: transactional BPO and strategic BPO.

- Transactional BPO is mainly focused on cost reduction. Transactional activities, as described earlier, offer potential improvement through econo- mies of scale and scope, expertise, and automation. Through streamlining processes, the associated costs can be significantly reduced. Therefore, consolidation of transactional activities and outsourcing to a specialized contractor who has the ability to set best- in-class processes in place and to apply state-of-the- art IT infrastructures improves cost efficiency. Especially in economic downturn situations, companies are more strongly attracted to outsource these activities.

- Strategic BPO comes into play as soon as companies use BPO as an explicit business tool. In this case, emphasis is put on more effective processes and improved Organizational Effectiveness. Companies pursuing strategic BPO start by identifying the true core processes of the business. Similar to understanding the purpose of the organization, they would first like to pinpoint precisely what should be the core of their existence as an enterprise. Is it, for example, "making" cars or "designing" or "engineering" them? The German automaker Porsche has made a bold step by outsourcing all activities except designing, engineering, and marketing for its model Boxter to third parties. As a result, a way to use BPO strategically is to outsource noncore activities in order to be strongly focused on the really important core activities. The senior management team can definitely free their agenda to focus on the strategic direction of the business if they can delegate certain non- or low-strategic processes to third parties. But the strategic use of BPO can work exactly the other way around, too: it can be an important strategic decision to decide that customer management activities will be outsourced to external service providers. For example, improved 24/7 service, 365 days a year, a better-skilled call center workforce and leading-edge technology are strategic reasons to contract with a third-party provider. In this case, BPO can also be used as strategic weapon. Overall, enhanced business value is certainly one important driver for strategic BPO.

There are certain business drivers on a macro-perspective level that have made BPO a increasingly attractive option these days:

- A slow economy is forcing corporations to focus on core competencies and search for cost-cutting opportunities in many areas simultaneously.
- Corporations now understand outsourcing and are becoming comfortable with outsourcing more complex functions.
- Enablers, such as Internet/Intranet technologies and ERP, are eliminating information and technology obstacles to BPO.
- Multi-national corporations need to provide consistent service across the globe, but without the massive capital investment and associated challenges.

Besides the macro level, there is a whole set of arguments that is internally business driven, the so-called micro-perspective level:

- There is a strong trend to focus more on strategic issues and reap the best return on assets/dollars invested.
- Companies are ensuring total customer focus by concentrating on core business processes and outsourcing the rest.
- A compelling drive to minimize cost of transactional services through upper quartile process excellence is aimed at maximizing efficiencies.
- Many CEOs/CFOs want to create a back office that provides insight for critical decision making.
- There is a growing need to ensure processes are operated in a scalable and modular fashion to accommodate future growth.

- Companies feel the need to dedicate assets invested in core competencies.

Last, but not least, the BPO provider market has reached a level of maturity that has reduced the risk of outsourcing entire business processes significantly. There are plenty of successful BPO cases that can be used as reference points. Companies that decide to outsource certain business processes always have to find the appropriate balance between cost advantages and service improvement and the risks associated in contracting out internal activities. Since BPO typically focuses on back-office functions, an insufficient outsourcing solution can hurt the business significantly, as the following examples illustrate:

- Delays in order fulfillment, wrong invoicing, and insufficient customer support are definitely a threat to the external client relationships. If external service providers do not comply with company standards in terms of customer management like, for example, friendliness and supportiveness, this can create confusion and irritation in the marketplace, too.
- The fact of moving the company's greatest asset – the customer files – tens of thousands of miles away in a developing country is an emotional obstacle that is hard to overcome for some companies.
- Internal customers such as employees will get annoyed through wrong or delayed paychecks, bad quality of training, and confused benefits administration. The employees have probably witnessed the pain and headcount cuts associated with the outsourcing decision. The reduced services through an outsourcing provider will even increase their anger and discomfort with the decision. Consequently, the general acceptance of commission-

ning third parties to take over more control of business processes remains low.

Companies that nevertheless pursue BPO strategies have to manage the issue of control very closely. Thus, from a company's perspective, the issue of control is very important. They have to make sure that the end-customer service levels and employee service levels are at least equal to a potential in-house solution or, ideally, even better. Performance metrics have to be defined that help to pinpoint reliability and on-time delivery of services. Outsourcing of processes provides the perfect opportunity to map the as-is processes accurately and to define state-of-the art processes. Consequent benchmarking of process performance versus best-in-class benchmarks ensures that the outsourced activities are performed on extremely high-quality levels. Another risk-mitigating activity is to transition key process owners to the new service provider. Through this, internal knowledge can be leveraged and continuity ensured. Moreover, transitioning employees to a service provider avoids the bad taste of massive layoffs. Although still a substantial number of employees will lose their jobs, for some of them it will appear as just a switch of the employer. But it shouldn't be downplayed that outsourcing of business processes is mostly driven by cost advantages, which means, consequently, that job cuts will take place. From an external and internal perspective this can be seen as distinct downsizing with all negative by-products as discussed earlier. Especially the decision to move labor-intensive work offshore raises eyebrows when the domestic economy is in trouble anyways. It can create the so-called double-dip recession effect. As a result, probably the most important decisions for a company that moves to the BPO stage are to decide upon the magnitude of outsourcing that is appropriate for the business and the level of control that will be given away.

But the business risk and issues with employee satisfaction are not the only barriers that hold back companies from BPO. The BPO service providers still need to convince the market space that they can handle the BPO challenge. Thus far, no mega-deal has happened and none of the major corporations has decided yet to outsource multiple end-to-end back-office operations to one distinct service provider. Most companies have already bits and pieces contracted out to specialized vendors such as payroll, credit and collection or help desks but the case of a company giving away the entire finance and accounting organization, HR, procurement, and customer contact management in one BPO contract package has not happened yet and probably never will. The market is currently fragmented into functional specific solutions and some providers offer a wide variety of support functions while others prefer to operate in niches and are holding significant shares in their functional space. Nevertheless, certain multi-functional players are dominating the BPO market. The following exhibit provides and overview of selected multi-functional players and the functional specialists in particular for HR and finance and accounting.

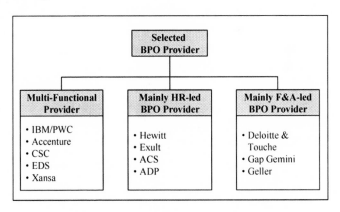

Exhibit III-22: BPO Providers - Examples

Business Process Outsourcing is often confused with IT outsourcing. The IT outsourcing market is clearly more mature and players such as IBM/PWC, EDS, CSC, Perotsystems, Sapient, and Cap Gemini operate considerable IT centers, lots of them offshore. There are major differences between BPO and IT outsourcing:

- Business process capabilities cannot be assessed as easy as IT capabilities. The Software Engineering Institute Capability Maturity Model allows the precise assessment of offshore capabilities. Service providers who come close to the highest score of 5.0 points on average quality of IT development staff are very likely to perform the assigned development tasks at a sufficiently high level. For BPO capabilities, a comparable assessment model does not exist yet and probably never will – at least not one as reliable as in the IT environment.
- Business processes can be quite complex and hard to comprehend. There are various qualitative skills such as communication, initiative, and relationship building involved that make a process successful. These factors are neither easy to measure nor can they be controlled if performed in a remote location ten thousand miles away from the business.
- At the moment, there are still concerns whether offshore BPO providers do have all the capabilities and skills to effectively perform complex business processes such as HR, finance and accounting, or customer contact management. Providers with roots in the IT environment have purposely created a strong technology-centric culture, which has to be transformed if they would like to succeed in the BPO space.[38]

- BPO engagements are much more complex than IT development projects. Business processes normally span various business units and functions, which means that the service provider needs to manage an entire network of business contacts. This is fundamentally different from IT projects in which foremost interaction takes place between the developer and single contact persons in the client company, such as IT architects and IT managers. As a result, the Gartner Group, like many other research firms, advises corporations in the U.S. and Europe not to rush into BPO offshoring as long as the decision is mainly cost-driven. The immaturity of potential offshore service providers is still a major risk. This is probably the key reason why only less than five percent of the U.S. companies with revenues ranging from $100 million to $4 billion have chosen to outsource back-office operations offshore.

In addition to the still existing maturity gap to IT outsourcing, there are a number of other specific risks that need to be addressed and overcome if BPO providers would like to get stronger traction in the marketplace.

- *Business Case: In-house Versus Outsourcing*
  BPO providers can offer compelling business cases that are mostly based on the same criteria as every captive Shared Services initiative: cost efficiency through consolidation and technology leverage, lower labor cost through attractive low-cost location, standardized and harmonized high service levels, and continuous improvement. If companies execute their Shared Services programs effectively there is actually no need to turn to a BPO provider. The cost

attractiveness of a BPO solution often looks even worse than the in-house solution because the provider still adds a margin on the cost basis for the center. Also, the distraction of migrating people and assets to a third-party provider can cause more harm than establishing owned Shared Services. BPO providers need to overcome these arguments with clear benefits, such as:

o Leverage of technology platforms is easier to realize for a specialized vendor who already operates an existing platform and adding another client is far less costly and complicated than the greenfield solution.

o New clients can be located in already existing near- or offshore facilities. No need to find or build a new location, no hassle of hiring the required staff.

o Expertise and best practices are likely to be more effectively leveraged in a center that is serving multiple clients. In-house solutions have a tendency to show less productivity improvements than constantly market-facing BPO Centers.

o Up-front investments can be avoided if a long-term contract is signed and the BPO vendor agrees to cover the start-up investments and to realize the payback over the length of the contract. The client can deal with a convenient service price or fixed price without worrying about the capital requirements for a Shared Service Operation.

• *Control: Regulatory Requirements and Sarbanes-Oxley*
Companies that contract with third-party providers give away a substantial amount of control over their

back-office operations. This is not only a challenge mentally for the senior management, it also has implications with regard to corporate responsibilities and accountabilities. Independent from the contractual agreement with the BPO provider, the executive managers of the company are still responsible for data accuracy, compliance with regulatory requirements, and service execution. If the service provider fails to provide services at contractual levels it will lead to penalties and probably even the termination of the contract. The damage caused by missing service targets, however, has to be dealt with by the company's leadership team. Some examples:

o Wrong or missing paychecks: the BPO provider has to pay penalties or accept price rebates but any legal action from the employees will be addressed against their employer – not the BPO provider.

o Inaccurate financial statements: again, the BPO provider will be penalized according to the contractual agreement. But the company's leadership is liable for the compliance consequences as addressed by regulatory authorities. In simple terms: the BPO provider has to pay; the CEO and CFO go to jail.

In particular, the latter example has become an entirely new dimension in the U.S. with the Sarbanes-Oxley act. The act was a result of the collapse of companies such as Enron and WorldCom due to accounting inaccuracies. It has made 'whistle-blowing" (section 301) and internal control systems (section 401) part of regulatory requirements. In particular, section 401 that requires companies to establish and certify a system of internal controls and processes used to obtain financial results has made CFOs become more suspicious with regard to outsourcing finance and accounting and payroll operations. It is expected that the act will slow down the drive for finance and accounting BPO until 2005 in the United States. Section 401 is effective June 15, 2004, and companies would like to ensure their internal control systems work effectively and are positively audited before they will consider broader BPO solutions. Until then, the BPO finance and accounting market will remain a very fragmented and niche-driven solution. Stronger scrutiny through regulatory authorities will be a roadblock for European corporations as well. BPO providers need to highlight the following benefits and strategies to overcome these concerns:

o BPO providers can be contracted for processing simple and low-risk transactional functions only. For most accounting or administrative HR processes, the amount of transactional activities is significant, and a specialized BPO vendor with a sophisticated IT platform can offer these services more cost efficient without adding any substantial risk. As long as activities such as data entry, reconciliation, file updating, and standard reporting are closely checked and appropriately audited, companies can comply with control issues as addressed by Sarbanes-Oxley.

o Operating advanced technologies is one of the key differentiators offered by BPO vendors. Since IT systems are often an important compliance enabler, the sophistication of a third-party provider can even strengthen alignment with various regulatory requirements.

o To foster the compliance aspect, most BPO providers are currently seeking certification of their service offerings with regard to compliance. If an independent audit firm confirms that a BPO platform conforms with regulatory requirements, the CFO's concerns should be addressed.

Although these arguments are quire compelling, it should not be downplayed that the reduced control and manageability of services provided by a BPO provider will remain a key obstacle, especially in areas that are critical and need to be audited.

Independent from the location of service providers, there are general models in which BPO solutions can be designed:

- *In-Sourcing*
  In-Sourcing is a model in which no external service provider is involved. In this case, all business processes remain in ownership of the company but, in addition, certain activities of the company's customer and/or supplier will be taken over. The company acts as a quasi-BPO provider itself. This solution can often be found in situations in which customers and/or suppliers to the company are fairly small players with limited bandwidth to perform certain back-office tasks on their own.
- *Business Process Management*
  The Business Process Management model is the classic model of BPO. Single- or multiple-business processes are outsourced to one service provider who performs them on behalf of the client. The provider owns the entire process; services and prices are contractually agreed and fixed.
- *Shared Utility*
  The Shared Utility model is the next logical step to set up efficient BPO solutions. In this model a service provider agrees with multiple companies to set up a utility that takes care of certain back-office functions

by using one common infrastructure at same time. The BPO provider is generally the owner of this "business process factory" but often the partner companies hold equity in the utility, as well. They operate based on an agreement that the third party jointly takes care of the companies' transactions for predefined business processes. The common infrastructure providing the services runs according to defined service level standards, and prices for services are standardized and consistent. From the perspective of each single partner company, this model is not significantly different from the Business Process Management model. The only difference is that, instead of having one exclusive infrastructure to operate the business process(es) for the company, the infrastructure is shared between multiple companies to further gain economies of scale and scope as well as cost advantages.

From a strategic perspective BPO comes into play as soon as companies seek cost advantages. For those pursuing the plain cost-leadership strategy, BPO is a tool that surely should be part of the organization management toolkit. While cost savings could be realized through internally-built and centralized Shared Services as well, the argument of improved service levels is another driver of BPO. Companies could use BPO strategically as a twofold weapon: First, outsourcing of so-called low-value-added activities gives more room to focus on the core activities. If senior management does not have to worry about the latest ERP and CRM technology or compliance to the latest pension and benefit reporting requirements, they have much more time to focus on other areas. Senior management time can be used to work on customer and market challenges, product strategies, partnerships, and market entry strategies. For companies following a differentiation strategy, this is certainly a plus.

But as discussed above, BPO can be used as a differentiator itself. Commissioning a high-service-level customer contact center provider will certainly improve the way customers are managed. And this can be a differentiator as well. Even small niche players will benefit from BPO. Due to their strategic focus these companies often don't have the bandwidth to perform efficient back-office operations. Outsourcing of back-office processes such as accounting or HR will help them focus more closely on their niches.

Offshoring

The term offshoring has already been used in particular as a cost-savings opportunity for Shared Services and BPO. To begin, some clarification around the terminology is needed:

- Offshoring refers to the relocation of work to another continent, in particular to leverage lower labor costs.
- Nearshoring refers to the shift of work to another – lower labor cost – country to leverage lower labor costs but also to be in better control due to the geographical vicinity and basically the same time zones than in an offshoring solution.
- Onshore solutions describe Shared Services or BPO centers within the main country of a company's operations.

The business case to move operations to offshore solutions is absolutely compelling. Primarily driven by the labor cost arbitrage, net savings of thirty-five to forty-five percent are possible especially if North American or West European companies are compared with countries such as India, the Philippines and China. On top of the labor cost advantages usually come the impacts of consolidation and process reengineering. In order to be successful, a Shared Service Initiative or a BPO contract should ensure that processes get reengineered before operations are moved to an offshore location. The simple principle, "your mess for less"— meaning offshoring broken processes without any major technology upgrades and process reengineering — would be a recipe for disaster. Dut to the physical distance from the business with its core processes, it would be almost impossible to drive process reengineering efforts from a remote Shared Services or BPO center in an offshore country. Some of the labor costs, consolidation, and productivity savings will be offset by additional travel costs, telecommunication costs, and the new infrastructure. Technology and facilities need to be built or reconfigured, and the capital requirements related to this can reduce the business case by one-third. The savings and cost categories for a captive Shared Service operation are summarized in an example below:

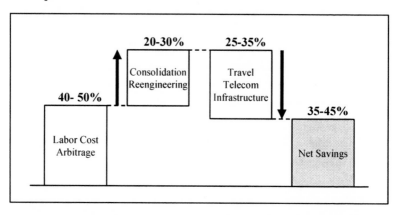

Exhibit III-23: Offshoring Business Case for captive Shared Services

But not only the cost argument is compelling for offshore solutions. In some cases the quality provided by an offshoring center is even better than in the home markets. The example of call centers will highlight why:

Especially in India, China, and the Philippines, jobs in call centers are considered high status and high earning. Almost every call-center agent has a college degree. In the U.S. and countries in West Europe, by contrast, call center jobs are perceived as mediocre paying, dead-end assignments that are taken more and more by college dropouts, students, retirees, and housewives who would like to earn some extra money. Turnover in some US call centers for example can be as high as one hundred percent and absenteeism reaches a somewhat incredible fifteen percent. As a result, quality in U.S. call centers has eroded substantially in the last couple of years. This is a real chance for offshore providers to step up and compete with the quality argument, besides their already convincing cost structure. In addition, 24/7 service on 365 days a year is not a big challenge for offshore countries. Workers, even with college degrees, have no problem working in shifts or over the weekend, and unions are not in place and won't create issues from a workers' contract perspective. For some companies, the move to an offshore place is mainly driven by the around-the-clock service argument. And, although business and industry knowledge still have to be built up in these countries, there is already capacity for offshore outsourcing in place. The following exhibit displays the various countries with offshore capacity in IT-related tasks that are the backbone to support any kind of back-office operation in finance and accounting, HR, procurement, and customer contact management.

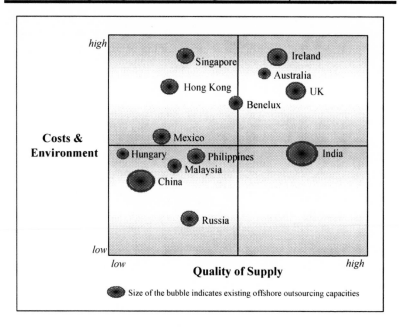

Exhibit III-24: Offshore Capacity for IT-related BPO Activities

India certainly leads the pack. Its more than half-million IT-knowledge workers and 75,000 IT graduates from colleges each year are a cornerstone of their leading position in the IT industry. But regions like China and Eastern Europe are catching up and leveraging the cost advantages while improving quality of supply. Some countries, such as the Philippines, pursue focus strategies in the battle for offshore business. The more advanced telecommunication infrastructure and the lighter accent of their English-speaking people compared to India makes them a strong contestant in the call center arena. Additionally, the Philippines are culturally closer to the U.S. than other parts of the Asian mainland, which is an advantage, especially in customer-contact activities. India, in this respect, has some advantages in the UK market based on their cultural history as former colony.

Skilled labor, however, is also one of the major concerns of offshoring. Although India produces a highly skilled IT workforce and the Philippines has made progress in training and educating call center personnel with regard to other support function qualifications, there are still gaps: Offshoring finance and accounting activities requires knowledge of U.S. and/or European accounting principles and laws. The same applies to HR: payroll, recruiting and employee data management have to be executed within the boundaries of local laws and regulatory requirements. But, as Ireland has proactively addressed the qualification question in the late 1990s and launched large-scale accounting programs subsidized by the government to increase the attractiveness of Ireland as a Shared Service location, most key offshoring countries are currently underway with plans to ramp up their international functional-specific skill base. India, for example, lures well-educated young Indians with college and/or MBA degrees and CPAs earned in the United States or Great Britain back to India with top local salaries. However, it needs to be acknowledged that in the main hubs for offshoring, especially in India, turnover rates start to increase extraordinarily. Young, well-educated intellectual workers have multiple opportunities to work in a wide variety of call centers, data centers, accounting centers, and so on. In the mid-term, meaning the next five to ten years, there is no expected shortage of skilled labor in the offshore countries. Language capabilities are absolutely required as well, and offshore players such as India and the Philippines have no challenge to cope with this, as long as the business language is English. As soon as multiple languages are required – which, in particular for international corporations, is often the case – there are limits in these countries. Eastern European countries such as Hungary, the Czech Republic or Poland offer a much wider variety of languages and a high-quality workforce and still offer substantial labor-cost savings. Especially for European companies, Eastern Europe has the chance to evolve to a highly-attractive nearshore solution.

But lower labor costs are not only possible through offshoring or nearshoring. There are some onshore alternatives that can help with the cost argument and high-quality standards all at once. In the U.S., so-called American Native tribe-owned businesses have emerged that offer various outsourcing services at substantially lower cost levels than most U.S. corporations can perform them. Lakota Technology Inc. is one example of a technology firm owned and operated by the Cheyenne River Sioux Tribe that offers services such as data processing, document imaging, on-line information services, and telemarketing. The advantages compared to remote offshore providers are: no time differences, less logistical efforts, and a stable political environment. Additionally, there are no issues with language and accent, familiarity with American culture, and accessibility – because they are based right in the middle of the U.S., in South Dakota. As in the U.S., such low-cost regions receive government support and tax breaks in Europe as well. Bari in southern Italy or eastern Germany are regions that have battled high unemployment rates for quite a while. Financial support programs by the local government and the EU make these locations very attractive if onshore outsourcing is the targeted strategy. This is often the case when data privacy, security, or legal requirements around intellectual capital are highly ranked criteria and the need for country-specific accounting, HR or law knowledge is very high. Moreover, companies with high corporate social responsibility and government agencies often prefer onshore solutions due to political pressure.

The offshoring market is clearly on the move as some facts will underscore: in 2000, roughly $4 billion in labor costs in the United States related to back-office operations were offshored. This number is expected to increase to $50-65 billion by 2010 and to more than $100 billion by 2015.

Also, almost two-thirds of the Global Fortune 500 companies have already started an offshore initiative. The focus of these initiatives are mostly the typical offshore candidates, such as India, the Philippines, China, or Eastern Europe. But how to identify which location will be right for a specific company? The country-scoring model provides helpful guidelines. It is comprised of three major categories: financials, environment and people:

- Financials
  o Cost of labor
  o Cost of management and infrastructure
  o Tax and treasury impacts
- Environment
  o Political and economic risk/stability
  o Country infrastructure
  o Cultural compatibility
  o Geographic proximity
  o Security of intellectual property
- People
  o Outsourcing process experience, expertise
  o Size of labor market
  o Education level of workforce
  o Language barriers and literacy rates
  o Employee retention

The financial category usually counts for the lion's share in this model and is often weighted at 40-50%. People and environment aspects are typically weighted equally, but in offshoring situations with high emphasis on functional specific knowledge, the people part is often rated higher (30-40%) than the environment (20-30%). It depends on the specific situation of a company (e.g. already existing locations in offshore places), types of functions that should be offshored, and how importantly the various categories and subcategories in the scoring model are weighted by the company's leadership.

From a strategic perspective offshoring supports both cost leadership and differentiation strategies. Cost leaders are very attracted by the concept of offshoring because of its compelling business case. Companies that already operate major parts of their core manufacturing and supply-chain processes in low-cost countries such as China or Taiwan often see offshoring of back-office operations as the next logical step to further drive down the cost structure. But differentiation leaders will find it attractive, too, because of the opportunity to customize service levels according to their customer groups. A major credit card company has recently moved large parts of their call center and accounting solutions to India in order to serve the mass-market customers with a more cost-efficient solution. The premium customers, however, are still served through the U.S.-based and specially trained call center agents to ensure utmost quality, responsiveness, and problem-resolution capabilities. Overall, offshoring of support functions is another concept that enhances strategic flexibility.

Conclusion

A chosen organizational structure is neither engraved in stone nor made for eternity. In fact, the design is one of the most important strategic levers of doing business overall. Managers need to proactively review the current organizational model they have set in place and monitor it with regard to its strategic effectiveness and the leverage of existing capabilities and strengths. Changes to the design are part of the organizational toolkit and should not be seen as scary restructuring efforts associated with crisis management. Research has shown that organizational redesign in crisis situations can be much less effective than the proactive approach of designing the most effective organization as part of the strategic management cycle. Consequently, companies *must* change their design as the competitive landscape and internal capabilities change to be able to leverage their full potential. However, in today's business world, many reasons still hold companies back from pursuing the most effective structure:

- *People-driven Organizational Designs*
  Organizational designs are often defined around persons. It's not necessarily a bad thing to assign organizational responsibility according to the capabilities and skills of those in charge of the tasks, but this should not prevent designing the most effective and rational structure. A typical example would be maintaining a regional structure because somebody would like to remain the regional head, although the business already takes place on a global basis and allocation of work according to divisions is clearly the most effective guiding principle. If the senior manager – as described in this case – is powerful and influential, he can delay and postpone the urgently required redesign. Preservation of power bases is quite often the reason why organizational designs are people and not strategy driven.
- *Increase of Complexity*
  Moving to an advanced organizational model like a Matrix Organization, Network Organization or BPO is often seen as an unnecessary addition of complexity. The fact that complexity increases is true, but, in most cases, there are some good reasons. Complex organizational designs are required because the business has become more complex! Today, some companies still try to operate with outdated functional structures although their business takes

place in multiple product groups across the globe. This is an issue mid-sized emerging companies are often faced with. Or, companies struggle to keep back-office costs on competitive levels without considering Shared Service or BPO as a real option. No wonder they have a hard time keeping up with competitive cost structures. As business grows more complex and challenging, so must the internal structures – and organization management in the new millennium can offer effective design alternatives, as discussed in this chapter.

- *Power Shifts and Decentralization*
  While companies reach out to multiple regions, new countries, or even continents in order to grow the business, they often remain quite centralized. Having central control over certain activities such as marketing, finance, or supply-chain management is useful to maintain consistency and compliance as the business grows. However, the fear of giving too much control to the emerging regional or divisional units is often too strong to move to an effective organization. As a result centralized leaders remain in power and the decentralized units struggle to customize the business according to regional or product group-specific requirements.

- *Fear of Redesigns and Business Interruption*
  Eventually, most companies still consider an organizational redesign as a painful, highly disrupttive, and distracting exercise. True, each change-management initiative distracts, but it does not have to be painful or disruptive. Changes or refinements to existing organizational structures should become an integral part of the strategic direction-setting process. Each strategic move triggers organizational effects. Effective organizations have picked this up quickly

and created a flexible organization culture that allows adapting designs according to strategic directions. Organizational redesigns are no longer the groundbreaking, seldom occurring, company life changing, crisis-like events; they are part of the strategy process. If the strategy changes, the structure changes; sometimes more, sometimes less. It is certainly not a good idea to turn the whole organization upside down each year, though. But first, radical strategic changes usually occur in cycles of more than a year, and second, not every strategic move requires a new basic structure but only some refinements. If organization management is done on a strategic level, the fear of redesigns should be considerably reduced.

Part 2:   Organizational Infrastructure

Organizational Infrastructure is the second major category of key design and delivery elements. The term illustrates that the focus is now on "flow": flow of information, decision-making, work, goods, services, documents, and other elements in business transactions. To use an analogy: the organizational design and structure provides the framework for how companies operate, the system of "streets" that has been laid out. The infrastructure describes how individuals interact, cooperate, and decide to deliver the final product to the customer and generate shareholder value. The infrastructure determines "how" the streets are used, which route will be chosen, which detours and shortcuts will be taken, and the speed with which information, goods, and services travel. The discussion on Organizational Infrastructure will be fourfold:

- *Process Management*
  Traditionally, organization management consisted of an organizational design part (the structure) and workflow management (the flow). Since the late 1980s the term "process" has begun to replace the traditional workflow thinking and has introduced the concept of Business Process Reengineering –an entirely new approach on process management. The discussion on process management focuses on company-spanning Core Processes and functional-specific Subprocesses, as well as the task of coordination across processes.
- *Decision-Making Capabilities*
  The effectiveness of process management depends to a vast degree on the assigned decision-authorities within the company and the effectiveness of their

execution. The RACI Matrix is an important tool to facilitate decision-authority allocation.

- *Information Technology*
  Technology has drastically improved the information flow and decision-support within companies. It has enabled companies to be more closely interlinked with business partners and provides the framework for entirely new business models. Even more important from an Organizational Effectiveness perspective, Information Technology opens new opportunities for improved internal information flow, information sharing, and coordination.
- *Capabilities*
  Organizations are made up of people. The capabilities of the various layers of management with regard to effectively applying the organizational management toolkit have a major influence on the success of a company.

13   Core Processes

Introduced and marketed by **Michael Hammer** in 1990, Business Process Reengineering (BPR) turned existing business organization models upside down. Traditional organizational models and their vertical hierarchical structures were seen as the major cause for the entire business crisis at the time and companies were urged to turn their focus solely on process management and, respectively, on process reengineering. BPR is characterized as a fundamental, radical, and dramatic change of processes to focus on customer value.[39] In essence, it introduces the Core Process idea that emphasizes the cross-company, customer-focused, end-to-end processes. Hammer bases his approach on the overriding mission of the company to create value for the customer.[40] Customer needs are the center of the business universe. Back in 1994 more than three-quarters of the U.S. corporations were reported to have gone through a kind of BPR initiative. The innovative idea of BPR is that processes are defined horizontally, cutting through departmental boundaries, and eventually will make vertical departmentalization obsolete. Customers see the company only through a horizontal perspective.[41] How the work is actually allocated and which departments are involved in the value-creation process are not visible to them. In fact, vertical departmentalization will be perceived as a barrier, especially if the customer is deflected from one department to another because the product is not working as expected. Processes are defined as much more than just the workflow that primarily takes place within the departmental walls.[42] The doom of the functional allocation of work was predicted. Processes would dominate the structural building block of organizations as well. Hammer even called one of his chapters in *Beyond Reengineering* "The End of the Organizational Chart." Instead of functional or divisional unit heads, "process owners" and the "VP for Business Process Reengineering" would be be quite common positions. And companies would be process-centered, flat and streamlined. Eventually, people would go through their entire business life with a maximum of one to two job titles.[43] It did not quite happen as predicted by Hammer. But why?

In fact, the principle of Core Processes doesn't address something else besides the cross-functional corporation. Pulling the functional barriers apart sounds truly revolutionary and like a new and potentially successful concept. But what are the consequences? Process focus would create a different organizational layer that could fall into the same trap as vertical functional silos, as the following example illustrates:

A process-oriented company runs the three Core Processes "Product Development", "Business Development and Sales," and "Supply Chain Management." The product development team is underway to develop a new service that optimally fits the needs of the current customer. The business development team, however, intends to drop this current customer segment due to predicted profitability issues. Same with supply-chain management. Although the product-development team has developed a smart new technology to serve the customers it creates headaches for the supply-chain team because appropriate suppliers are not readily available or have an overwhelming negotiation power that diminishes the value proposition. The solution for the first problem could be a marketing process that coordinates future product/market segmentation strategies and links technology needs with business plans. The second issue could be solved through a procurement process that integrates sourcing needs for product development projects and evaluates the sourcing opportunities for mass production in parallel. The consequences: Welcome back to the functional organization! The challenge for organization management remains to coordinate different organizational units. It doesn't matter if they are built according to processes, functions, regions, or divisions.

Process Management, though, helps to make a chosen operating design more effective. A Core Process should be a process that goes across multiple functions or units and is closely related to the Strategic Capabilities of the company. If a company is well known for its superb product development capabilities, one Core Process should be "Product Development" or "Innovation Management." If a company is a great marketer, one

Core Process should be dedicated to "Brand Management" or "Strategic Marketing." These processes could potentially go across the entire company. But in some cases there are limits, such as assigning responsibility for "Brand Management" to somebody in the procurement department. In a one-dimensional functional organization, the overlaying Core Process structure can easily be applied. Besides the functional heads, the respective process owners will be installed and report directly to the CEO as well.

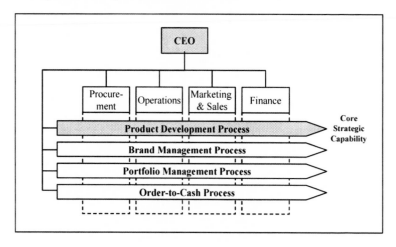

Exhibit III-25: Core Processes in Functional Organizations

Structurally, it depends on the reporting relationship how the matrix of processes and functions interacts. If functions are at the superior level, employees will be assigned primarily to functions and will secondarily report to a process team as in a Hybrid model, with solid reporting lines to the functions and dotted reporting lines to the processes that have been created. Another common way to set up cross-company processes is the differentiation in "Delivery Processes" and "Customer Processes." While the latter ones primarily focus on interaction with the customer, assessment of market potentials, negotiation of deals, and marketing of the products, the delivery team works around the product. They connect with suppliers, design and develop the product, manage the supply chain, ensure quality, and eventually deliver the final product to the retailer or directly to the customer. To mitigate the potential disconnect between the delivery team and the customer team, a "Portfolio Management Process" could be installed to ensure company-spanning coordination.

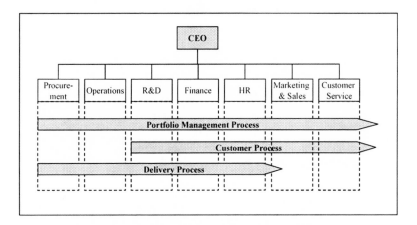

Exhibit III-26: Delivery and Customer Processes

Promoting a process approach in a functional environment is simple and easy to comprehend. However, most corporations today are mostly not functionally driven. Allocation of work has been made to a vast extent according to divisions and geographies. Hybrid models are probably the most common organizational practice, with one superior and one subordinate organizational dimension. Managing this complexity is already quite a stretch for the employees.

Processes, even cross-company ones, do not add a new structural dimension. They organize the workflow. Structure and flow are two different things. Each company needs a structure to allocate work and it needs processes to work within its structures. So, introducing processes is not adding a new structural dimension and won't necessarily add additional complexity. It is a consequence of organization management that provides the workflow perspective. And Core Processes, as defined above, enable a flow perspective that cuts across the organization. The Core Processes are basically a framework for cross-company cooperation.

In a Hybrid Organization with superior divisions, Core Processes need to be defined for each division. It depends on the level of independence if the divisional processes will have linkages to processes in other divisions.

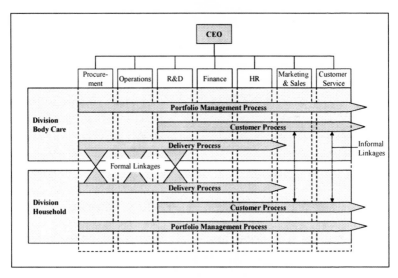

Exhibit III-27: Core Processes in a Hybrid Organization

In the example above, cooperation of body care and household products is useful for operations and procurement activities. Raw materials are relatively similar and can be sourced jointly. Manufacturing processes are similar, as well, and plants can produce a cleaning substance with basically the same production line as for shampoo or soap. However, due to the significant market differences, process linkages between the customer processes on an informal basis will be sufficient. From a workflow perspective, employees are part of a process, meaning they are integrated in a network of information, product, and service flow. The Core Process determines from whom employees get what type of information or unfinished work to which they have to add value by working on it further. The process also determines which type of decisions have to be made along the workflow:

- *Quantitative Decisions*
  These decisions are made based on certain thresholds that must be surpassed before an unfinished product or information gets worked on further.
- *Qualitative Decision*
  These decisions are based on managerial skill, experience, and rational.

Core Processes are a cornerstone to improve Organizational Effectiveness. Through cross-departmental cooperation, the customer perspective can be maintained throughout the whole company. Additionally, process teams help to overcome departmental boundaries and are an enabler to company-wide cooperation. If they are involved or even empowered in the crucial decision-making activities, Core Processes will have a significant contribution to successful strategy execution.

14   Subprocesses

It is important to have distinct processes running across the entire company, or at least across multiple functions. However, not every process has by nature a company-spanning scope. Processes that take place only in one part of the company and do not run across several functions are called Subprocesses. To avoid having the Subprocesses defined as isolated and disconnected from other processes, it is important to develop first a comprehensive process landscape as shown in the following example:

- Core Process: Delivery Process
  - o Subprocesses
    - Sourcing and Procurement
    - Operations Management
    - Product Development
    - Supply Chain Management
    - Logistic Management

- Core Process: Customer Process
  - o Subprocesses
    - After Sales Management and Customer Service
    - Brand Management
    - Sales Management
    - Business Development
    - Offer Development

- Core Process: Portfolio Management
  - o Subprocesses
    - Strategy Development
    - Strategic Planning
    - Market Research

- Core Process: Support Process
  o Subprocesses
    ▪ Information Technology
    ▪ Finance and Accounting
    ▪ HR

Since the Core Processes are operating company-wide, their design should be the starting point for the process landscape. The structure illustrated above is very common, but variations due to company- or industry-specifics are possible. The process landscape is a supplement to the chosen organizational design; it makes the design work and determines how goods and information flow and how decisions are made within the chosen structure. Thus, it's much easier to change and to adapt if required. And it's very unique to each company.

As soon as the Core Process and Subprocess landscape is drafted, all processes eventually need to be linked to each other. The high-level process flow highlights the sequence of all Subprocesses, how the different processes interplay, and how the interface with the customer is arranged.

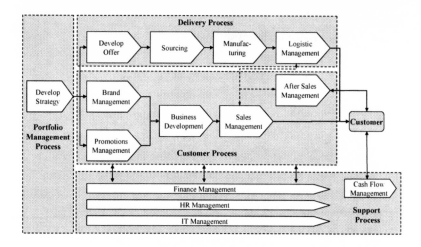

Exhibit III-28: Process Landscape - Example

Subprocesses need to be identified, and general rules and principles how to coordinate and interact need to be developed. Ideally, for each Subprocess a process map is drafted that contains a description of the workflow, coordination principles with other Subprocesses, decision rules, and assignment of responsibilities and accountabilities. Additionally, performance metrics have to be assigned to each process and its respective activities. By regularly monitoring the performance indicators, process performance, stability, and risk to the business will be assessed. Leading indicators are those metrics that provide insights about the expected process performance. They are forward-looking predictors for the expected process performance. Lagging indicators, by contrast, measure the process output. They are solely focused on the actual result and, hence, are backward-looking metrics that are reported too late to actually influence the ongoing process. However, with regard to the future process quality, these indicators provide valuable insights on how to improve and redesign the current process flow.

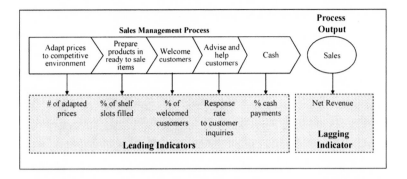

Exhibit III-29: Leading and Lagging Indicators – Retail Example

As indicated the net revenue reported, for example, on a monthly basis will reveal the sales management process performance for the past period. A well-designed performance management system will provide not only lagging metrics that require a detailed root cause analysis first to be able to react; It will also consist of leading indicators to balance forward-looking and backward-looking information and lay ground for effective and timely decision-making.

Six Sigma

There are structured ways to determine process performance. The Six Sigma approach was first successfully applied by GE and has helped many companies since to optimize their processes. It is an approach that enables companies to eliminate costly defects in their processes and realize substantial cost savings. Profitability is often referred to be the core of the methodology. The improvements will be achieved in sigma shifts: a sigma shift of one can lead to a twenty percent gain in margin improvement.[44] The "sigma rating" pinpoints the number of defects-per-million-opportunities in any manufacturing, service, or support process.[45] Although the basic principle is relatively simple, the Six Sigma approach is a complex and holistic process-management approach to either improve profitability, increase customer satisfaction, or enhance employee satisfaction. To be able to implement the Six Sigma approach, the company first has to identify its Core and Subprocesses and link them in a process map. Subsequently, clear responsibilities for all processes will be assigned. Since Six Sigma is a comprehensive and company-spanning philosophy, the whole management team and the high-potential management trainees will be involved. Depending on their functional role, skill and expertise, selected individuals will be trained and developed to take over distinct process responsibilities. The Six Sigma principle differentiates several types of process owners that carry names associated with the martial art Karate. Similar to Karate, process owners need focus and strong discipline to execute their assigned Six Sigma responsibility:[46]

- Green Belts: Highly talented staff or junior managers. These employees can belong to each part throughout the whole organization. They execute Six Sigma projects as part of their job. Thus, the respective projects that they are involved in are closely related to their day-to-day activities. Within the larger Six Sigma project they are normally assigned to lead small-scale improvement projects. In some cases Green Belts work one hundred percent for Six Sigma, in other cases they are assigned on a part-time basis only.
- Black Belts: junior or middle managers that have been identified as high potential. They work under the Master Black Belts and are assigned to specific projects. They work one hundred percent for the Six Sigma project meaning they are freed from any

others tasks. Besides managing their distinct large-scale Six Sigma projects, they are committed to train at least one hundred Green Belts per year.

- Master Black Belts: managers in senior management positions who are assigned by a senior executive, who acts as Six Sigma Champion, to work full-time on the Six Sigma initiative. The Master Black Belts devote all their energy on Six Sigma and are freed from any other operational and leadership responsebility. They train and coach Black Belts and Green Belts intensively. Their core functions are organizing people, coordinating projects, and ensuring cross-company cooperation. Eventually, it's their task to transform Six Sigma into the culture of the organization.

To implement the Six Sigma approach, the company's potential Green, Black, and Master Black Belts will be coached by a group of experts consisting of Black Belts and Master Black Belts. Mostly, Six Sigma trainers have proven track records within a particular function or process for at least ten years. They work jointly with the company to identify current process performance, assess actual error rates, and determine ways to reduce process defects. Eventually, responsibility for process management will go exclusively to the assigned process owner who will continuously focus on his or her own process. The process will gradually be further optimized until a target defect range is achieved. Usually, the target is defined at Sigma 5; approaching Sigma 6 would be considered as world class. Performance will be measured on metrics according to the Six Sigma quality levels. These levels define, for example, Sigma 1 performance at 697,700 defects per million opportunities and Sigma 6 performance (the highest level possible) at 3.4 defects per million opportunities. The opportunities paraphrase the number of process repeats.[47] So if, for example, the billings-to-cash process produces only 3.4 potential errors per one million invoices, it can be seen as Sigma 6 performance. This sophisticated statistical metric approach is a cornerstone of the Six Sigma philosophy.

Six Sigma represents a unique philosophy. The success of frontrunners such as GE, DuPont, Allied Signals, Invensys, and Eastman Kodak proves the robustness and effectiveness of this approach. By applying Six Sigma, the whole company turns to a process focus with a zero error mentality. The leadership team is fully engaged with designing effective processes and puts a clear emphasis on cost effectiveness, customer satisfaction, and its employees. However, on the flipside, Six Sigma is a complex method. Especially with regard to process performance, the methodology is based on a rigid statistical approach that clearly defines variation ranges, capability and performance indices.[48] Implementation requires a major effort. The entire management team has to be coached and trained; high-potential and strong-performing managers have to be assigned fulltime to the effort; processes and performance metrics have to be identified on a very granular level. Furthermore, Six Sigma is not the first concept to re-emphasize the importance of process quality.[49] Other approaches like Total Quality Management (TQM), Kaizen, or Lean Management have targeted process performance explicitly, too. And they were also announced and introduced with a big hooray. They are mostly gone like a fashion of yesterday. Very often, if not communicated and played right, the Six Sigma initiative is mistaken as another kind of "quality management" approach and managers promoting the error-free, high-performing processes are seen as quality auditors only. Eventually, Six Sigma ends up somewhere in the corporate closet driven by some headquarters staff that operates quite remotely from the operational processes of the business.

International Standardization Organization (ISO)

Another tool that has survived different "fashions of the day" approaches over the past fifteen years are the generic management system standards developed by the International Standardization Organization (ISO). Introduced in more than 430,000 organizations in 158 countries, the ISO standards are probably the most widespread process-quality systems around the world. The great success of the ISO standards can potentially be traced back to the fact that ISO is not a consulting approach. Although founded in 1947 and well known by engineers for decades for their work to keep industry standards conforming, ISO standards have gained broader awareness in the business world since 1987 when it released the ISO 9000 standards family. In 1997 the ISO 14000 standards family was released and has gained significant popularity, too. Both families are called generic management standard systems because it doesn't matter if a company provides a product or a service to the market. ISO standards provide a guideline on how to organize processes, assign responsibilities, systemize the network of interrelated activities, and utilize resources efficiently.[50] The management system standards provided by ISO is seen as a state-of-the-art model because experts in the field have basically defined it as a leading practice.

The ISO 9000 addresses whether everything has been done to ensure that the product meets the customer's requirements. The ISO 14000 focuses on whether everything has been done to ensure a product will have the least harmful impact on the environment, either during production or disposal, by pollution or depletion of natural resources.

ISO doesn't issue any certificates. Although the standards are basically used and accepted worldwide, there is no "official" certificate. However, companies applying the standards generally request a proof of their compliance to the principles. Hence, third parties, such as specialized registration firms and governmental bodies, are issuing verifications of compliance to the ISO 9000 and ISO 14000.[51] Companies also often use internal audits to avoid costly "tollgate" inspections. These audits are also explicitly used to address process effectiveness and process optimization.[52] Another advantage of ISO standards is that they provide a proven framework and solid principles to effectively monitor and improve the process performance. In some industries it is a competitive advantage to be compliant with the ISO standards and to provide evidence through a registration firm. Internal audits can be applied to further stabilize and enhance existing processes.

ISO standards are, however, only generic standards. Companies in search for optimizing process improvement will have difficulty deriving performance-boosting ideas out of the general process models provided by the standard. Since the purpose of the ISO standards is to ensure minimal process requirements, they won't provide industry-specific or even company-specific recommendations for highly effective process designs. A company will use ISO standards to compare its current operations with the generic state-of-the-art model to make sure that it's basically on track to perform on the same level as its industry peers. But since the process models are so general and generic, the ISO standards are not a source for detecting distinct industry leadership capabilities. Additionally, ISO audits focus on documented procedures and determine if the company operates in compliance with its own standards rather than providing best practices.[53] From a historical perspective, ISO standards have evolved through the mostly technical driven need for standardization across countries.[54] The variety of different national technical standards was and still is today a major obstacle for companies that operate across borders. Harmonization of technical standards – even though today a vastly unresolved issue – has put additional emphasis on ISO standards. Thus, application of these standards is often seen as a technical, design, or engineering exercise only. In other cases, the use of ISO standards is simply required by the customer. In the automotive industry, being compliant to ISO standards is a simple necessity of doing business within the industry. Similar to the Six Sigma approach, there is a certain risk that ISO standards are just seen as another kind of quality auditing system. Having them is just a necessity and employees carrying the task of conducting ISO audits are seen as a necessary evil rather than as process coaches who manage and orchestrate large-scale process redesign programs.

In spite of the issues of Six Sigma and ISO standards, they are effective tools to facilitate the important task of identifying and designing Core and Subprocesses. They both provide useful frameworks to start with and guidance to design effective processes. Before reinvent-ting the wheel, it is very effective (re)visiting these approaches before starting major business process redesign initiatives.

15   Decision-Making Capabilities and RACI Matrix

Eventually, process performance depends vastly on the quality of decisions that are made along the process flow. Even if processes are designed to be very stream-lined and efficient, and even if excellent coordination is ensured, there are still many managerial and operational decisions to be made to actually execute the process.

Decision-making in organizations has generally three dimensions:

1. Strategic decision-making
   It illustrates the *strategic decisions* to be made by the top management on purpose, mission and overriding strategic goals of a firm. Based on these decisions it will define the appropriate corporate and business unit strategies to pursue and strategic capabilities to focus on.
2. Hierarchical decision-making
   These decisions are *hierarchical decisions* because they are pre-determined through the organizational structure of the company. The hierarchical superiors execute certain decisions to organize and execute the work in their immediate area of responsibility.
3. Process decision-making
   These decisions are not necessarily associated with hierarchical structure because they focus on processes and their cross-functional interfaces. They are more complex because there is little guidance about whom to assign and how to execute them efficiently. In particular for process decisions, the concept of empowerment is often applied. Through empowerment, decision rights will be pushed down into the organization.

The decision making itself is driven by certain basic models. There are some distractions such as love, anger, envy, or self-esteem that will influence decision quality but the underlying principle can be categorized according to the following basic models:[55]

- *Rational Choice Model*
  This decision model is based on the principle that there is always a logical way to solve even complex organizational decisions. It uses mathematical and statistical evidence to derive the only correct, because

scientifically proven, decision. Rational decisions are never based on random or accidental inputs. All goals are clearly defined and different alternatives to reach the goals are outlined and fact-based.

• *Political Behavior Model*
The Political Behavior Model basically describes exactly the opposite of the Rational Choice Model. The underlying assumption is that decisions are made based on political influence of certain stakeholder groups and not based on valid and reliable information. The company is seen as a fragmented organization with different interest groups who do not pursue agreed upon and consistent goals. Each group has its own agenda and tries through political power and bargaining to influence decision making in their interest. In these organizations, detailed information to increase quality of decisions is often – although available – neglected.

• *Carnegie Model*
The so-called Carnegie group, headed by James March, Richard Cyert and Herbert Simon, has developed an organizational decision-making model that focuses on consensus building. While previous models were focused on decisions made by key executives or managers who are basically provided with all required information to come up with an either rational or politically driven single decision, the Carnegie Model assumes that decisions are made in coalitions of managers. The coalition basically has agreed on the organizational goals and has a clear idea how to prioritize decisions according to current strategies. Usually the group consists of cross-functional managers to be able to deal with competing goals within the firm and to identify appropriate solutions. Thus, the Carnegie Model is not aiming for

the ultimate best decision to an organizational issue. It is trying to find the most satisfying solution. The coalition is used to reduce the uncertainty through limited information provision. Managers are humans with limited capacity to store and process information. The group decision allows information spreading and helps the managers to formulate their opinions based on various perspectives and inputs.

- Garbage Can Model
  The Garbage Can Model takes an entirely different approach on organizational decision-making. Based on the idea that many companies operate in unstable environments and are forced to come up with reasonable decision-making under extreme uncertainty, this model provides a framework for effective and frequent decision-making practices under these conditions. The uncertainty is driven by the so-called organizational anarchy that emerges if strategic goals are not clearly defined and broken down, relevant markets and technologies are poorly understood, and companies are hit by high employee turnover that diminishes the skill, knowledge, and expertise base of the firm. The term "Garbage Can" describes exactly this situation; everybody is basically throwing ideas, issues, information, and solutions into a garbage can in hopes somebody who can use them will pick them up.

RACI Matrix

So far, the discussion has focused on the *theory* in organizational decision-making. But how does it work in business *reality*? A simple but very effective tool is the roles and responsibilities matrix. The basic principle of this matrix is to identify and categorize all business decisions. To identify all decision situations, it is necessary to analyze each Core and Subprocess in detail. By analyzing the information flow within the processes, the decision gates have to be highlighted to derive the explicit decision. The following table provides a list of selected typical organizational decisions linked to the Core Processes as discussed earlier.

Core Processes	Organizational Decisions
Portfolio Management Process	Corporate Strategy
	Business Unit Strategy
	Strategic Plans
	Product Portfolio
	Capital Investment
	Core Technologies
	Strategic Partnerships
Customer Process	Sales Channels
	Marketing Plans
	Product/ Market Segmentation
	Market Entry
	Product Launch
	Pricing
	Sales Channels
	Customer Service/ After Sales Services
	Distribution Network
	Marketing Investments
Delivery Process	Production Concept
	Inventory Levels
	Product Development
	New Product Concept
	Product Features
	Supplier Selection
	Supply Chain
	Plant, Property & Equipment Investments
Support Processes	Budgets
	Compensation

Table: Typical Organizational Decisions

Since most of the decisions cross the Core Processes or even impact all Core Processes, it is important to involve different parties across the firm in the decision-making process. The different types of involvement can be categorized as follows:

- *Responsibility*: This is the most important and active role in the decision process. Individuals are responsible for certain decisions because they fall right in their immediate organizational function.
- *Accountability*: Although somebody makes a decision and takes full responsibility, another individual is in charge, too, and carries the accountability for the decision. Especially if decision rights have been delegated down the hierarchical chain, the superior must be accountable for decisions made and executed on his behalf. There are two different forms of accountability: the direct accountability requires an immediate approval of each decision made by a subordinate before it will be executed. The indirect accountability comes into play if a superior has empowered subordinates to make and execute decisions independently and without any further approval. However, if subordinates come up with obviously wrong and strategically non-compliant decisions, the superior has to take full accountability.
- *Consulting*: As already indicated, decisions that go across major functions and processes of a company are generally not simple, linear, and easy to make. Substantial information, data, and knowledge input are required to ensure the high level of quality that's needed. Thus, sufficient decision-support and advice have to be involved in each organizational decision. These groups are neither responsible nor accountable for the impacts of the decision. And they are not confronted with any consequences.
- *Information*: Independent of how decisions are made and executed, it is required to inform other

individuals about the outcome. This can be required simply to keep other managers up to date so they can incorporate a certain solution in their decision-making tasks. In some cases, individuals are only slightly impacted by the decision's outcome, but since it has at least some relevance to their immediate area of responsibility it's certainly worthwhile to keep them in the loop.

Responsibility, **A**ccountability, **C**onsulting, and **I**nformation are the building blocks of the RACI Matrix.

Who Decisions	Executive Team	Procure-ment	R&D	Operations	Marketing	Sales
Product Portfolio	R/A	I	C	C	C	C
Product/ Customer Segmentation	C	I	C	I	R/A	C
Pricing	A	C	C	C	C	R
Sales Channels	A	I	I	C	C	R
Marketing Investment	A	I	I	I	R	C
Inventory Levels	A	C	C	R	I	C
Product Development	A	C	I	C	C	C
Supplier Selection	A	R	C	C	I	I
PP&E Investment	A	C	C	R	I	I

Table: RACI Matrix in Functional Organizations - Example

The exemplified version of a RACI Matrix in the table above illustrates that decisions like pricing and product development very often cut across the entire company. In addition, it displays the accountabilities of the executive team. Basically, in all core decisions the C-level holds the accountability. Sometimes, as indicated for the product portfolio decisions, the responsibility resides with them as well. Allocating RACI roles is simpler and more straightforward for Functional Organizations than in other organizational models.[56] Applying RACI Matrices in

Divisional Organizations or even Hybrid Organizations is far more complex. However, the technique works in divisional structures, too, but on another level of decisions.

Who Decisions	Executive Team	Alcoholic Beverages	Soft Drinks	Snacks
		Divisions		
Corporate Strategy	R/A	C	C	C
Business Unit Strategy	C	R/A	R/A	R/A
Product Portfolio	A	R	R	R
Capital Investment	R/A	C	C	C
Brand Management	A	R	R	R
Shared Resources	A	R	R	R

Table: RACI Matrix in Divisional Organizations

It depends on the corporation's philosophy how to manage the divisions and, therefore, the assignment of decision-rights looks different from company to company.

The process to develop and implement a RACI Matrix is challenging and often underestimated because it surfaces almost all implicit existing role assignments of the corporation's managers and institutionalizes "fuzzy" decision areas. Very often decisions rights are not explicitly addressed and need to be clarified while completing the matrix.

Effective organizations use the RACI Matrix to manage their decision-allocation processes. They use the advantages of categorizing recurrent key decisions and assign them clearly to selected individuals within the firm. In this way, they clarify ambiguous decision areas and solve decision conflicts upfront. People have a clear understanding about their roles and know exactly how they have to contribute to the various organizational decisions. A RACI Matrix should not only exist on the top of the company. It is a useful tool that should be rolled out over the different layers of the organization. As indicated in the two examples above, the real strength of the matrix comes into play as soon as process coordination across functions has to be made.

Incentive Systems

Ideally, individual goals are harmonized with those of the firm; however, for almost all decision situations displayed in the RACI Matrix examples above, there will be at least one conflict between various managers, as the following examples will stress:

- The Chief Operating Officer (COO) often assumes responsibility for management of inventory levels. Since working capital is important to keep cash flow up and capital commitment low, there is a high level of interest to keep stock levels down. Often it is one of the core objectives of the operations department to manage inventory levels at the lowest level possible. The marketing and sales department, by contrast, has different objectives with regard to inventories. For them it is a major threat to face bottlenecks in efficient market provision. Thus, they will advocate "safety" stock levels to ensure responsiveness to customer needs.
- Pricing has been emphasized as one of the true cross-company processes. The ultimate responsibility mostly resides with the sales and/or marketing team because they are interacting with the customer and have market visibility. The sales team in search of market share and revenue growth often tends to lower prices or to ease up payment conditions. Especially

sales teams with objectives based on revenue growth or market share show this behavior. The executive team or the strategy department in charge of managing the overall product portfolio often has issues with this pricing practice because, strategically, certain products should be positioned purposely as "high-price products" while other products are positioned at lower price ranges. The Portfolio Management team will find its objectives often defined as market penetration by product group, which will get in trouble if the sales team operates its own pricing scheme.

Both examples stress the importance of the Incentive System. The Incentive System is the ultimate vehicle to transfer company goals into day-to-day decision-making practices.

Basically, the Incentive System determines how performance within the company will be rewarded. The system can be quite complex, offering different components such as financial compensation, retirement plans, early retirement, company cars, use of company facilities, and memberships in clubs, etc., to reward outstanding performance. The cafeteria approach is used as a synonym to highlight the various compensation alternatives besides money. It is designed to meet the varying needs of employees.[57] To design Incentive Systems to optimize decision-making quality, two basic principles are important:

- Not all decisions can be made jointly. The principle of allocating work to different functions, divisions, and geographies simply requires the *decentralization of decision power*. Otherwise the functioning of work allocation would be contradicted. Usually, understanding, insights, and assessments of market conditions are better on decentralized levels and, therefore, decisions tend to have a better quality if made by the ones who have closest access to the issue. Additionally, consensus-based and central decision-making practices lead to delays and fuzzy decisions. In summary, decision rights have to be consequently assigned according to the chosen organizational model. And that means as decentralized as possible. The routine decision-making practices should follow the organizational model and be linked to the incentive system to be effective.

- *Decision rights have to be closely aligned with the organizational role* of managers. A useful way to ensure this is the case is to treat an organizational function as a business on its own. To avoid having a sales force in search of market share and revenue growth pushing products with unreasonable price levels into the market the sales force should be treated like a "profit center" to make sure that the growth achieved is profitable. The sales force will be measured according to two major goals: "revenue growth" and "profit per unit." Ideally, both are equally weighted and are directly linked to the Incentive System.

These examples illustrate how to principally align decision-making rights with organizational roles. It depends on the general business model, the chosen organizational structure, short-term and long-term strategic goals, and the competitive landscape how to allocate decision rights in detail. As stated, treating the various functions, divisions, and/or geographies as quasi "profit centers" is the first step to get fair and understandable allocation of accountabilities realized. The Incentive System should focus exactly on rewarding performance closely related to the organizational role and subsequently assigned decision-rights.

16   Information Technology

Technology plays a significant role in effective Organizational Infrastructures today. The remarkable developments in Information Technology (IT) over the last two decades have heavily impacted the way corporations do business and organize themselves internally. There are basically three Information Technologies that have improved Organizational Effectiveness drastically:

1. Enterprise Resource Planning systems
2. E-business
3. Intranet solutions.

Enterprise Resource Planning (ERP) systems evolved in the 1980s as a key enabler to create sound business infrastructures. Companies like SAP, Oracle, J. D. Edwards, and PeopleSoft are well known for their contributions in this field. In general, an ERP system can be summarized as the structured approach to optimize a company's internal value chain.[58] The basic idea of these systems is to provide a company with consistent sets of data throughout all business and internal activities. To do so it organizes, codifies, and standardizes all the company's business process data. ERP systems focus on the transactional data that will be turned into information to support the business. Consequently, as soon as data enter the system, such as sales data, they will be used to initiate multiple transactions: activating the distribution department to prepare and execute the delivery, letting inventory management know that certain items are scheduled for delivery, and informing manufacturing that warehouse space needs to be replenished. Moreover, accounting will be informed that a receivable is outstanding and that collection after a certain period of time has to be ensured. In an ERP environment, data are integrated and consistent, which means that data concerning amount of goods, delivery mode and time, price and payment conditions will be used throughout the entire business transaction as they were initially entered into the system. Manual intervention is not required and data are not compiled from different IT systems. Sources of potential errors are reduced to a minimum and, as a result, once data are made available to the system, it literally executes the transactions without any human action needed. At least that is the basic idea. In reality, a system without any manual activity or interfaces to adjacent systems can rarely be found.

If companies switch their structures from functional or divisional models to multilevel structures such as Matrix, Hybrid, or Tensor Organizations, major adjustments have to be made. Corporations transform their structures to a Geographic or International Organization as soon as they turn the business towards multi-regional or even international activities. With regard to the ERP solution, it has to be determined if the company still can operate with one overall integrated system or if the autonomous units require their own ERP solutions. If underlying business models of the geographic regions are significantly different, maintaining just one harmonized ERP system will end up in a mess. The case that one region operates with a key account sales process while the other operates with a product-driven sales approach illustrates the challenge of integrated and consistent data structures across the entire corporation. If supply chain, manufacturing, and market conditions are different, separate ERP solutions by subsidiaries are more beneficial.[59]

E-business is the second radical new development in IT that has significantly changed today's business models. It actually consists of three perspectives:[60]

- **E-commerce**
  Focus of e-commerce is reaching customers through Internet-based sales channels and to purchase via the Internet goods and services more efficiently. Since e-commerce just uses the Internet as an additional sales and/or sourcing channel it does not interfere with given organizational structures.

- **E-business**
  E-business cuts deeper into the structures and cultures. E-business circumscribes the ability to use electronic means to connect with customers and suppliers along all steps of the value chain. Through understanding and optimizing the entire business process from customer requirements through supplier capabilities, e-business has become the most important tool to streamline businesses. Cost reductions and improved customer service are further important advantages of e-business that indicate the differences from e-commerce. Therefore, e-business undoubtedly has considerable effects on organizational designs, cultures and processes.

- **E-partnering**
  E-partnering is eventually the perspective of new technologies that deals with industry supply-chain optimization through Vertical Networks. These networks have already been discussed as the advantageous cooperation among companies of the same industry but on different supply levels. In these networks each partner focuses on its core strength and cooperates closely with its customers and suppliers. Therefore, functional activities such as marketing, sales, manufacturing, assembling, and product development are clearly assigned to certain network partners that have the strongest capabilities to perform them. As a consequence, a Vertical

Network is able to generate higher returns than the isolated activities of each network partner. E-partnering is the technological mean to manage, facilitate, and coordinate those networks. It ensures that customer inputs and requirements will quickly find their way over the multiple levels of the industry supply chain to the respective supplier who is in charge of it. And e-partnering enables Vertical Network-wide supply-chain management. Companies strive to use the Internet to implement e-customer relationship management (eCRM) and e-supply chain management (eSCM) capabilities.[61] These two seamlessly connect operations of all network partners with each other and the final customer. This perspective is much more strategically oriented than the other two perspectives and has, as a consequence, substantial impacts on Organizational Effectiveness.

ERP systems are foremost internally focused and put strong emphasis on process efficiency, data integration, and consistency. E-business, by contrast, is focused on the external relations of the company. It deals with Vertical Network coordination, and connecting business partners, third parties, and customers via the Internet with the company. Although some argue that, with increased use of e-business applications, the time of ERP systems will be over soon, there is still long-term sustainable value to them. Business transactions will always generate masses of transactional data that have to be processed, analyzed, and reported. Goods, information, and money flow need reliable tracking systems independent of whether they are Internet or ERP system based. To be able to process, store, and manage all transactional data, an integrated system will continually be required. The following exhibit summarizes the interplay of ERP and e-business.

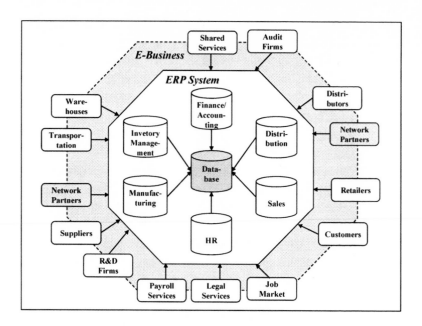

Exhibit III-30: ERP Systems and E-Business

As a consequence, both information technologies will be part of an effective organization. And both have an extensive impact on Organizational Effectiveness: introduction of ERP systems increases transparency of information throughout the whole company. In addition, since data are integrated and consistent, lots of manual work, reconciliation activities, and report generation can be reduced drastically. Thus, ERP systems have led to flatter organizational structures with fewer layers of managers and, as a result, have notably lowered overhead costs. On the other hand, working with ERP systems requires a different mindset among employees. To ensure consistency, data have to be updated regularly and administered very carefully. Only if data are inputted correctly into the system can the full potential of integrated systems be utilized. Additionally, ERP systems require certain standardizations because the system structure is based on an ideal business process. Thus, short-term changes are not easiy to realize and analyses and reports have limits. Effective organizations use ERP systems and have created an e-enabled business environment. The new technologies provide significant potential to reduce costs, streamline and accelerate processes, and improve the overall quality. ERP systems are important to master the transactional data masses. They help to organize, to categorize, and to integrate data for more efficient internal processes. The times of isolated IT islands should definitely be over, as should the times of hundreds of homegrown and high-maintenance IT systems. Especially in terms of e-business, new technologies elevate traditional businesses to entirely new levels. New e-business models have emerged and proven to be successful in most industries. Organizations can be connected directly with their environment and network of stakeholders, which certainly increases effectiveness.

Historically, information flows have been physical, either paper-based or through voice, mainly via the telephone. Computers have enhanced this information flow through structured messages via electronic data interchange (EDI) and unstructured messages via e-mail. Technologies like e-commerce have evolved to combine and integrate these messages and to facilitate the exchange and distribution of information within and across organizational boundaries. Intranets are another group of significant IT developments since the 1980s. IBM's Professional Office System PROFS and early versions of Lotus Notes were forerunners at that time. The initial idea of intranets was enhanced office productivity by allowing employees to communicate over the network, share documents, retrieve and review reference materials, and administer jointly used calendars.[62] As a result, the intranet can be defined as a system consisting of networks, client, servers, and applications to support internal communication. Today, all major corporations around the world use intranets. The intranet works in general like the Internet with the exception that it is accessible to employees and selected guests only. Because of the access restrictions it can be used to exchange and publish information that is proprietary and confidential. Although websites on the Internet can be set up with restricted access, an intranet provides a much safer environment that is protected against unwanted visitors. Companies today have produced and possess tremendous amounts of documents and electronic information. All different kinds of documents related to the business activities, internal processes, policies and procedures, manuals and handbooks, forms and templates, product design specifications, financial data, and so on are available somewhere in the organization. The real challenge is to find a way to bring these pieces of information in front of those who need them. And the intranet is the most efficient and economic tool to make this possible without requiring an unreasonable amount of training.[63] Document and knowledge management as a whole has become a new dimension since intranet solutions were put in place. To differentiate clearly with ERP systems or e-business it has to be stressed that the intranet is not only meant to be a tool that streamlines business processes or enhances coordination with customers and suppliers. It sure does, but its main goal is increasing internal communication and information flow that supplement business processes in terms of quality, speed, and reliability. If intranets play a role in improving business transactions they do it mostly in terms of quality (additional, explanatory, more reliable information) or time (on time, no delays through inner-office mail). Intranets are much more than just e-mail. Intranet solutions include communication of updates and key decisions, interactive websites, employee surveys, file transfer, video conferencing, and training and learning applications. They are the platform for internal bulletin boards and corporate information such as phone and mailing lists, human resource databases, and forms and templates. Moreover, intranets help with sharing best practices, sales presentations, proposals, market research, and serve as a search engine to pinpoint the individual responsible for creating the materials.

With regard to Organizational Effectiveness it is obvious that intranets are important contributors to improve it. Companies use them to decentralize decision-making practices as far as possible into the organization. The individuals with the closest access to the market can quickly be provided with all essential decision support. And decentralized decisions can easily be coordinated and confirmed with corporate functions. The communication culture within firms using intranets has been revolutionized. Cross-departmental and cross-process information and communication flow is easy and quick. Employees are able to share issues with a broader audience and to seek advice. Employees do feel better informed about corporate decision-making, policies, and strategies. They will develop a better understanding on strategy, mission, and goals if they are explained on an intranet web page and Question and Answer (Q&A) sections help to comprehend them better.

The technology aspect and its impact on Organizational Effectiveness, however, were overvalued during the technology boom of the late 1990s[64]. Information Technology features should be analyzed in detail before adopting them. A lot of the so-called state-of-the-art Information Technology is not really required and just nice to have. It won't add significantly to the effectiveness.

17   Team and Individual Capabilities

Organizations are made and run by humans. Thus, the first and most important driver of Organizational Effectiveness is the Executive Team and the CEO. Another important driver is the middle management. Since the group of middle managers is very diverse and a strongly sought-after resource, there is always the risk of overstretching this group. Middle managers are often key influencers of the Organizational Culture and need to be managed proactively and very sensitively at the same time.

Executive Teams

The single great leader is dead. Although distinct individuals have dominated the business history of the last century, effective teams of managers control the major corporations today. **Henry Ford** and **Alfred Sloan** were great entrepreneurs, innovators, managers, and leaders that have almost single-handedly excelled the growth of the U.S. automotive industry. The German **Werner von Siemens**, who invented the pointer telegraph in 1847, was the driving force behind the electronics giant of today, **Gerard Philips** who, in 1891, established a small electronics products and lamp company in Eindhoven, laid ground for another major player in the electronics industry of today. **William Procter** and **James Gamble**, a candle and a soap maker who started their business in 1837, were the driving forces of today's consumer goods giant Procter & Gamble. They all had in common that they turned innovative ideas into sustainable business models and pushed their companies through charismatic leadership to the dominant roles they play in today's business. However, becoming an industry leader today can rarely be attributed to just one outstanding individual. **Bill Gates** is often seen as an exception.

However, even his success was born through a team of talented and like-minded individuals that jointly crossed the one million dollar threshold in 1978 to achieve their dream of having a computer on each desk and in each home. Gates has neither named the company Gates-Software, nor has he been the only and charismatic leader. He has fueled the innovative energy of Microsoft, coined the name, and opened the world for personal computers. However, it was a team that has driven the overall success of the firm. No wonder Microsoft today has the highest percentage of millionaires amongst its employees. In contrast, the wealth created by the "old economy" has been basically accumulated within the founders' families. The same applies to another software giant: SAP. Created by a team of ex-IBM system engineers, the firm has gained an industry leadership that is not rooted with just one charismatic leader. The name of the firm is quite practical (**S**ystem, **A**pplications, **P**roducts) and to recall the names of the founders (Hasso Plattner, Dietmar Hopp, Hans-Werner Hector, Klaus Tschira, and Claus Wallenreuther) is, for most people, a real challenge. Another example is Amazon.com. The online-bookseller is one of the survivors of the Internet boom and it still thrives. Founded by Jeff Bezos in 1995, it has gained significant brand value and brand recognition within its short tenure. Bezos has created an industry marvel with a revolutionary business model, but his name is not used as the company's name and the majority of Amazon's customers probably won't be able to recall it. The success of Amazon.com is not only based on his charismatic leadership but moreover on the great team consisting of talented programmers, creative marketing experts, and leading-edge retail industry experts.

Today, neither "new economy" nor "old economy" firms rely on distinct and charismatic leadership personalities anymore. Teams of managers that are mostly not related to the founders' families manage the major corporations today.

The lonely great man is dead; long live the team!

- The **composition of the executive team** is the first cornerstone of successful teamwork. Some simple groundrules can help to identify improvement potentials for executive teams. With regard to the leader of the team, it is extremely important that he or she is able to facilitate the group effectively and to integrate with the group. The selfish and eccentric CEO can distort the entire group harmony and create severe communication and coordination roadblocks among the members of the team. An executive team that does not communicate effectively and is not coordinated well will create confusion in all layers of the organization. Additionally, confidence and trust in broadly accepted strategic goals will erode further down in the company if contradicting statements and opinions by the members of the executive team are spread around. Conflict around these topics should be resolved in the boardroom. Since managerial tasks on the top are generally more complex than lower in the organization, the chief executive has to spend a significant proportion of time with the team to discuss and agree on objectives, compare actual performance with targets, and coach and advise them. Hence, a span of control exceeding ten executives is unreasonable and distracts the CEO from other important tasks. A span of less than three executives is too small to be efficient. In particular in Hybrid and/or International Organizations, some Leaders find themselves in situations with more than twenty direct reports due to functional, divisional, and geographical dimensions that have to be managed at the same time. Ideally, the group of direct subordinates to the CEO stems only from the leading organizational dimension. That means if divisions have been chosen to be the guiding principles and regions report in dotted line to divisions, the executive team should consist of the CEO, the divisional heads, and selected functional officers only. The regions report either in the CMO or COO depending on their core tasks ("selling" or "manufacturing"). In this way, the number of team members can be kept below ten and remain manageable for the CEO.

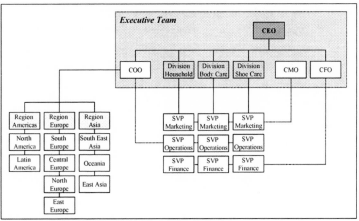

Exhibit III-31: Composition of the Executive Team - Example

- Besides the span of control, **allocation of responsibilities** is another cornerstone of Executive Teams. Each executive should have main responsibilities for decisions that are under his or her functional, divisional, or regional control.[65] The marketing strategy will be intensively discussed within the executive team and the CEO will provide advice, but execution and implementation of the strategy will take place under full responsibility of the CMO. It is important that responsibilities be clearly assigned to avoid lengthy decision periods and administrative efforts to coordinate the decision-making process. Thus, each team member has to make decisions based on his or her area of expertise, which should match with the organizational role. Effective Executive Teams have, in general, clearly allocated responsibilities. Even though they act normally as a team, most of the day-to-day decisions are clearly assigned.

• The third cornerstone of effective executive teamwork is clear **governing principles** for the team. As a general groundrule, the Executive Team should meet at least once a week to coordinate day-to-day activities. Performance reviews should be conducted in at least monthly meetings and planning/forecasting reviews should take place at least on a quarterly basis. The strategy should be reviewed twice a year. All other non-routine subjects, such as M&A activities and technology decisions, should be added as needed to the agenda of the meeting schedule. The framework of the meetings can be different: the Executive Team may be supplemented by the group of Senior Vice Presidents in the monthly meeting, or the broader management team may be invited to discuss strategic plans in bigger settings on a biyearly basis. It doesn't matter which schedule, list of attendees, or format (conference call, video-conference, in person) has been chosen. What matters is that frequent communication and coordination are institutionalized and topics to be discussed and decided on the agenda of the relevant meeting to be effective as an Executive Team.

CEO selection and succession is probably the most complex area of Executive Team effectiveness but the most influential on effectiveness as well. The effectiveness of the CEO is difficult to assess: personalities, leadership styles, talents, and characteristics cannot be consolidated into one sounding framework of the "effective CEO."[66] Since the chief executive is the key facilitator and coordinator of the Executive Team, his or her role is exceedingly important. And so is the succession. As a matter of fact, succession planning in most companies is still very much focused on the model that the current chief executive will leave the job at a pre-determined point in time, mostly defined as the start of retirement. These companies are often hit by surprise if the CEO unexpectedly leaves, gets fired, becomes severely ill, or suddenly and unexpectedly dies.[67] Effective organizations will apply succession planning as part of their talent screening and development management. This process identifies, over years and years, high-potential employees and systematically develops their leadership skills by assigning new and challenging tasks to them. Ideally, each company has several highly trained and well-developed candidates who are basically ready to take over the CEO role immediately. But this is not always the case. Some chief executives have emotional problems with appointing a "stand-by" successor because it confronts them with the issue of mortality.[68] In normal succession cases, there is no need to select under time pressure the new leader who has been, ideally, developed over years internally. It is often the case to consider outside candidates as potential successors, as well.

- The first selection criteria are skills and expertise. The potential new leader has to have outstanding management capabilities; he or she has to facilitate and integrate the Executive Team and should be able to make quick and confident decisions. The CEO has to cope with the immense responsibility related to the task and should have no problems at all making and being accountable for difficult decisions. Furthermore, he or she should be an expert in the core business of the firm.

- The new chief executive should fit into the Organizational Culture. Internally developed CEO candidates are generally stamped by a particular culture, but if external candidates are part of the search, they should be screened to see if they would fit into the environment. This is even more important if candidates from different industries will be considered. Although experience and knowledge from different industries can be refreshing and lead to more diverse management practices, the personal fit of the candidate with the – unwritten but nevertheless existing – culture is vital for a smooth transition to new leadership.

- The candidate should fit the so-called "strategic situation." The strategic situation comprises the current business conditions and current and future strategic direction. Potential candidates are screened if they will fit the strategic situation of the company. The potential strategic situations vary widely and depend heavily on the current business conditions of a company and the particular environment.[69]

Alternative Strategic Situations:

- o Startup
- o Turnaround
- o Profit Improvement / Rationalization
- o Dynamic Growth – existing business
- o Dynamic Growth – new business
- o New Acquisition
- o Liquidation / Divestiture

Other criteria besides the three groups mentioned above focus more on "soft factors" that characterize ideal CEO candidates. However, to use them in real selection processes has limitations. A study, for example, of the education and social backgrounds of two hundred chief executives in America has revealed that they are mostly public-college educated, married, have religious commitments, and are basically in better physical conditions than non-CEOs.[70] To use these criteria in selection situations would be a stretch and, hence, they can be considered only indirectly.

Middle Management Teams

Within major corporations the middle management is one of the most important groups, too. Major restructuring efforts or integration of acquired companies are heavily dependent on the support of the middle management. The middle management significantly coins the culture of the firm and this group enables (or hampers) all communication and coordination across the company.

The middle management carries all managerial functions within the firm that don't have executive responsibilities and decision rights. Broadly defined, that means everybody from staff supervisor and junior manager to the senior vice president without executive power belongs to this group. This definition already highlights the immense size and importance of middle management. These are the leaders of the firm on all levels except the executive level.

Since basically all leaders except the Executive Team are part of the middle management, this group is the connection between top management and staff level. Through their managerial capabilities, the company's mission, strategy, and strategic goals get converted into day-to-day activities. Thus, they need a good understanding and buy-in of strategic goals and, in addition, great capabilities and personal characteristics to make those objectives comprehensible and plausible for the entire company. Furthermore, it depends very much on the individual leadership styles of the middle management if the workforce is loyal, highly motivated and committed, and strong performing. But, in reality, the middle management especially is often a source of cynicism and demoralization, which can send out dangerous signals for the performance of the whole workforce.[71] As illustrated in the "Dilbert" cartoons, the middle management can easily turn well-intended management practices into absurdity and severely damage communication flow and coordination. Eventually, they can create a poisoned work atmosphere that leaves the workforce unmotivated and insecure. Due to the size and composition, the middle management consists of different individuals with different backgrounds and different individual goals. The new entrant to the middle management group is typically the highly energized junior manager in his or her first supervisory role. These individuals are both challenged and motivated through their new role. If they are ambitious they consider this position as an intermediate step to a more senior leadership role. If they pursue more moderate career goals they will focus on control and master their newly appointed managerial tasks. Managers on the senior manager or director level can be split into basically two groups as well: the group of relatively young managers and directors that are still pursuing promotion goals, and those settling on this level as their ultimate career goal. The same essentially applies to the non-executive vice president level.

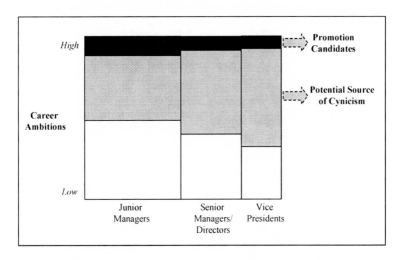

Exhibit III-32: Composition of Middle Management

The simplified composition of the middle management illustrated above indicates that on each level a substantial group of ambitious leaders won't be able to pursue its career goals. Although once highly energized, they get stuck on their career path and find themselves in roles that don't match their expectations. This group is a potential source of cynicism and demoralization whose impact can be even stronger than from the group of relatively low-ambition leaders who have settled happily in their current positions. With increasing tenure and experience on certain management functions and without having career prospects, middle managers tend to get frustrated and overly critical towards each attempt to redesign the organization, adjust strategic goals, improve the work atmosphere, and implement new management techniques. Admittedly, in stagnant industries in particular, not everybody can fulfill his or her intended dream career. People simply have to accept the fact that, when the time comes, they have probably reached the end of their individual career path. Most middle managers have realized this and live with it quite comfortably.

Middle management team building is one approach that attempts to develop a cohesive and effective "team" of managers, although they all have their individual areas of responsibility. It is important to create a team spirit among the middle managers even if they are part of different functions, divisions, or regions. The middle management team needs to comprehend its important role to foster Organizational Effectiveness.

Middle managers are the communication interface to the organization. Close communication among middle managers will help cross-functional and cross-divisional coordination without having explicit Councils and Committees or Project Teams taking care of it. Thus, middle managers should have the capabilities and interests to share information not only along their reporting lines. They should be open to cross-company information sharing and seek ways to realize it.

Middle managers are the most demanded resource for cross-company project work. Therefore, they are often distracted from their routine work and have difficulty balancing project requirements and their regular jobs. However, middle managers are crucial for the project's success: in most cases they have the required experience, expertise, company insights, and eventual decision-power to implement project efforts. Hence, there is no way to conduct successful project work without involving a substantial number of middle managers.

The middle management is not easy to handle and it can be a dangerous source of cynicism. It's very diverse, with individuals who have highly ambitious career goals and those who are heavily frustrated due to limited promotion prospects. The art of managing effective organization includes the capability of the top management to create a team spirit among the group of middle managers.

Talent Management

The patterns of Individual Performance have already been exhaustively discussed in chapter I. Individual performance and the willingness of the individual employee to contribute effectively to the firm's business activities is undoubtedly a key to Organizational Effectiveness. Attracting and keeping talented individuals and offering them appropriate development opportunities are extremely important to strengthen Organizational Effectiveness. Talent Management has become a discipline of its own with two core tasks:

- **Attracting and keeping sufficient expertise.**
  Certain industries are, dependent on their growth patterns, continuously in search for highly qualified young business professionals to provide the expertise requested by their clients.[72]
- **Talent Management.** There is a constant need to identify, develop, and nurture high potential employees who possibly will be the successors to the senior leadership team.

It is quite common that effective companies use integrated Talent Management systems that process systematically all data concerning expertise requirements, management succession needs, development stages of high potentials, and performance appraisals. These systems help the HR department to facilitate the Talent Management process, keeping files up to date, and maintaining a consistent set of sensitive data.

- **Attracting expertise**
  As long as required expertise can be hired right away from universities, business schools, institutes, or other educational institutions, targeting specific schools is proably the best approach. Examples of differentiating factors to attract talent from schools, as well asexperienced hires, are listed below:

  o Compensation
  o Profit sharing
  o Stock options
  o Career prospects
  o Working conditions
  o Memberships
  o Company cars
  o Vacation days
  o Balance of work and social life
  o Perceived Organizational Culture

  In terms of "hard facts" such as compensation and vacation days competitors are often comparable, therefore "softer" criteria such as social life and Organizational Culture will make the difference.[73] Each potential employee assesses the new position from the perspective of whether he or she will fit in the new environment. Inviting prospective new employees to social events of the firm, offering them the opportunity to speak with a broad variety of employees, and meeting in private settings are opportunities to demonstrate certain cultural strengths of the organization – and eventually convince a candidate to sign the contract.

- **Retaining employees**
  Effective employee retention is vital for keeping customer and technology knowledge within the firm. Often employees possess tacit knowledge concerning customers that can hardly be replaced. Specific customer behaviors, their individual needs and desires, and preferred styles are implicitly understood but nowhere documented or tracked in the systems. Executing effective employee retention can be achieved by simple groundrules:

  o Make work fun
  o Maintain open communication
  o Encourage camaraderie
  o Be fair and honest
  o Create desirable work areas
  o Allow personalized work areas
  o Hold individual meetings
  o Express confidence in people
  o Fight boredom

  Roger Herman presents and thoroughly discusses three hundred different strategies to be applied to retain people.[74] It catches the eye that those groundrules are closely related to the Organizational Culture. Maintaining a balanced, attractive, and fulfilling culture is obviously key to keeping the crucial talent on board.

But retaining talent should also be supplemented by **leadership succession planning.** Potential Leaders will be selected meticulously and early to give them enough time to further develop leadership capabilities and gain experience. It is recommended to use in-depth trainings or assessment centers to detect the strongest candidates. And it is useful to inform leadership candidates about their potential career path. It will point out the pre-requisite of superior performance, provide further sharpening of management skills, and allow international and cross-company experience. Subsequently, leadership candidates should be exposed on their way to senior leadership positions to assignments that provide international experiences, give insights into corporate headquarters functions, familiarize them with divisional leadership challenges, and provide cross-functional experiences. Hence, the leader of tomorrow will have an in-depth understanding of the firm from all different angles. Middle managers who are not selected as the future top leaders of the firm should not be left in the dust. Career goals should be openly discussed with them as well. This group can be a threat if cynicism takes over – as illustrated earlier. If these managers are aware of their role and do not have to "suspect" that there won't be any significant promotions for them, it is easier to deal with them. Opportunities for part-time work or early retirement can be discussed to give them the opportunity to pursue other objectives in life.

[1] David A. Nadler, Marc S. Gerstein, and Robert B. Shaw, *Organizational Architecture, Designs for Changing Organizations* (San Francisco, CA: Jossey-Bass Publishers, 1992), p.4.

[2] Chris Sauer and Leslie P. Willcocks, "The Evolution of the Organizational Architect," *MIT Sloan Management Review*, Vol. 43, No. 3, Spring 2002, pp. 41-42. Highlights the need for an Organizational Architect, in particular with regard to e-business.

[3] Stephan B. Bradley, Jerry A. Hausmann, and Richard L. Nolan, *Globalization, Technology, and Competition* (Boston, MA: Harvard Business School Press, 1993), p. 3.

[4] William A. Pasmore, "Creating Strategic Change: Designing the Flexible High-Performing Organization," 1994, pp. 24-25.

[5] Lawrence E. Koslow and Robert H. Scarlett, "Tips to Take Your Company Worldwide," *Global Business*: 308, Houston, TX: Cashman Dudley, 1999, pp. 3-5.

[6] Jay R. Galbraith, *Designing the Global Corporation* (San Francisco: Jossey-Bass, 2000), p. 4.

[7] "Waging War on Complexity: How to Master the Matrix Organizational Structure," A.T. Kearney Whitepaper, 2002, Chicago, IL, pp. 2-6.

[8] Fritz Kroeger and Graeme Deans, *Merger Endgames*, New York: McGraw-Hill, 2002.

[9] Richard L. Daft, *Organization Theory and Design*, 6th ed. (Cincinnati, OH: South-Western College Publishing, 1998), pp. 214-215.

[10] Geary A. Rummler and Alan P. Brache, *Improving Performance: How to Manage the White Space on the Organization Chart* (San Francisco: Jossey-Bass Publishers, 1990), pp. 6-7. Highlights the functional silo phenomenon.

[11] Nick Sternberg and Scott Heil, *Organization Charts: Structures of 230 Businesses, Government Agencies, and Non-profit Organizations*, 3rd ed. (Farmington Hills, MI: The Gale Group, 2000), p. 92-94

[12] Soeren Dressler, "Closing the Gap Between Managerial Accounting and External Reporting," *Journal of Cost Management*, Vol. 16, No. 1, 2002, p. 20.

[13] David A. Nadler and Michael L. Tushman, *Competing by Design, The Power of Organizational Architecture* (New York: Oxford University Press, 1997), p. 121.

[14] Frank Ostroff, *The Horizontal Organization: What the Organization of the Future Looks Like and How it Delivers Value to Customers* (New York: Oxford University Press, 1999), p. 70.

[15]Frank Ostroff, *The Horizontal Organization: What the Organization of the Future Looks Like and How it Delivers Value to Customers* (New York: Oxford University Press, 1999), p. 70.

[16] Leslie Bendaly, *Organization 2005: Four Steps Organizations Must Take to Succeed in the New Economy* (Indianapolis, IN: Park Ave. Productions, 2000).

[17] Freek Vermeulen and Harry Barkema, "Pace, Rhythm, and Scope: Process Dependence in Building Profitable Multinational Corporations," *Strategic Management Journal*, Vol. 23, No. 7, July 2002, pp. 637-638.

[18] James McGrath and others, *The Value Growers: Achieving Competitive Advantage Through Long-Term Growth and Profits* (New York: McGraw-Hill, 2000), pp. 15-19.

[19] Freek Vermeulen and Harry Barkema, "Pace, Rhythm, and Scope: Process Dependence in Building Profitable Multinational Corporations," *Strategic Management Journal*, Vol. 23, No. 7, July 2002, pp. 640, 648-649. Provides considerations on speed of internationalization activities.

[20] David A. Nadler, Marc S. Gerstein and Robert B. Shaw, *Organizational Architecture: Designs for Changing Organizations* (San Francisco, CA: Jossey-Bass Publishers, 1992), p. 23.

[21] David A. Nadler, Marc S. Gerstein and Robert B. Shaw, *Organizational Architecture: Designs for Changing Organizations* (San Francisco, CA: Jossey-Bass Publishers, 1992), p. 23.

[22] Richard Daft, *Organization Theory and Design*, 6th ed. (Cincinnati, OH: South-Western College Publishing, 1998), p. 259.

[23] Timothy Blumentritt and Douglas Nigh, "The Integration of Subsidiary Political Activities in Multinational Corporations," *Journal of International Business Studies*, Vol. 33, No. 1, 2002, p. 61.

[24] Bruce A. Pasternack and Albert J. Viscio, *The Centerless Corporation: A New Model For Transforming Your Organization For Growth and Prosperity* (New York, NY: Simon & Schusters, 1998), pp. 24-25.

[25] Larraine Segil, *Intelligent Business Alliances: How to Profit Using Today's Most Important Strategic Tool* (Toronto, Canada: Times Business, 1996), pp. 184-185.

[26] Jeffrey J. Reuer and Africa Ariño, "Contractual Renegotiations in Strategic Alliances," *Journal of Management*, Vol. 28, No. 1, 2002, pp. 47, 58-65.

[27] Michael Y. Yoshino and U. Srinivasa Rangan, *Strategic Alliances: An Entrepreneurial Approach to Globalization* (Boston, MA: Harvard Business School Press, 1995), p. 110.

[28] Richard Daft, *Organization Theory and Design*, 6th ed. (Cincinnati, OH: South-Western College Publishing, 1998), pp. 256-257.

[29] Michael E. McGill and John W. Slocum Jr., *The Smarter Organization: How to Build a Business That Learns and Adapts to Marketplace Needs* (New York: J. Wiley, 1994), pp. 108-109.

[30] Robert F. Freeland, "When Organizational Messiness Works," *Harvard Business Review*, No. 5, 2002, pp. 24-25.

[31] Kathleen Goolsby and Eric Simonsen, "To Share or Not to Share, an Analysis of the Effectiveness of a Shared Service Strategy vs. an Outsourcing Strategy," Everest Group White Paper, www.everestgrp.com, May 2002, p. 4.

[32] Marcie Krempel, *Shared Services: A New Business Architecture for Europe*, London, UK: The Economist Intelligence Unit, 1998

[33] Jane Linder, Susan Cantrell and Scott Crist, "Business Process Outsourcing Big Bang, Creating Value in an Expanding Universe," Accenture White Paper, www.accenture.com, 2002, p. 1.

[34] Romala Ravi et al., "Worldwide Business Process Outsourcing Forecast and Analysis, 2002-2006," IDC, 2002, p. 10.

[35] Knowledge@Wharton Special Section: The Rush to Send Back-Office Business Overseas – Part 2: Managing the Extended Organization: Handling the Risks of BPO Relationships, 2002, p. 2.

[36] Peter Bendor-Samuel, "Finance and Accounting Outsourcing Set to Explode as Stable Service Provider Base Develops," *Outsourcing Journal*, July 2002, pp. 1-2.

[37] Rebecca Scholl, "Business Process Outsourcing at Crossroads – Market Trends," Gartner Group, January 31, 2002, p. 1.

[38] F. Karamouzis, "Buyers Beware: Indian IT Service Providers to Foray Into BPO," Gartner Group, research note, December 2002, p. 3.

[39] Michael Hammer and James Champy, *Reengineering the Corporation: A Manifesto for Business Revolution* (New York: HarperBusiness, 1993), pp. 32-36.

[40] Michael Hammer, *Beyond Reengineering: How the Process-centered Organization is Changing Our Work and Our Lives* New York: HarperBusiness, 1996), p. 97.

[41] Dan Dimancescu, *The Lean Enterprise: Designing and Managing Strategic Processes for Customer-Winning Performance* (New York: American Management Association, 1997), p. 5.

[42] Peter G.W. Keen, *The Process Edge: Creating Value Where It Counts* Boston, Mass: Harvard Business School Press, 1997), p. 17.

[43] Michael Hammer, *Beyond Reengineering: How the Process-centered Organization is Changing Our Work and Our Lives* New York: HarperBusiness, 1996), p. 61.

[44] Mikel Harry and Richard Schroeder, *Six Sigma: The Breakthrough Management Strategy Revolutionizing the World's Top Corporations* (New York: Doubleday, 2000), pp. 2-3.

[45] Six Sigma Academy website, http://www.6-sigma.com.

[46] Mikel Harry and Richard Schroeder, *Six Sigma: The Breakthrough Management Strategy Revolutionizing the World's Top Corporations* (New York: Doubleday, 2000), pp. 193-195.

[47] Mikel Harry and Richard Schroeder, *Six Sigma: The Breakthrough Management Strategy Revolutionizing the World's Top Corporations* (New York: Doubleday, 2000), p. 145

[48] Forrest W. Breyfoggle III, *Implementing Six Sigma: Smart Solutions Using Statistical Methods* (New York: John Wiley & Sons, 1999), pp. 186-190.

[49] Michael Hammer, "Process Management and the Future of Six Sigma," *MIT Sloan Management Review*, Vol. 43, No. 2, 2002, p. 26.

[50] International Standardization Organization website, http://www.iso.ch

[51] Donald A. Sanders and C. Frank Scott, *Passing Your ISO 9000/QS-9000 Audit: A Step-by-Step Guide* (Boca Raton, FL: St. Lucie Press, 1997), pp. 93-96.

[52] Tom Taormina, *Successful Internal Auditing to ISO 9000* (Upper Saddle River, NJ: Prentice Hall, 1999), p. 5.

[53] Tom Taormina, *Successful Internal Auditing to ISO 9000* (Upper Saddle River, NJ: Prentice Hall, 1999), p. 1

[54] Kenneth L. Arnold, *The Manager's Guide to ISO 9000* (New York: The Free Press, 1994), pp. 2-4.

[55] Ben Heirs and Gordon Pehrson, *The Mind of the Organization: How Western Organizations Can Sharpen Their Thinking*, (New York: Harpers & Row Publishers, 1982), p. 21.

[56] Geary A. Rummler and Alan P. Brache, *Improving Performance: How to Manage the White Space on the Organization Chart* (San Francisco: Jossey-Bass Publishers, 1990), pp. 181, 184-185.

[57] Burton T. Beam Jr. and John J. McFadden, *Employee Benefits*, 6th edition (Chicago, IL: Real Estate Education, 2001), p. 431.

[58] Norris Grant et al., *E-Business and ERP: Transforming the Enterprise* (New York: John Wiley & Sons, 2000), p. 12

[59] Norris Grant et al., *E-Business and ERP: Transforming the Enterprise* (New York: John Wiley & Sons, 2000), pp. 73-74.

[60] Norris Grant et al., *E-Business and ERP: Transforming the Enterprise* (New York: John Wiley & Sons, 2000), p. 14.

[61] Norris Grant et al., *E-Business and ERP: Transforming the Enterprise* (New York: John Wiley & Sons, 2000),, pp. 19-20.

[62] James Ware et al., *The Search for Digital Excellence* (New York: McGraw Hill, 1998), pp. 20-21.

[63] Ronald L. Wagner and Eric Engelmann, *Building and Managing the Corporate Intranet* (New York: McGraw Hill, 1997).

[64] Harold J. Leavitt, "Technology and Organizations: Where's the Off Button," *California Management Review*, Vol. 44, No. 2, Winter 2002, pp. 126-127, and Bert Rosenbloom, "The Ten Deadly Myths of E-commerce," *Business Horizons*, Vol. 45, No. 2, March-April 2002, pp. 62-65.

[65] Dennis A. Romig, *Breakthrough Teamwork: Outstanding Results using Structured Teamwork* (Chicago: Irwin Professional Publishing, 1996), p. 159.

[66] Peter F. Drucker, *The Effective Executive* (New York: Harper & Row, 1985), pp. 22-24.

[67] Dennis C. Carey and Dayton Ogden, *CEO Succession: A Window on How Boards Can Get It Right When Choosing a New Chief Executive* (New York: Oxford Press, 2000), pp. 2-3.

[68] David Nadler, Marc S. Gerstein and Robert B. Shaw, *Organizational Architecture: Designs for Changing Organizations* (San Francisco, CA: Jossey-Bass Publishers, 1992), p. 206.

[69] David Nadler, Marc S. Gerstein and Robert B. Shaw, *Organizational Architecture: Designs for Changing Organizations* (San Francisco, CA: Jossey-Bass Publishers, 1992), pp. 196-197.

[70] *CEO: Who gets to the top in America* (East Lansing, Michigan: Michigan State University Press, 1989), pp. 181-185.

[71] Ron Ashkenas and others, *The Boundaryless Organization: Breaking the Chains of Organizational Structure* (San Francisco, CA: Jossey-Bass, 1995), p. 101.

[72] Charles Woodruffe, *Winning the Talent War: A Strategic Approach to Attracting, Developing and Retaining Best People* (Chichester, UK: John Wiley & Sons, 2000), pp. 16-17.

[73] Jim Harris and Joan Brannick, *Finding and Keeping Great Employees* (New York: AMACOM, 1999), pp. 103-105, 161.

[74] Roger E. Herman, *Keeping Good People: Strategies for Solving the #1 Problem Facing Business today* (Winchester, VA, Oakhill Press, 1994).

"The new strategic weapon"

Strategic Control: Performance Management and Target Setting

Strategic Control focuses on **monitoring** Organizational Effectiveness. Senior executives need to understand how and if organizational improvement activities have been implemented. Strategic Control explains target setting, controlling, and managing the process towards a fit of the organization with its strategic goals. Key Performance Management has taken on a different meaning, especially with the introduction of the Balanced Scorecard in 1992. It is no longer focused primarily on financial metrics but has become a strategic dimension that is widely applied to monitor strategy execution. The role of Strategic Control is now taken more seriously and advanced Performance Management systems are used as strategic weapons in order to achieve competitive advantages.

Different Approaches to Performance Measurement

Management reporting is an important source of the company's performance and displays the true ability to generate operative returns that are required to cover the costs of capital. There are certain trends that highlight the changes in Performance Management over the past decade:

- Management accounting reveals the accurate financial conditions through its focus on the "**economic**" capabilities of the business that are not constrained by generally accepted accounting principles. Hence, the internally driven management reporting should be the primary source for perfor-mance measurement and not the far more restricted reporting according to certain external regulations.
- Historically, management accounting has faced **less scrutiny** than financial accounting.[1]
- Effective reporting today puts an emphasis on **leading metrics** that are early warning indicators or predictors to help the management understand and anticipate the performance to come. Instead of backward-oriented analysis of the reasons for variances, the reporting provides upfront insights and reliable predictions – and makes variance analysis of actual and planned figures easy and comprehensible. These primarily nonfinancial predictors monitor, for example, quality metrics that display the current performance in process management. If quality falls short or error rates surge it certainly will have an impact on the cost of goods sold.
- Performance Measurement and its management reporting have become today more **holistic and comprehensive**. Top Managers don't want to work through thick piles of financial data to understand key issues of the business. They require a more complete picture that pinpoints almost self-explanatorily where the business stands and what financial impacts to expect.
- Managers often struggle to keep their eyes permanently on the **overriding strategic goals** while they are screening and analyzing the details of their man-

agement reports. The strategy should be the driver to select performance indicators.

- Top management would like to ensure that, on **all layers** across the firm, decision-making practices comply with the overall strategic direction. Thus, advanced performance management systems need to be integrated, cascaded, and eventually rolled-out across the entire organization.

In recent years various new approaches to Performance Management that address the new trends have emerged.

- *Balanced Scorecard* - This is a management system that attempts to translate the company's strategy into measurable indicators and make strategic goals plausible for each individual within the firm. Scorecards should be balanced because performance indicators are covering four different fields: financial metrics, customer metrics, internal business process metrics, and learning and growth metrics. Balanced Scorecards focus strongly on the strategy. It is the guiding principle. Although shareholder value can be derived as one core financial measure, it is possible that it won't appear on the scorecard because measures like profitability or revenue growth are higher prioritized. Shareholder value is not the explicit focus of Balanced Scorecards.

- *Value-Added Measurement* – This approach declares optimizing shareholder value as the top priority. Based on shareholder value as the leading metric, the composition of value generation will be broken down into the value tree. This tree consists of major revenue, cost, and capital drivers to increase shareholder value. Through refinement of the value-tree the most important value levers can be identified, performance indicators can be derived, and accountabilities can be assigned. These approaches operate with the assumption that shareholder generation is always the predominant strategic goal.

- *Integrated Strategic Measures* (ISM) – This Performance Management approach combines strategy focus and shareholder-value focus in one integrated system. The key performance metrics, as defined by the top management, will be cascaded through the entire organization. The reporting format is the "management dashboard" that summarizes and categorizes the indicators according to the financial perspective, customer and market perspective, opera-tions perspective, and resource perspective. Each indicator must have either a strong correlation to the strategic goals or to shareholder value; ideally, they have both. While cascading the performance metrics to the next layers of the organization, each indicator will be scrutinized in detail as to whether it's linked to those of the top management dashboard.

18   Balanced Scorecard

The Balanced Scorecard was born when a breakthrough article by **Robert S. Kaplan** and **David P. Norton** appeared in the *Harvard Business Review* in 1992.[2] Kaplan, a Professor of Leadership at the Harvard Business School, was, prior to his work on Balanced Scorecards, already well known for his contributions to the activity-based cost management and the subsequent challenges for effective management reporting. Based on their year-long research, both authors invented the core principles of the Balanced Scorecard:

- A set of measures that gives top management a fast but comprehensive view of the business.
- Operational metrics on customer satisfaction, internal processes, and innovative capabilities that are primarily forward looking should supplement the financial metrics that are backward focused.
- Monitoring indicators from various dimensions to ensure the company is on its way to achieve the strategic targets.

Kaplan and Norton used the very vivid analogy of an airplane dashboard. For a pilot it would surely be fatal if he were to rely only on one instrument. Hence, to safely fly a plane from one location to another the pilot has to track continuously a whole set of parameters such as course, altitude, speed, fuel, oil and hydraulic pressure, temperature, and so on.

The Balanced Scorecard consists of **four different perspectives**:

- Financial perspective
- Customer perspective
- Learning and growth perspective
- Internal business processes perspective.

The selection of these four perspectives basically demonstrates the "balancing" aspect of the approach. The Balanced Scorecard brings together in a single report the elements that are urgently important to improve competitiveness: Financial results will rely heavily on success in the market, which is primarily driven by the customer. Customers will be satisfied if product, service and price make a good value bundle. Financial results will also depend on efficiency of the internal processes. Internal processes are strong if the company is continuously learning and innovative. To effectively improve financial perfor-mance, successful management of customer relationships, internal processes, and innovation is required.

To understand how to identify and select the appropriate performance measure for each perspective, the following questions guide the way:

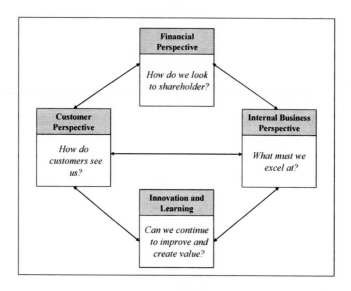

Exhibit IV-1: The Four Perspectives of Balanced Scorecards

Defining the appropriate set of key performance indicators for the customer perspective starts with the question of how the customers actually see the performance of a company. Usually price, service, quality, after-sales services, and delivery speed are the main elements to rate a company's service. Therefore, these categories play an important role to derive the appropriate customer-related performance indicators.

Internal efficiency measures will subsequently be identified and selected on their importance to achieve customer satisfaction. If a customer values after-sales services as the most critical capability to differentiate between several suppliers, indicators such as response time have to be monitored. The Balanced Scorecard has introduced the perspective of innovation and learning to monitor future competitiveness. Tangible metrics that provide insights into innovation are, for example, revenue with new products or new patents. Learning can be monitored through indicators such as training days per employee.

On the financial side, profitability is the overriding goal. Revenue growth is often also part of the financial indicators because it highlights how a company keeps up with market growth. The shareholder value category monitors if reasonable payback to the shareholder can be achieved.

Ideally, a Balanced Scorecard contains, overall, not more than fifteen performance indicators to be easy and quick to read. The measures are derived from the goals and allow a feedback loop to the strategic direction, as the following example stresses:

Perspective	Goals	Measures
Customer Perspective	Win new key clients	Revenue with target key clients
	Reliable delivery	% on-time delivery
	Best after sales services	% of solved customer requests
Internal Business Perspective	Reduce response time to customer request	% of immediately solved customer claims
	Continuous cost improvement	Cost per unit
	Operational excellence	% of assembly line outages
Innovation & Learning Perspective	Innovation leader	# of new patents
	Market success of new products	Revenue with products introduced in the last 24 months
	Highly skilled workforce	Average training days per employee
Financial Perspective	Keep pace with market growth	Revenue growth relative to competition
	Generate Shareholder Value	Economic Value added
	Reduce capital intensity	Working Capital

Strategy

Exhibit IV-2: Example of a Balanced Scorecard

Although a final Balanced Scorecard often looks relatively simplistic, it is a significant effort to create one. Detailing the strategy and consensus building consumes the bulk of the time. Therefore, the success of the Balanced Scorecard relies heavily on abilities to detail the strategy. **Strategy Maps** have been developed as a supplementing tool that will help to translate strategic goals into tangible results and will help to execute them.[3] The strategy map approach by Kaplan and Norton uses the concept to illustrate how a company converts its various assets into desired outcomes. The functioning is based on the cause-effect relationship between the different perspectives of the Balanced Scorecard. The following exhibit illustrates the logic of a strategic map:

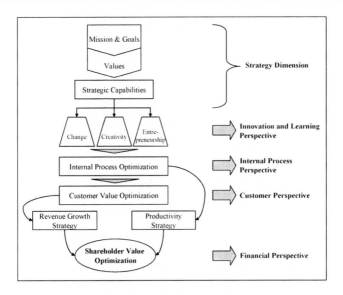

Exhibit IV-3: Strategy Map

The ultimate goal of a strategy map is to create the link between the actions of individual employees and the overall objectives of the firm. It will make visible how intangible assets such as knowledge, innovativeness, and skills are related to shareholder value creation. Employees will understand their contribution and will feel energized to play an important role in achieving strategic targets.

Since 1992 Balanced Scorecards have had a triumphal procession around the globe. In research and business, the idea of integrating various performance indicators on one quick and easy-to-read scorecard resonated with both top managers and academics. A study of 194 German companies, for example, revealed that two-thirds of them are familiar with the concept and that, in some industries like electronics and telecommunications, almost ninety percent know Balanced Scorecards.[4] However, although Balanced Scorecards are today a widely accepted top management reporting method, companies still have difficulty entirely applying the principles of Balanced Scorecards. The reasons are deeply rooted in the traditional ways of management reporting but could certainly be overcome.

- Reporting was historically purely financially driven. The profit and loss statement and the balance sheet were starting points of each type of management report. Financial metrics dominated the reports and, thus, managers have developed distinct skills and capabilities to read, interpret, and construe financial metrics. Some top managers today still believe that they can pinpoint every major strength or weakness of the company by simply screening and analyzing financial data they are provided with through the financial systems of the firm.
- It is a significant challenge to identify, detail, and prepare predictions of nonfinancial performance metrics. To segregate strategic goals in order to derive the exact financial metrics is already a stretch. But to create the link between strategic goals and nonfinancial metrics still appears for many companies insurmountable.
- Most companies' reporting systems already consist of multiple performance indicators, both financial and nonfinancial. Although they are often not explicitly linked to a particular strategy, they are useful and proven to monitor and control the tactical activities of departments or groups. Independent from what the current strategic directions are, these operational drivers are perceived as extremely important to run the day-to-day business. With implementation of a Balanced Scorecard there is the fear that these metrics could be deemphasized.
- The efforts to implement Balanced Scorecards are significant. Senior executives feel that, to run through

the painful exercise to operationalize the strategy, break it down into financial targets, and link it to the subsequent drivers for financial and nonfinancial performance just to get an enhanced reporting system in return is not a worthwhile investment.

To address the concerns mentioned above, Kaplan has further evolved the concept of Balanced Scorecards to an entire management system. The Balanced Scorecard management system puts stronger emphasis on the **strategy focus**. The goals and the metrics of Balanced Scorecards should be more than just an ad hoc collection of financial and nonfinancial performance metrics. By using the Balanced Scorecard as a management system, the inability of managers to link long-term strategies with short-term actions is addressed explicitly.[5] The management system approach should help top managers get started with implementing a scorecard. Since it is one of the core strengths of the approach to make strategies visible and translate them into actionable items, the actions of each individual in the firm should be oriented towards the long-term strategic goals. To make this happen, new business processes are required. Four different business processes should help to realize a Balanced Scorecard from the company's vision to communication until precise business planning and performance feedback loops.

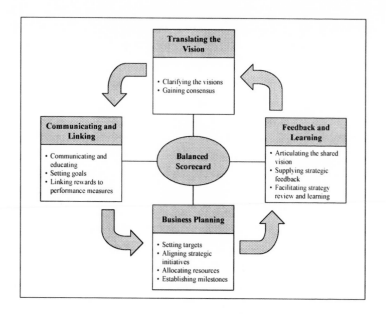

Exhibit IV-4: Balanced Scorecard as Management System

- Translating the vision – As already highlighted, visions, strategies, and their respective mission statements are often vague and very generally stated. For example. a plant manager needs some clarifica-tion what it means for him if the company pursues the strategy of "being the technology leader of the industry." The activities to translate the strategy are basically twofold:

  o Clarification of the strategy: All different facets that the strategy can potentially carry have to be specified. The true linkage between strategy and performance indicators needs to be created. The process will uncover some undefined parts of the strategy or even competing elements of strategies, as well.

o Consensus building: Detailing the strategy will very likely surface competing objectives and conflicts of interest within the management team. It is vital for the process of building Balanced Scorecards that all competing goals are balanced and univocal, strategic subgoals are derived.

- Communicating and linking – Now the strategy will be broken down into the organization. Managers will have to communicate their specified strategic goals. People will be educated about the strategic direction and how it relates to their particular work places. Additionally, the appropriate performance indicators will be addressed that have to be monitored to ensure that each employee's actions are aligned with the overall long-term strategic direction.

- Business planning - After the performance metrics have been derived, they have to be linked to the financial plans. Appropriate targets for the performance metrics have to be defined and the resource allocation to pursue the strategic goals has to be determined. Eventually, every strategic action needs to be considered in the business plan. The detailed breakdown of strategic actions into business plan elements will enable the company to understand the realistic financial impacts of the long-term strategy and will direct the activities of each individual manager and employee towards the strategy.

- Feedback and learning - The monthly, quarterly, and yearly reviews of business plan goals will reveal how well a company pursues the strategic direction. These insights will be used to provide strategic feedback and learning. Typical elements of feedback are:

o Has the strategy been clearly translated?

o   Are the set goals realistic?
o   Are funds and resources optimally allocated to pursue strategic initiatives?
o   Is the company able to achieve the strategic goals?
o   What has to be done differently to achieve the strategy?

The Balanced Scorecard provides a framework that integrates goal setting, strategic initiatives, resource allocation, and performance feedback. Prior to the Balanced Scorecards these processes were uncoordinated and short-term focused. Now, they are aligned and integrated with the overall strategic direction. Additionally, companies introducing Balanced Scorecards identify that their current strategic direction is not articulated clearly and crisply. They use the Balanced Scorecard initiative to reformulate or clarify strategic goals.

19   Value-Added Performance Measurement Systems

Value-Added Performance Measurement Systems use a different guiding principle than Balanced Scorecards. Whereas Balanced Scorecards are always built around the strategy first, this approach to Performance Measurement starts explicitly with shareholder value creation. The rise of the shareholder value movement in the 1980s was led by **Alfred Rappaport** and **Thomas Copeland** and pushed by the large institutional investors, in particular in the U. S. One can argue whether a rigid shareholder value orientation is useful or not. The fact of the matter is that managing the shareholder value closely is well justified: large institutional investors still build the capital backbone of most publicly listed corporations and, as a consequence, their foremost interest is shareholder value. Also, weak stock price performance makes companies easy M&A targets. For private companies, managing the shareholder value is important, too, because they can easily be compared and benchmarked with public companies. Even Kaplan and Norton stress the importance of the shareholder value in their Balanced Scorecard approach: if strategies and their derived operational goals are not reflected in increased shareholder value, management should reconsider the strategy.[6]

There are basically four **concepts of shareholder value measurement**:

- Economic Value Added (EVA)
- Market Value Added (MVA)
- Total Shareholder Return (TSR)
- Cash Value Added (CVA).

The concepts of EVA and CVA are based on the philosophy of monitoring returns in invested capital. They put a strong emphasis on the profitability: EVA is working with adjusted accounting profits and CVA with cash flows to illustrate the contribution to the bottom line.[7] Both approaches compare the earnings performance with the capital invested in the business. EVA operates with adjusted book capital as the capital base, and CVA focuses on the invested capital in the business evaluated with the acquisition values. Although the technical differences of both approaches are significant, the general principles in terms of measuring the performance towards shareholder value creation are very similar. The two other approaches, MVA and TSR, have a different focus. They both have a market perspective rather than a company-internal perspective. The MVA concept uses the stock evaluation as the key measure to assess if shareholder value has been created.[8] The TSR concept includes at least the dividends as an indicator for profitability and earnings generated. But both neglect the internal strength to generate returns in invested capital. Hence, they both have limits to be used as Performance Management systems. In essence, the EVA and the CVA approach are better suited to be combined with a Performance Measurement system.

Criteria	Economic Value Added (EVA)	Cash Value Added (CVA)	Market Value Added (MVA)	Total Shareholder Return (TSR)
Leading Metric	Economic Earnings	Cash Flow Return on Investment	Market Capitalization	Market Capitalization + Dividends
Profitability Measure	Net Operating Profit After Tax (NOPAT)	Cash Flow	-	(Dividends)
Capital Investment Measure	Economic Book Capital	Invested Capital	-	-
Shareholder Value Creation Perspective	Internal	Internal	External	External (internal only dividends)

Attachable to Performance
Measurements Systems

**Exhibit IV-5: Comparison of Shareholder
Value Management Approaches**

Although the EVA and CVA vary with regard to the key profitability metric, they both have the **value tree** principle in common. The value tree deconstructs all value drivers (revenue, cost, capital) that impact shareholder value. Economic earnings are on top of the tree in the EVA approach, capital value added as a result of CFROI, and capital charges are on top in the CVA approach. The principle to deconstruct the tree is, in both cases, the same.

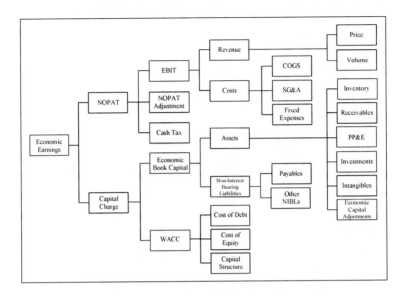

Exhibit IV-6: Value Tree Example (EVA)

The value tree deconstructs all financial drivers that ultimately lead to economic earnings. Therefore, one core branch deals with profitability and one with capital charges. The profitability, measured in the EVA approach accordingly as "Net Operating Profit After Tax" (NOPAT) deducts taxes and considers economic adjustments like, for example, capitalizing leases. The main driver, however, is "Earnings before Interest and Taxes" (EBIT). The further breakdown differentiates major revenue and cost components. The revenue per product and product group is broken down by price and volume. The same applies to the cost items. The entire cost structure will be broken down to the smallest increments possible to understand the importance of each driver. The breakdown of the capital charge is different in particular for the "Weighted Average Cost of Capital" (WACC). The WACC can be calculated by using different methods, but the main drivers will be the cost of debt (interest rates for debt), the cost of equity, and the capital structure. The WACC characterizes the minimum required rate of return or the opportunity cost of capital.[9] Whereas the cost of debt can be found in the financial statements the cost of equity has to be determined specifically for each company. The Capital Asset Pricing Model (CAPM) provides the framework.[10] Depending on the capital structure and the company-specific risk assessment, the expected return rate on equity for investors can be calculated. Although the CAPM has been proven as the best approach to determine the cost of capital, it is not flawless. The model operates with expected returns that typically rely on historical or realized returns. However, markets are not efficient and subsequently, these returns are for the most part not the future returns.[11] Since no better proxy for future returns is currently available in finance theory, the CAPM model is still the best model of choice.

The formula to determine the cost of equity is based on the company-specific risk rate that has to be multiplied with the difference between the risky investment alternative (S&P 500 return rate) and the safe investment alternative (government bonds), which is called the market risk premi-um.[12] The result will be added to the risk-free rate. It basically expresses the payback each investor would expect for the investment under current risk assessment, cost of debts, and deducted tax payments. Predominantly, investors investing in stocks expect higher return rates than the long-term government bonds, which are considered to be safe. In addition, investors would like to earn a premium that covers the risk of investing in a particular company that carries a specific competitive risk. Since the stock prices of single companies are very likely more volatile than the S&P 500 index, each investment has to be weighted. This weighting factor is the Beta factor. If a company's stock price, for example, is ten percent more volatile than the S&P 500 index, the Beta factor would be 1.10. The following formula illustrates the principle:[13]

> Cost of Equity = (Risk Free Rate + Risk Premium (S&P500 Return Rate – Government
> Bond Return Rate))
> = Risk Free Rate + Beta (Market Risk Premium)

To calculate the weighted average cost of capital (WACC), the cost of debt will be multiplied with the marginal tax rate since interest payments are deductible from the taxed income. The interest minus the tax rate and the cost of equity will be subsequently multiplied with their respective percentages to calculate the WACC.

> WACC = (Percentage Debt * Interest (1-t) + (Percentage Equity * Cost of Equity)

In managing the capital structure there are certain limits: since liabilities appear to be "cheaper" compared to the cost of equity, EVA-minded financial managers are inclined to leverage the capital structure towards liabilities. Capital markets, however, won't like this strategy because a high debt/equity ratio increases the risk of paying back interest. Thus, the rating will worsen, accessibility of liabilities will be limited, and, subsequently, conditions for interest rates will go up. As a consequence, optimizing capital structures can basically only take place within the industry debt/equity benchmark.

The economic book capital can be broken down into more actionable drivers. The asset base will be structured into its major balance sheet items such as plant, property and equipment, inventories, accounts receivable, and intangible assets. Another group of assets will be analyzed separately: the non-interest-bearing liabilities consist of capital that is currently used by the company but for which it has to pay neither interest nor generate a return. Accounts payable often makes the majority of this group.

The **link to the Performance Measurement system** is usually be done in two different ways:

- *Significance-based Approach*

  The revenue components and cost drivers as identified through the value tree analysis are selected based on their significance. That means focus will be on the product groups with the highest relative revenue proportions. Accordingly, the cost items with the biggest impact on the cost of goods sold will be highlighted on the cost side. The same applies also to the capital charges: major drivers will be determined and specifically monitored. Performance measures will be developed and regularly analyzed for major revenue, cost, and capital charge drivers only. The management can consequently compress the number of performance indicators and focus on the most important ones to monitor shareholder value. The biggest advantage of this approach is its simplicity; the biggest shortcoming is that it does not reveal any more details than the in-depth analysis of the profit and loss statement and balance sheet.

- *Sensitivity-based approach*

  The goal of this approach is to understand thoroughly the value creation potential associated with each revenue and cost driver. Therefore, the value tree will be populated with the planned figures for the upcoming period instead the actual data. By applying a comparable approach as described above, the most significant value drivers will be pinpointed. As the next step each of the identified drivers will be increased by a percentage range that is seen as realistic fluctuation (mostly determined through analysis of historic plan – actual deviations) for the respective driver. To be able to run the calculation now requires in-depth knowledge of the cost structures, especially the differentiation between variable and fixed costs. Eventually, the impact of the changes to revenue, cost and capital change drivers on the shareholder value will be measured and will determine the set of the most important performance indicators. The example below illustrates the principle. The unexpected overachieve-ment of the revenue goal for "Alcoholic Beverages" by 5% has created $80 million in extra shareholder value:

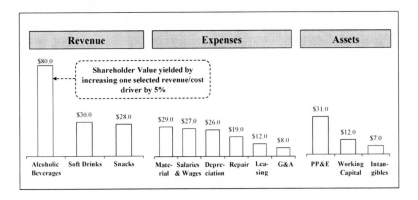

Exhibit IV-7: Shareholder Value – Sensitivity Analysis

The biggest advantage of this approach is its forward-looking perspective through the use of plan data. Additionally, the sophisticated sensitivity analysis method reduces the number of potential key performance indicators drastically. The firm is truly pursuing a value-oriented strategy. The major bottleneck to this method is the availability of relevant data. Most companies have difficulty clearly splitting variable and fixed cost proportions over all cost items. The relationship between certain variables can't be analytically proven, which raises concerns about the applicability of the approach, too.

Companies that get attracted to a Value Added Measurement System put strong emphasis on the shareholder. To link the shareholder-value metric with the operational business and with value drivers and, ultimately, with performance measures that monitor the operation business is fairly complex. As a result, the Value Added Measurement Systems are mostly applied in industries with relatively simple value chains and business models. Divisional or Hybrid Organizations that operate with distinct and very different types of businesses on a global basis are challenged to apply the value tree approach and often find it too complex. Also, outside the U.S., the rigid shareholder value principles still carry a slightly negative image because they are associated with reckless job cuts and "old capitalism."[14] Thus, some major corporations, particularly in Europe, have abandoned shareholder value indicators as leading key performance metrics.

Even though the Value Added Measurement approach is based on plan figures it will only reveal the effectiveness of the organization in terms of shareholder value. There is no doubt that strategy and organization need to be linked to the EVA creation, but the "EVA-optimal" organization does not exist.[15] The Value Added Measurement Systems are very much result-oriented and have to be supplemented by a Performance Management approach that is strategy focused.

20   Integrated Strategic Measures (ISM)

The approach of Integrated Strategic Measures was developed by the consulting firm A.T. Kearney. It is an approach that explicitly targets the issues of both value-driven Performance Management and the deployment of strategic goals. In some cases the approach is called "Strategic Performance Measurement" to highlight the combination of financial, strategic, and operating business measures to gauge how well a company meets its targets.[16] Consequently, ISM basically pursues three objectives of effective Performance Management:

1. ISM promotes **alignment** throughout the organization with the strategy and the ultimate goal of value creation. It attempts to integrate strategic goals and business initiatives through the translation of strategic direction into guidelines for day-to-day activity.
2. ISM ensures **focus** on actions with the highest impact on strategy execution and value creation. It tries to identify and define indicators that monitor the strongest levers with respect to strategy and shareholder value. By doing this, the number of performance metrics can significantly be reduced and the management can concentrate on the most important ones.
3. ISM provides **insight** into past and future organizational performance. Depending on the chosen strategic direction, certain elements of Organizational Effective-ness have to be prioritized (simple example: technology leadership as a core strategic goal requires sufficient talent and skill recruiting). The relevant drivers will be monitored through selected performance indicators.

Through cascading of shareholder value targets over the various levels of the organization, each manager and, ideally, even each employee will develop a better understanding of the direct contribution to shareholder value. Companies that emerge from private ownership to public ownership are often in search of better understanding of shareholder value among their employees. Typically, these companies have strong family roots and have probably operated over decades with a small- to medium-size business scale and mentality. Goals like "job safety" and "good corporate citizenship" are frequently pursued but are not aligned with shareholder value targets. The ISM approach is the middleman and mediator between these extreme positions that helps to develop integration between "soft" strategic and "hard" shareholder value goals.

Hence, ISM operates with both dimensions: strategic and value orientation. It applies a value-tree concept to clearly carve out the shareholder value focus and it maps the strategy to derive a set of strategy-oriented indicators.

Value-Based Measures	Measures Derived From Strategy
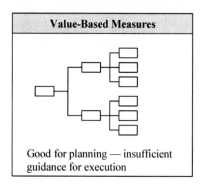	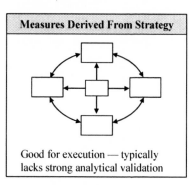
Good for planning — insufficient guidance for execution	Good for execution — typically lacks strong analytical validation

Exhibit IV-8: Balancing of Value and Strategy

- The **value-based measurement approach** is good for planning purposes. It pinpoints the target ranges for the value drivers to ensure sufficient value creation. As long as each manager and employee fulfill their respective objectives, the firm will create value. However, managers are left alone on how to execute their objectives. It is basically up to them to define actions in order to achieve their shareholder value goals. Clearly, objectives can be competing and, by strictly pursuing individual value goals, a manager can significantly reduce the likelihood that other colleagues will meet their targets. In summary, shareholder value can erode instead of rise.

• The **strategy-driven measurement approach** introduced with the Balanced Scorecard earlier is easier to execute. Through the four perspectives (1. learning and innovation, 2. internal process efficiency, 3. custom-mer, 4. financials), the strategy is broken down into cause-effect structures that highlight the contribution of each individual within the firm to achieve the strategic goals. People understand the strategy better and will receive tangible objectives to contribute to it. However, it remains, to a certain extent, unclear if and how strong individual activities will help to strengthen shareholder value. There is little analytical validation of the effects to shareholder value creation.

The key steps to develop an ISM Performance Measurement System are:

• *Key Performance Indicator Selection*
• *Designing Dashboards*
• *Cascading of Dashboards*

The **Key Performance Indicator Selection** is subsequently driven by the philosophy of combining value and strategy orientation. Therefore, ISM applies the same method to deconstruct the value tree and to break down the distinct value drivers as the Value Added Measurement approach does. Another core element is the *strategy breakdown*. The breakdowns are supposed to close the gap between the company's strategy and the corresponding performance measures. Strategy breakdowns provide a visual representation of a company's strategy, critical objectives and the crucial relationships among them that drive organizational performance. The primary goal of a strategy breakdown is to derive candidate measures that are tightly linked to the company's business vision and strategic objectives.

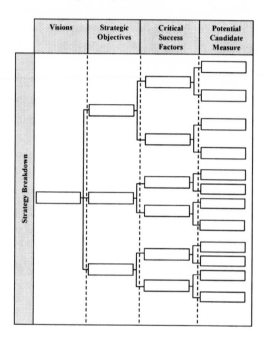

Exhibit IV-9: Strategy Breakdown

As soon as the management team has detailed the vision into clear strategic objectives, critical success factors will be determined. If, for example, the strategic goal of "**technology industry leadership**" has been defined, the corresponding critical success factor candidates are:

○ *Develop and retain technological capabilities*
○ *Provide sufficient funding for technology projects with market potential*
○ *Accelerate the market readiness of development projects.*

Through the critical success factors, the link to the potential candidate measures is closed. For each success factor at least one candidate measure will be developed. In the example above, critical success factors and performance measures could be linked as follows:

Critical Success Factor	Candidate Measure
"Develop and retain technological capabilities"	• Open R&D positions • Offers sent out • Accepted offer ratio
"Provide sufficient funding for technology projects with market potential"	• R&D budget/Revenue • % Under funded projects • % Revenue with products younger than 24 months
"Accelerate the market readiness of development projects"	• Time-to-market span • % Milestone compliance

Table: Critical Success Factors and Candidate Measures

As this example demonstrates, the strategy breakdown eventually leads to tangible performance indicators that are directly related to the strategy. Ideally, the strategy breakdown produces a list of thirty to sixty potential performance indicators.

The next step is the prioritization of all measures: those that have been identified through the **value tree analysis** and those that have been defined through the **strategy breakdown**. The combination of value and strategy focus will be realized through assessment of each potential indicator in regard to its value contribution *and* strategic importance. That means all indicators that have been derived from the value tree will be analyzed for their compliance to the strategy and vice versa.

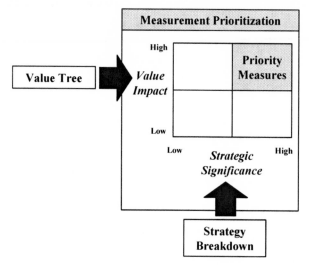

Exhibit IV-10: Measurement Prioritization

Additionally, the criteria "measurability" and "controllability" need to be tested.

    o Measurability - Ability to be measured in order to ensure clear target-setting and performance measurement. In some cases, the internal information systems are not advanced enough to extract the data needed which is often the case for detailed cost breakdowns on the product and customer dimension and for operational metrics such as department specific work-in-progress inventories. Some indicators, such as the relative market share, are not accessible because data concerning the overall market volume are not available. Also, if performance indicators are conceptually too complex, reliable measurement is exacerbated.

o Controllability – Managers would like to be measured only against a target they can actually influence. Measuring the performance of a manager in relation to the GDP growth and/or the Dow Jones development, for example, is difficult because they certainly have no direct control over these metrics. But relative indicators like company revenue growth/GDP growth or company stock price growth/Dow Jones growth will work because they contain at least one controllable variable.

The following prioritization table will guide the selection process:

Potential Candidate Measures	Criteria				
	Strategic Importance	Value Impact	Controllability	Measurability	Prioritization
Revenue with new products	●	◑	●	●	◕
R&D budget/revenue	◕	◑	●	●	◕
Market share growth	●	●	○	○	○ ⇦
Revenue growth/industry growth	●	●	◕	●	●
Economic Earnings	◕	●	●	●	◕
Cash Flow	◑	●	●	●	◕
COGS reduction	◑	●	●	●	◕
Inventory reduction	◑	◕	●	●	◑
Work safety ratio	◕	◐	◕	◕	◑
Training days	●	◑	●	◕	◕
...	□	□	□	□	□

●= Very high   ○= Very low

Table: Prioritization Criteria

The controllability and measurability criteria will not count for the prioritization ranking. However, if these criteria are not in place, a potential measure will fail the selection process automatically (indicated in the example above for the "Market share growth").

The process of assessing each indicator with regard to the strategy impact will very likely lead to a list of 30 to 60 potential measure candidates. Potentially, 10 to 15 potential measures are usually added due to their shareholder value significance. The prioritization process, if rigidly applied, will bring down the number of key performance indicators to 10 to 20. More than 20 indicators for the corporate dashboard are not very useful.

Designing Dashboards is the next step. The corporate dashboard needs to contain all measures the CEO has to monitor closely and which are related to the CEO's compensation. Consequently, the higher the number of indicators, the lower the likelihood that the CEO will stay in control of all of them. Additionally, breaking down the performance-based compensation to more than 20 indicators will have each indicator carrying less than five percent of the variable compensation, on average. This is neither practicable nor manageable. The calculation of the variable remuneration will become mostly an accounting exercise and will not emphasize the strategy and value focus it should carry. Ideally, the corporate dashboard has 10-15 indicators (basic rule should be "the fewer the better"). To design a balanced corporate dashboard, indicators will be allocated according to four different categories:

1. The **value category** displays all the indicators selected to closely monitor and control the financial development of the firm and the creation of shareholder value. That means, besides information on profitability such as operating profit or net income, metrics on shareholder value generation will appear here. Additional value indicators are often dedicated to monitor cash flow, liquidity, and the stock price development and dividends.
2. The **customer/market category** focuses on all indicators that report on revenue, revenue growth, and market penetration. Revenues by major product, product groups, or important customers, market share and market share developments are typical examples here.
3. The **operations category** turns the focus to the internal operational perspective. Information on the efficiency of core processes are the indicators typically used in this category. Another important group of

metrics deals with quality indicators and cost per unit indicators. Cost efficiency of products, parts, components, or processes is a matter of effective internal operations. Thus, cost per unit metrics belong to the operations category.

4. The **resource** category summarizes indicators around all the assets a company needs to acquire, develop and nurture to be successful in the future. Therefore, some assets are tangible and will be monitored with indicators such as asset productivity and inventory turnover; other assets are intangible, such as innovativeness, creativity, learning, and talent retention.

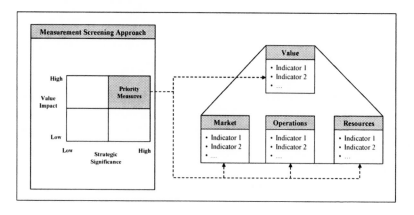

Exhibit IV-11: Priority Measures and Dashboard Categories

An effective framework to allocate the indicators in the right category is shown below. Based on the response to the question posed in each category the indicators will be aligned accordingly.

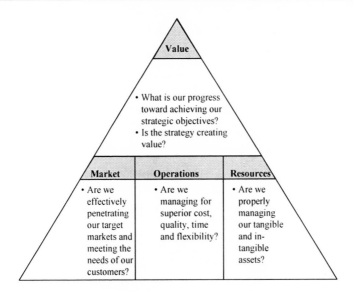

Exhibit IV-12: Dashboard Categories and Core Questions

Cascading of Dashboards to the next level of the organization is the next step. While a Balanced Scorecard is unique to one company and stays the same on all levels of an organization, the ISM approach advocates specific dashboards for each layer, function, and division of the firm. The trick is integration of performance indicators. As soon as the corporate dashboard has been designed, each indicator will be broken down to the next level. For example if "revenue growth" is a core indicator on the CEO's report, it will be cascaded to "revenue growth by key account" on the Chief Marketing Officer's (CMO) dashboard. Operational indicators will typically find a cascaded version on the Chief Operating Officer's (COO) report. In general, indicators should only appear on the dashboard of a manager if he can effectively influence them. Eventually, each indicator from the corporate dashboard will be displayed in a cascaded version on the dashboards of the next organizational layer as long as the accountability for the cascaded version resides on this level.

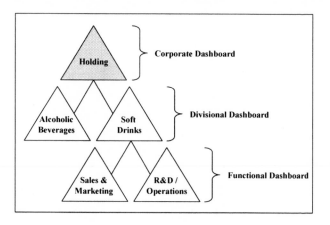

Exhibit IV-13: Cascading of Dashboards

Since the 10 to 15 indicators provided by the corporate dashboard are not sufficient to populate all dashboards on the next level, supplementing indicators need to be defined for each division and function. The process to develop additional indicators on the next layers is similar to the process to define the corporate dashboard. Ideally, according to the ISM approach, each manager has his "own" unique dashboard. As a consequence, the entire company consistently pursues the overall strategic direction and focuses on shareholder value creation at the same time.

The ISM approach works best for companies that are typically swamped with various kinds of reporting information. Especially in industries such as airlines, railroads, telecommunication, or utilities in which loads of data have to be tracked for regulatory reporting purposes anyway, ISM is the optimal approach to facilitate a strategy-guided and value-oriented streamlining of reports. Also, industries like retail that operate with a tremendous number of items are often attracted to the basic principles of ISM. In these industries in particular, reporting appears to be an "indicator jungle," and ISM provides a comprehensive framework to effectively navigate through it.

Through its bifocal approach on strategy and shareholder value, ISM is very useful to measure Organizational Effectiveness. The strategy focus makes sure that strategic goals are translated into comprehensible, actionable, and manageable performance indicators. The cascading logic reinforces the rollout of strategic goals to the entire organization. The combination with the consequent value focus enables strategic directions to be revisited and continuously assessed for their impact on value creation.

21   Best Practices in Reporting

Management reporting is the key to clear communication of performance indicators to the organization. Whereas the Balanced Scorecard, Value Added Measurement systems, and ISM are addressing the content of management reports, the vehicle to deliver the messages is almost equally important. Best Practices in Reporting focus on "how" to display and communicate information and, thus, can basically be applied to all different concepts of Performance Management as discussed above.

For many firms the way of reporting is still old-style and traditional:

- Paper-based – Each month a stack of paper is produced with numerous tables and with more or less useful rows and columns. Management reports are neither accessible via the Web or intranet, nor do recipients have the ability to customize their own reports.

- Outdated data – Information on the previous months is constantly part of each monthly report. Data sets are partly outdated. Instead of summarizing previous performance in trend lines, the details as presented earlier are simply repeated.
- Lack of illustration – Rarely does a graph or exhibit aerate the readability. Information is not prioritized or highlighted and explanations to understand figures and the background on variances and deviations from target are not provided.
- Information overkill – Reporting packages sometimes contain more than 1,000 pages each month. The experienced manager flips directly to the one or two pages that are of interest and pinpoints intuitively the few performance metrics that have to be monitored. The rest of the reporting package will be neglected or just confuse the inexperienced reader. For new managers or new hires the reporting appears to be a mess: reports are complex, overloaded with useless information and data, and very hard to comprehend.
- Non-focused information – In lots of cases, reporting packages have evolved over years rather than being the result of structured initiative. Consequently, new indicators and reporting pages have been added without ever cleaning up the packages in terms of information relevance and strategic importance. To filter important information has become a challenge.

Implementing a new Performance Management approach provides the opportunity to clean up the reporting environment as well. Best Practices to be considered are as follows:

- **Information Provision via Electronic Means**
  E-mail, intranet, and Internet sites are standard in most companies. Also, there is no reason why reporting still has to be paper-based. Although some managers still prefer the touch and feel of paper because it's more convenient for them to take notes or to flip through the reports while they are away from their desks, the standard reporting should be provided via electronic means. The manager who still likes paper can print out selected pages or entire reports if he wants to do so. Software packages can automatically generate reports and send them to pre-determined distribution lists. Data provision through Internet/intranet sites enables monitoring real-time data and self-service.[17] Self-service means that recipients can customize their specific reports and formats by using Internet/intranet-based raw data.

- **Easy to read formats**[18]
  o Graphically supported – even if the reports are prepared and distributed electronically, they should be graphically supported.
  o Standard Formats and Layouts – using standardized templates makes it easier to find and to highlight variances. Standard formats ease navigation through reports and make it easier to find certain information.
  o Scanable Information – information must be easy and quick to find; lengthy data columns or written notes make it more difficult to scan a report. Scanable information means that the report should be prepared in a way that the reader can detect useful information with just a glance.

○ Bold Settings – important information and/or variances and deviations need to be highlighted; bold setting is an easy and pragmatic way to get started.

○ Use of Abbreviations – abbreviations make reports quicker to read but not necessarily easier to read. They should be used frequently but not excessively to make reports comprehensible for relatively new employers and outside stakeholders (such as Board Members).

○ Verbal Comments and Summaries – major variances and deviations from plan should briefly be commented upfront to avoid lengthy research activity. Proactive reporting software packages will automatically prompt the manager in charge to key in a comment for major deviation.

○ Traffic Light/Red Flag Reporting – as an advanced version of bold settings, the definition of performance ranges or thresholds makes it easier to focus on the really important plan versus actual deviations. Traffic lights are helpful to indicate the severity of plan deviations: green – in range; yellow – still in range but needs close monitoring; red – out of range, requires immediate action.

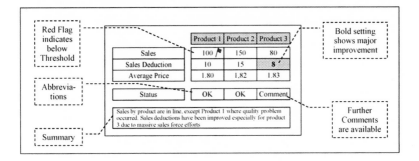

Exhibit IV-14: Easy-to-Read Reporting Principles

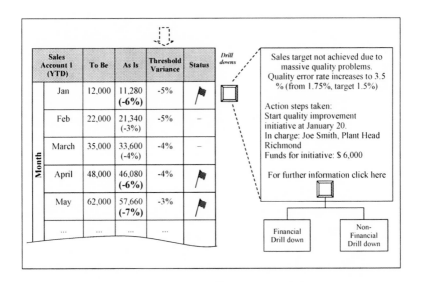

Exhibit IV-15: Effective "Red Flag" Reporting - Example

- **Timing**

   Timing of reporting can be influenced through various process and system changes:

   o Quick closing process - all financial, cost, and revenue performance metrics are reliant on the closure process of the respective financial systems (which happens mostly in monthly cycles).

Best Practice companies are able to close their books in less than a day after a monthly period is completed. Consequently, the reporting is available in a matter of one to two days.

o Monthly soft close/quarterly hard close – the common practice of a monthly hard close is not required in all cases. A monthly soft close is often sufficient: major revenue and cost components will be determined and updated with real figures for the monthly period. Minor positions will be averaged; positions that need to be accrued because they occur only in yearly cycles such as, for example, pension fund charges, will be averaged based on plan assumption as well; the same applies for other accruals like, for example, warranties: instead of determining in great detail the exact amount of money that needs to be accrued for warranty, standard accruals will be calculated based on historic data and current revenue and automatically captured during the monthly soft close. The use of standard costs instead of "as is" costs and the reduction of consolidation levels are additional measures to simplify the monthly closing routine. There is no need for cumbersome and lengthy analysis of each line item; the month will be closed based on averages and standards. The quarterly (or even bi-yearly) close replaces the assumptions with the real data. As a result, the workload for the monthly close is minimized and time can be freed up for value-added analysis and decision-support.

Best Practices in Reporting work literally in all different kinds of businesses and can be applied independently from the strategic direction. The right mix between streamlined standard report packages and customizable web-based self-service solutions enables the maximum effective provision of decision-support relevant data – at any time. In conjunction with a content-driven approach as discussed in the previous chapters, and under consideration of basic design principles, the reporting can emerge to a competitive advantage and increase Organizational Effectiveness significantly.

22   Planning and Target Setting

The generation of performance targets is the result of the planning process. For most of the major corporations it has become a yearly or seasonally recurrent ordeal to develop revenue and cost targets, budgets, capital plans and profit plans for the upcoming planning period, which is mainly the fiscal year. In some cases, entire back-office functions – in particular the finance and accounting function – are overloaded through planning activities, which last in a fiscal-planning cycle sometimes from as early as March until the very end of year. Multiple top-down and bottom-up iterations of various versions of the budget are developed, revised, re-revised, pre-confirmed, and eventually passed by the senior management team. Instead of focusing on current performance, planning consumes the vast majority of managers' time. There are good reasons to put high emphasis on planning; however, execution should generally be more important than meticulous efforts to develop a plan. Reasons for precise planning are manifold:

- The **shareholder and analysts community** requests detailed insights on the company's future development. They have a legitimate right to understand the planned course of their investment. And, to be able to present a reliable, trustworthy, and stable outlook, plans are questioned, revised, and questioned again, over and over again. However, there is a dilemma of planning for shareholder information purposes: if plans are too conservative and probably sandbagged, shareholders feel enticed to cut back their investment due to short-profit outlooks. On the other hand, if plans are too aggressive and optimistic, shareholders often overreact if results turn out to be not in line with expectations and try to sell the stock. As a consequence, the attitude towards planning has changed significantly. Historically, plan-ning was conducted to justify major investment decisions or to prove credit-worthiness for banks and other creditors. The plan was intended to serve as a mid- and long-term business case that revealed how a company would pay back its debt. The spread of corporate equity to the public has introduced a much stronger short-term orientation and a strong emphasis on profit generation. Publicly listed companies today are challenged to deliver accurate planning and to present a highly reliable picture to their shareholders.

- The goal of a plan is to **convert strategic goals into operational execution**. Planning is indeed the major lever to align business activities with the overall strategic direction.[19] With the emergence of the Balanced Scorecard and Integrated Strategic Measures that enable the linkage between planning and strategy, companies in recent years have put strong emphasis on strategy-oriented planning. While in 1997, 51% of the major U.S. corporations had reported a significant and strong alignment between planning and business strategy, this number soared to 70% of the companies by 2002.

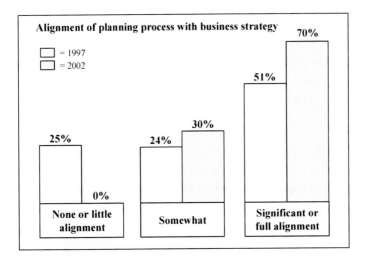

Exhibit IV-16: Planning and Business Strategy[20]

Some examples outline how the link between strategy and planning targets work:

- o If a company pursues an innovation strategy and approaches revenue growth through new products, for example, funding for R and D projects needs to be stronger than usual.
- o If a company pursues an internationalization strategy with multiple market entries abroad, the funding for new marketing activities in target markets needs to be promoted.
- o If a company drives a rigid cost leadership strategy, capital investments need to be monitored closely. Capital budgets will be scrutinized in great detail before they are confirmed.

- • Planning serves also for **"softer" purposes**: It is an inherent quest of humans to face the complexity of daily personal and professional life through anticipation of required actions and activities. Everybody has the tendency to "plan" his or her life. Scheduling and planning is part of life for kids and adults: kids need to arrange a short-term schedule to arrange school, homework, soccer practice, and other activities. Adults operate with longer-term schedules, as well, integrating aspects such as job, family, education, and even leisure time that are very often well planned. It is not rare that professionals today have "to-do lists" and work plans even for the weekend. Most people today have defined their own goals – careerwise and personally – that provide a strategic direction. It is the uncertainty of the future that drives people to plan every step in their lives well in advance. Consequently, people look for plans for their business activities as well.

The major challenge to assemble plans for businesses is two-fold: process and outcome.

- If the process is not well arranged, it can consume a significant amount of time and manpower to complete the planning.
- If the outcome is unreliable, shareholders will be dissatisfied as will employees who are remunerated based on performance targets defined by the plan.

There are four elements of an effective planning process: time horizons, coordination of goals, timeline, integration and software support.

- *Time Horizons* - Traditionally, plans are differentiated in:
  - o **Long-term plans (strategic plans)** for all time horizons above five years.[21] The usefulness of strategic plans has been controversial. Multiple rapid and unexpected changes of business landscapes for lots of industries have raised serious concerns about the ef-

fectiveness of strategic plans. The creation of long-term scenarios is a vital tool to detect future trends and possible development paths for the company. However, detailed long-term plans con-taining granular revenue projections, detailed cost estimates, and profit plans for a time period longer than three years ahead are often not worthwhile today. Thus, as long as they are not used to develop trend scenarios, long-term plans are dispensable. Tactical plans or rolling forecasts can cover a period of up to three years with financial figures. Planning activities keep entire departments busy, and consume significant amounts of meeting time and senior executive attention. Often, entire organizations are almost "paralyzed" because of non-value adding planning work.

o **Mid-term plans (tactical plans)** that cover a time period of more than one and less than five years. The plans should basically display a rough projection of the key planning dimensions: revenue, costs, invest-ments, personnel, cash, and profits. More than that is not required for a streamlined planning system. Accordingly, focus of the planning system should be the yearly and quarterly time horizon.

o **Short-term (operational plans)** that includes yearly budgets and forecasts with quarterly and yearly horizon.

  – **Budgets** should be updated on a yearly cycle to be in sync with the fiscal year and to give employees the opportunity to operate with them over the seasonality of an entire year. The budget is intended to serve primarily as a tool to convert strategic direction into business activities and to enable performance-based compensation. Bud-gets are normally released shortly before the budget period starts.

- The **forecast cycle** is shorter.[22] Since quarterly earnings have to be reported in quarters anyway, the forecast-update cycle should be quarterly, as well. The forecast should be more than the sophisticated econometric models such as statistical trend analysis.[23] It should be an updated version of the budget based on experience and insight gained through real, as-is data. In addition, a twelve-month rolling forecast is needed to extend the fiscal year perspective.

Both projections – the budget and the forecast – have different purposes. The forecast is intended to update the planned figures of the budget with more realistic predictions[24]. Therefore, the forecast is prepared with a shorter timeframe and is released just at the start of the forecasting horizon. Since budgets are fixed over the timeframe of a year, forecasts provide updates during the year based on actual developments. Changes in business conditions, unexpected price shifts, new business opportunities, and the gain or loss of mega deals can lead budget figures easily *ad absurdum*. Thus, in particular the shareholder community is looking for a more reliable and realistic prediction of the business. And that is the main purpose of the forecast.

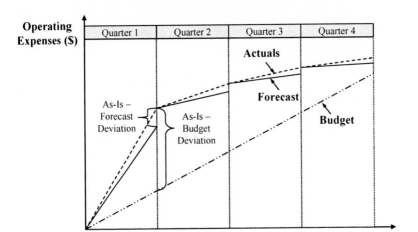

Exhibit IV-17: Budget and Forecast

As the exhibit above reveals forecasts should be, by definition, closer to the actual results because they consider changes to the planning assumptions that have occurred in the meantime. Forecasts serve as well as an early warning mechanism for the company to launch short-term actions against deviations from plan. The example in the exhibit highlights a typical operating expense development after an inbound-price increase in the first quarter. The cost explosion could be mitigated through aggressive cost reduction beginning in the second quarter. Eventually the operating costs are back on track and close to the budgeted figure. Without forward-looking forecasts, the cost increase would have been detected too late. The quarterly forecasts are also used to predict a more reliable and realistic year-end result. This prediction will also be updated on a quarterly basis and is, by far, more accurate than the initial budget-based estimate of the year-end result. The rolling forecast will help to keep track of the business development over the (fiscal) year end of the budget cycle. The yearly focus of the budget is a kind of "artificial" end point because business will not stop on December 31. The rolling forecast provides a continued and ongoing, twelve-month-forward view.

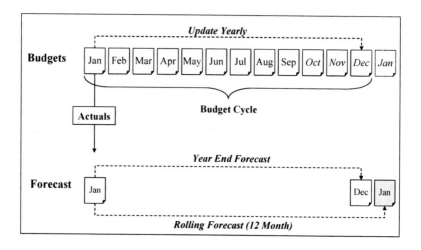

Exhibit IV-18: Rolling Forecast

The rolling forecast is produced on a quarterly basis to provide always a full-year outlook. The year-end outlook updated in October for example covers just the three remaining months of a fiscal year. The rolling forecast will already reach far into the following year and provide valuable market and cost data until October of the following year. In terms of content and level of detail the rolling forecast should be less detailed than the budgets or the quarterly year-end forecast. In order to manage performance and risks proactively, the rolling forecast is an essential tool of the planning toolbox.

- ***Coordination of Goals*** – Effective planning processes need close and effective coordination of top-down directive and bottom-up reality. Also, planning takes place in parallel in multiple places of the organization, and the various planning inputs need to be coordinated and reconciled.

The **carousel meeting** has evolved as the most effective tool to coordinate goals in the planning process. Among the biggest threats of effective planning are the multiple revision rounds, the so-called "iterations." There are basically two types of iterations:

o Top-down/bottom-up iterations. In a typical top-down/bottom-up planning approach, figures will be developed through continuous reconciliation of top-down targets with bottom-up budgets. After multiple rounds of negotiation, budget figures will be agreed upon that are acceptable for senior management and shareholders and that are realistic from a revenue generation and cost perspective, as estimated by the people in charge further down the organization. Under today's tough business conditions, these types of "negotiations" can rarely be found. Particularly for publicly listed companies, profit estimates are to a certain extent predetermined through industry benchmarks and the relentless investor community. Hence, the top financial objective is often externally given and the company has to figure out how to align revenues, costs, and assets to generate the required profit.

o Horizontal iterations do not take place in a top-down/bottom-up direction but in a horizontal way. In a divisional organizational structure, the various divisions and their business groups have to decide upon their profit contribution. On the next level, marketing/sales and operations have to coordinate contributions to the profit target. Coordination between divisions and/or functions causes multiple negotiation and iteration rounds. Whereas the operations department primarily seeks optimized asset utilization and economies of scale and urges the sales side to generate higher revenues, sales is focused on premium quality and continuous product provision at the lowest production costs possible. An oxymoron is created and it is up to the people in the organization to resolve it. Companies today spend month after month coordinating diametric interests of divisions and business units and the sales and operations sides of the business.

The carousel meeting's idea is to ease the time and energy consumed by the lengthy and cumbersome coordination of goals. The meeting takes place as a concerted action to gather the key decision-makers to run through all required iterations at once. The name "carousel" illustrates the meeting format: all parties involved have to circle again and again around various options until they have reached consensus on realistic revenue targets, operations costs, asset utilization, inventory levels, and so on. In essence, the carousel meeting will help to identify as quickly as possible the operating ratio that is required to hit the given performance objective.[25] And it will define the constel-lation of the major variables as well.

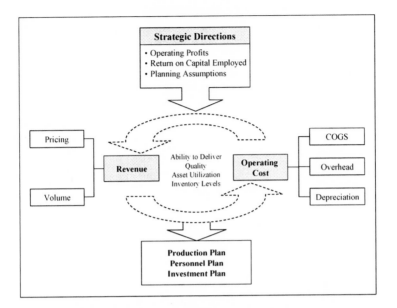

Exhibit IV-19: Carousel Meeting on Functional Level

Ideally, the carousel meeting takes place as soon as the senior executive team has decided on the strategic targets, planning assumptions, and the profit and return on capital employed goals. The meeting will be organized as an offsite event that lasts one to two days. All major decision makers from the division, marketing and sales, and operations need to be present. To facilitate an effective meeting, an integrated planning software tool and simulation tool should be used to compute a realistic and achievable budget plan. In corporations that consist of multiple divisional, subdivisional, and business group levels, the carousel meeting has to be repeated on each different level. The strategic targets and profit goals will get consistently broken down based on realistic budgets.

- *Timeline* - The accelerated timeline is the next cornerstone of the effective planning process.

It is implausible that some major corporations today start their budget planning process as early as March. Although economic developments and business condi-tions are vastly uncertain and most planning assumptions will change by the end of the year, the first pre-budget is sometimes released in April. And even detailed budget plans are often developed as early as mid-year although future developments of the upcoming year, multiple revisions, change of planning assumptions and strategic targets will make them obsolete anyway.[26] In a planning system that operates with rolling forecasts there is no need to start budget planning for the upcoming year earlier than late fall of the current year. The forecasts provide outlooks on performance well in advance and are sufficient to settle any uncertainties. By using rolling forecasts and the carousel meeting as planning elements, the timeframe to run through the yearly budget planning process can be reduced significantly.

o The ideal timeline starts with a **strategy meeting** of the senior management team in early October (assuming the budget will be developed for the upcoming fiscal year). This meeting should result in:
   - Overall profit targets
   - Return on capital employed target
   - Essential planning assumptions such as market growth, industry price development, economic outlook, foreign exchange rates, salary and wage increases, and employee numbers.
o In parallel, the operating units should produce **first estimates** for their budgets for the upcoming year based on preliminary profit targets and planning figures.[27] Preliminary profit targets can be derived from the rolling forecast.

o Senior executive directives and the first estimates are the input for the carousel meeting on a **divisional level**.

o As soon as divisions have agreed on how profit contribution should be allocated, carousel meetings on the **functional levels** take place.

o The results from these meetings are the major input for the **detailed budget plans** to be completed by the operating units further down in the organization. Basically, the units will take the carousel meeting results and update the first estimates.

o Eventually, detailed budget plans will be summarized and finally adjusted and submitted for **senior management approval**. Only one approval round should be required sometime in December. In any case only minor revisions should be required since targets have been provided top-down and have been broken down consistently through the organization. In addition, the timeframe from releasing strategic goals until completion of the budget is fairly short and should allow only minor changes to the planning assumptions.

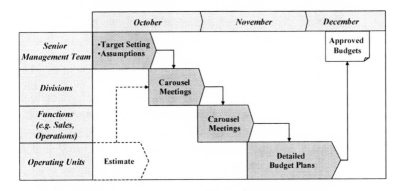

Exhibit IV-20: Planning Timeline - Example

Thus, the entire timeline to generate the yearly budget plan has been condensed to less than ten weeks. Best-Practice examples allow completion of the entire budget planning process in less than three weeks.

- *Integration and Software Support* - The last element of an effective planning process is data integration under use of adequate software support.

Planning processes often suffer from inconsistent data and planning assumptions. Although general guidelines are predetermined, each division still has to figure out the specific interpretation of general assumptions with regard to the following common reasons:

- o Specific competitive requirements require different planning assumptions (e.g., market growth).
- o Financial systems and planning systems of divisions are often not consistent. They are fed by different financial subsystems, HR systems, and manual inputs containing assumptions and other planning variables.
- o Plan data of divisions or functions are not comparable and can hardly be consolidated in one company-wide, consistent planning data set.

State-of-the-art planning software can help resolve these issues. In most applications, a specific planning database will be introduced that reinforces the particular planning structure and harmonizes the input data. These systems are only effective if rolled out across the entire company with its various management layers. As soon as all detailed plans have been developed, they can easily, and even more importantly, be consistently consolidated on the top level of the organization. Features such as central planning assumption administration and update as well as simulations will further support effectiveness of the planning process. As with the ERP systems to support effective and consistent information management, integrated planning tools streamline and harmonize the planning process. ERP system-providers offer integrated planning applications as part of their packages. Other providers offer planning tools that can easily be linked to existing ERP systems.

One of the major reasons for a thoughtful planning process is the definition of realistic and challenging performance targets. Without reasonable targets actual performance cannot be assessed and evaluated. Budgets will be derived out of targets as they get translated into quantifiable levels of desired performance during the budget process.[28] There are two principally different approaches on setting targets:

- External Target Setting - Targets are defined through shareholder expectations and industry benchmarks.
- Internal Target Setting - Targets are defined through internal goals and objectives. The Management-by-Objective (MBO) approach basically adds a certain percentage (mostly between five and ten percent) to past performance for the next year based on the negotiation between superiors and subordinates.[29] The positive aspect of MBO is that it indirectly fosters the search for continuous improvement. Additionally, through negotiation rather than predetermination of targets, subordinates generally show a higher level of acceptance. On the other hand, the MBO process can easily develop unrealistic targets simply because continuous growth (of revenue, for example) or reduction of costs cannot be realized by five percent and more on a yearly basis.

Target setting always requires sensitivity. It is inherent in human nature that nobody tries to overachieve without being challenged and stretched by hard-to-reach targets. On the other hand, goals should not be unrealistic. If individuals strongly believe upfront that there is no way to achieve the target, they will get unmotivated and perform at an average level or even below. There is no need for them to try hard. The MBO framework, however, provides a useful methodology to develop realistic targets through its emphasis on "negotiation."

Target setting explicitly approaches the challenge of common strategic goals and clear allocation of work to realize them. The overriding strategic direction needs to be clarified and articulated first before it can be broken down into subsets and cascaded over the several layers of the organization. If each employee focuses on optimizing individual performance, he or she needs a holistic framework to ensure the overall direction is still in line with the strategy. Balanced Scorecards and Integrated Strategic Measures (ISM) are proven concepts to facilitate the effective target-setting process through their strategic focus and integration of performance metrics. Integration of targets and coordination of performance are keys to success for effective Performance Management.[30]

23   Benchmarks and Best Practices

To ensure that targets are realistic, the outside comparison is mandatory. Cross-company benchmarking with competitors in the same industry or, in some cases, other industries is a practical and straightforward approach. The following principles need to be applied by working with external benchmarks.

- The **universe** of potentially comparable companies has to be defined. The starting point is the industry classification or the Standard Industry Classification code (SIC). These codes reveal the affiliation of a company to a specific industry group and are the first step to identify competitors and comparable companies. Another source to identify potential benchmarking candidates are analyst reports.
- Identified comparables need to be **screened** according to two perspectives:

  o Independence - If comparables are subsidiaries of holding companies, performance indicators can be misleading. The transfer pricing policies within the benchmarking candidate probably disregard corporate infrastructure and assets without extra charges or vice versa. In these cases, performance metrics reflecting the profitability will get distorted.
  o Type of Business - Comparability can only be achieved if companies are operating basically the same industry value chain. Indicators are not comparable if companies do most of their business in distribution, whereas others focus on manufacturing performance.

- Typical criteria to define a **homogeneous group** of benchmarking companies are:

  o Size in terms of revenue or
  o Number of employees.

Obviously, large-scale companies have better opportunities to leverage assets, infrastructure and back office operations than smaller players. As a result, growth and profitability patterns are different depending on size and, therefore, size ranges are essential to ensure reasonable comparability. Also, availability of financial data needs to be ensured. To develop comprehensive benchmarks, at least three consecutive years of financial data are required, which is not an issue for publicly listed companies in the U.S. However, disclosing requirements outside the U.S. are not that rigid and, additionally, benchmarking candidates can have a private company status and be required to disclose only limited financial data once a year. If data availability does not allow a thorough benchmarking, candidates have to be elimi-nated from the analysis.

As soon as comparable benchmarking candidates are identified, the financial data will be compiled to define benchmarks. Using quartiles to allocate the performance indicators is a common practice for cross-company benchmarking.

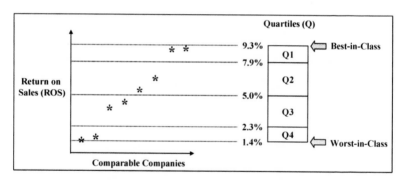

Exhibit IV-21: Cross-Company Benchmarking - Example

In terms of the metric to compare the benchmarking participants, there are various options:

o   Return on Sales – provides insights on the profitability; return can be defined as Net Income, Operating Profit or Earnings before Interest and Tax (EBIT).

All these financial data are accessible for publicly listed companies.

o Return on Assets – provides insights on profitability in regards to the invested capital.
o Return on Capital Employed – provides insights on shareholder value generation. Very useful indicator with limitations because of adjustment requirement to economic capital and profit.
o Sales Growth – provides insights on revenue generation potential.
o Cost of Goods Sold/Revenue – provides insights on operational cost basis.
o Sales, General and Administration/Revenue – provides insights on efficiency of support functions.

The selected benchmarking metrics need to be averaged over a period of at least three years to define reasonable target ranges. Also, the compound average growth rates $(CAGR = [(Last\ Year/First\ Year)^{1/N-1}] - 1 \times 100)$ over time should be compared to assess if targets are overly aggressive or extremely conservative with regard of the industry development.

Another important tool to derive applicable, realistic, and motivating benchmarks is a competitor database. Although detailed financial information and insights on specific process performance are often not accessible at all, there is other information that helps to track competitors' activities. The following categories need to be updated in a competitor database:[31]

o Competitor's history and key events (e.g., major mergers and restructuring activities)
o Products and services offered to the market and price ranges, including rebates and special promotions
o Product/Market Segments served and the relevant market share in target markets

- o Competitor's values and mission; ideally the current mission statement and written strategic goals
- o Address of headquarters and major divisional/regional centers
- o Partnerships, alliances, and networks the competitor is involved in
- o Senior executive officers and other key employees; number of employees in total and by major division/region
- o Competitor's current organizational structure and previous models
- o Summary of key financial performance, including development over time for major finance metrics such as revenue growth, net income growth, shareholder value growth, product development costs, overhead costs, spending for community and charities
- o Key strengths, weaknesses, opportunities and threats.

The information in the competitor database provides context for the quantitative benchmarking and will help to understand under- and overachievement of industry standards. Also, the qualitative assessment of the competitive environment will help to double-check performance targets. If an industry peer has gone through major restructurings, for example, that have limited its growth and profitability potentials, subsequently the same will apply for other players that are undergoing restructurings and will prevent unrealistic target setting.

The outside comparison provides both orientation and guidance. In addition, it should be used as a framework to facilitate the pursuit of industry leadership in the mid- and long-term. To strengthen elements of Organizational Effectiveness, Best Practices demonstrated by industry leaders should be copied or, even better, improved.

[1] Bob Eiler and Tom Cucuzza, "Crisis in Management Accounting," *Journal of Cost Management*, Vol. 16, July/August 2002, p. 29.

[2] Robert S. Kaplan and David P. Norton, "The Balanced Scorecard – Measures That Drive Performance," *Harvard Business Review*, No. 1, January/February 1992, pp. 71-79.

[3] Robert S. Kaplan and David P. Norton, "Having Trouble with Your Strategy? Then Map It," *Harvard Business Review*, No. 5, September/October 2000, pp. 167-176.

[4] Armin Toepfer, Gerhard Lindstaedt and Kati Foerster, Balanced Scorecards: Hoher Nutzen trotz zu langer Einfuehrungszeit, *Controlling*, No. 2, February 2002, pp. 79-80.

[5] Robert S. Kaplan and David P. Norton, "Using the Balanced Scorecard as a Strategic Management System," *Harvard Business Review*, No. 1, January/February 1996, pp. 75-85.

[6] Robert S. Kaplan and David P. Norton, "The Balanced Scorecard – Measures That Drive Performance," *Harvard Business Review*, No. 1, January/February 1992, p. 77.

[7] Bartley J. Madden, *CFROI Valuation: a Total System Approach to Valuing the Firm* (Oxford; Boston, MA: Butterworth-Heinemann, 1999), p. 79.

[8] Joel M. Stern and John S. Shiely, *The EVA Challenge: Implementing Value-added Change in an Organization* (New York: Wiley, 2001), pp. 16-17.

[9] Hazel Johnson, *Determining Cost of Capital: The Key to Firm Value* (London: Financial Times/Prentice Hall, 1999), p. 89.

[10] S. David Young and Stephen F. O'Byrne, *EVA and Value Based Management: A Practical Guide to Implementation* (New York: McGraw Hill, 2001), p. 165.

[11] Mary Kwak, "Recalculating the Cost of Capital," *MIT Sloan Management Review*, Vol. 43, No. 2, Spring 2002, p. 13.

[12] G. Bennett Stewart III, *The Quest for Value: A Guide for Senior Managers* (New York: HarperBusiness, 1991), pp. 436-437.

[13] Hazel Johnson, *Determining Cost of Capital: The Key to Firm Value* (London: Financial Times/Prentice Hall, 1999),, p. 73; G. Bennett Stewart III, *The Quest for Value: A Guide for Senior Managers* (New York: HarperBusiness, 1991),, p. 442.

[14] Peter Horvath and Lutz Kaufmann, Balanced Scorecards – ein Werkzeug zur Umsetzung von Strategien, in: Harvard Business Manager, No. 5, 1998, p. 40

[15] Joel M. Stern and John S. Shiely, *The EVA Challenge: Implementing Value-added Change in an Organization* (New York: Wiley, 2001), pp. 27-50.

[16] Stephen Gates, "Aligning Strategic Performance Measures and Results," *The Conference Board Research Report* 1258-99-RR, 1999, p. 4.

[17] Mark Graham Brown, *Winning Score: How to Design and Implement Organizational Scorecards* (Portland, OR, Productivity Press, 2000), p. vi.

[18] Mark Graham Brown, *Winning Score: How to Design and Implement Organizational Scorecards* (Portland, OR, Productivity Press, 2000), p. vi.

[19] Norman Moore, *Forecasting Budgets: 25 Keys to Successful Planning* (New York: Lebhar-Friedman Books, 1999), p. 9.

[20] The Hackett Group, "Book of Numbers 2002," http://www.hackettbenchmarking.com.

[21] Norman Moore, *Forecasting Budgets: 25 Keys to Successful Planning* (New York: Lebhar-Friedman Books, 1999), pp. 10-11.

[22] Robert G. Finney, *Essentials of Business Budgeting* (New York: AMACOM, 1995), p. 9.

[23] John A. Tracy, *Budgeting a la Carte: Essential Tools for Harried Business Managers* (New York: John Wiley & Sons, 1996), p. 5.

[24] Norman Moore, *Forecasting Budgets: 25 Keys to Successful Planning* (New York: Lebhar-Friedman Books, 1999), pp. 70-71.

[25] John A. Tracy, *Budgeting a la Carte: Essential Tools for Harried Business Managers* (New York: John Wiley & Sons, 1996), pp. 46-56.

[26] Robert G. Finney, *Essentials of Business Budgeting* (New York: AMACOM, 1995), p. 6.

[27] Robert G. Finney, *Essentials of Business Budgeting* (New York: AMACOM, 1995), pp. 88-89; Finney calls the estimate preliminary budget.

[28] Mark Graham Brown, *Winning Score: How to Design and Implement Organizational Scorecards* (Portland, OR, Productivity Press, 2000),, p. 49.

[29] Mark Graham Brown, *Winning Score: How to Design and Implement Organizational Scorecards* (Portland, OR, Productivity Press, 2000),, p. 50.

[30] Richard Y. Chang/ Paul De Young, Measuring Organizational Improvement Impact, Irvine, Calif.: R. Chang Associates, 1995, p. 29-30

[31] Mark Graham Brown, *Winning Score: How to Design and Implement Organizational Scorecards* (Portland, OR, Productivity Press, 2000), pp. 109-110.

"Best Practices applied"

Case Studies for Designing Effective Organizations

Measuring Organizational Effectiveness has been an ambitious objective for both academic research and business practice. Certainly, there is a link between Organizational Effectiveness and financial performance but the question is whether it is strong enough to conclude that financial performance will always improve as a result of improved Organizational Effectiveness.

The general assumption that companies with relatively low overhead costs will be more productive and yield better financial performance is a fact for many industries such as semiconductors for example. The lower the relative overhead costs, the better the companies perform in terms of Return on Sales (ROS) and Return on Assets (ROA). The correlation between relative overhead costs and ROS in the semiconductor industry is -0.80 for the year 2001.

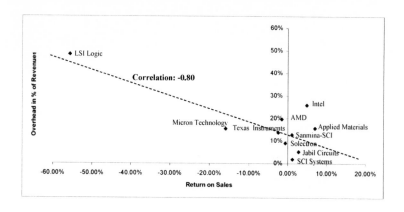

Exhibit V-1: Correlation Analysis of Semiconductor Industry

However, in other industries these correlations are not at all that strong or are even contrasting:

- Computer hardware industry (ten industry leaders) – correlation: –0.40
- Airline industry – correlation: –0.11
- Electronics and equipment industry – reverse correlation: +0.30.

Another assumption is that in today's fast moving and challenging markets, companies that devote a higher proportion of total costs to research and development are more successful than others. But, exactly the opposite is sometimes the case: the analysis of the top ten electronics and equipment industry leaders reveals that the better the financial performance in terms of ROS, the less money is invested in R and D. This is, of course, just a result of the untypical capital expenditure profile of the year 2001, which has led to reduced R and D budgets, but it illustrates how difficult it is to derive a general rule.

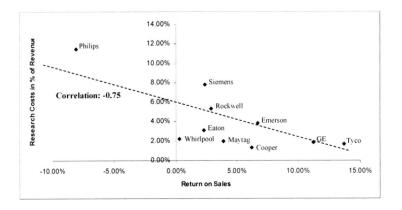

Exhibit V-2: Correlation Analysis Electronics Industry 2001

In fact, the analysis of development over time shows that the correlation is – as expected – positive. The same ten companies display a positive correlation of ROS growth and relative R&D costs growth over the period of 1997 to 2001 of +0.55.

As a result, the empirical evidence that certain patterns of Organizational Effectiveness are related to improved financial performance cannot be verified. Although researchers and business practitioners generally agree that effective organizations will positively influence the companies' financial performance and value creation, empirically proof of the hypothesis is still outstanding.

Consequently, case-based examples need be used to demonstrate evidence for the benefits of nurturing an effective organization. The following cases are based on real companies. In order to maintain confidentiality, some data and facts have been slightly modified and the company names have been disguised. All principles and solutions described have been implemented and helped these companies to significantly improve Organizational Effectiveness and overall performance.

24   More Entrepreneurship through Organizational Design
– The North American Railroad Case

Heavily regulated industries such as utilities, airlines, telecommunications, or railways are prone to be bureaucratic, slow moving and hierarchical in organizational design. Governmental regulation has protected the railroad sector from tough competition for decades and, over the years, the railroads have become lethargic and even more complex. The old basic principal that each administration tends to create its own justification can nowhere be seen as clearly as in the formerly regulated industries. In particular, the North American railroad industry carried significant burdens from former regulation, privatization, and union influence. Railroads have become heavily over-equipped with assets and manpower, which they had to drastically cut in order to sustain a brutal period of mergers and acquisitions while significantly boosting up competitiveness and maintaining the bottom-line. Market share and revenue growth, even in shrinking markets, proved to be key in order to survive as well as thrive at the end of the late 1990.

The case company is a North American rail company that has mastered these challenges. Their operating ratio is fourteen points above the industry average. In terms of free cash flow and earnings, the company has established a leadership position in the industry. Privatized in the mid-1990s, the company has grown substantially through strategic and targeted acquisitions. The firm is able to run approximately eighty-five percent of its business on its own network, which means they have direct control of origin and destination routes. Although economic upturns or downturns are impacting the rail business directly, the corporation has coped with the recent shortfall in transportation demand and has even used the situation to enlarge their market share since 1999.

The reason for the case company's tremendous success is basically twofold:

- Implementation of a rigorous Service Plan
- Introducing Regional Profit Centers

Both of these initiatives are innovative, unique, and excellent examples of thought leadership in the railroad industry. As the first railroad to implement this strategy, the company has developed a schedule, which ensures trains leave and arrive at terminals according to a published timetable. As a result, the railroad is able to guarantee its customers an unprecedented on-time delivery and has, therefore, gained significant operating advantages. Furthermore, since the firm applies the Service Plan on a "car and shipment basis," it needs fewer freight cars and, subsequently, fewer assets. Each single car has its own "trip plan" which enables the case company to reduce their safety stocks. Their car fleet has been reduced during the period from 1998 to 2001 by more than seven percent per year on average. And, on-time performance for 2002 is more than ninety-five percent, which exceeds the railroad industry performance rating overall.

While the Service Plan is a resourceful strategic move that has led to best practice service levels, the second initiative – implementing Regional Profit Centers – has strengthened the company in terms of Organizational Effectiveness. Before 1999, the company was like most railroad companies today – basically structured according to the Functional Organizational design. At first glance, this organizational design might be the logical framework for this type of business: One-product services (rail transportation), network-based operations (similar to one multiple assembly line manufacturing facility) and strategically focused on service (on-time performance) and cost reduction. The natural principles of an organization would be according to business functions such as operations, engineering, marketing, sales, and other back-office functions such as finance and HR. Responsibility for operating and maintaining the track systems, yards and terminals, and rolling assets such as locomotive and freight cars would reside with operations and engineering, whereas marketing and sales would primarily sell their services as provided by the network. Each function could basically act autonomously, in cross-functional coordination (e.g., for planning purposes or for overarching decisions, such as which trains to prioritize if a route is congested, would be covered by certain committees). Although the Functional Organizational design might be the obvious choice for railroads, it will automatically bring the drawbacks associated with this principle. Communication between operations and marketing lag – decisions are delayed, and optimal utilization of all railroad assets is hindered. Especially the latter example – asset utilization – is probably the biggest challenge railroads have to master: demand for rail-based transportation services follow certain patterns, with a peak demand between Sunday and Wednesday, and off-peak demand from Thursday to Saturday. However, railroads operate 365 days a year with no downtime, which means the vast majority of railroad assets are heavily underutilized during the latter half of the week.

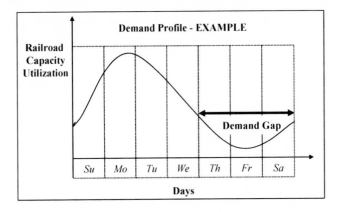

Exhibit V-3: Demand Gap in the Railroad Industry

The case company has targeted this demand gap with a smart organizational design that is unique to the railroad industry. National customers would like to move their inventory early in the week to create ample storage space for ongoing production and drive the peak performance mainly on Monday and Tuesday. The second half of the week is generally slower because only regional customers would like to haul goods over short distances. It is exactly this shortfall of demand the railroad has tackled with its regional organizational design approach. In the "old" organizational structure, the CMO and the majority of the marketing and sales force would have been headquartered in one major North American city with a primary focus on national accounts. Although some salespeople would have operated regionally, they weren't aware of spare rail transportation capacity inside their region, nor did they have the means to sell off this capacity. If they wanted to sell additional regional business, they either had to go up the functional ladder to find out if network operations would offer a train with open cars in a particular timeslot, or they had to convince a local operations superintendent to attach additional cars to a train, or possibly even run an extra train. Also, in the old structure, the superintendent would be responsible for smooth rail operations in his or her region and it might not be of foremost interest to change the system's configuration for "some" additional business. The "old organizational structure" is outlined below.

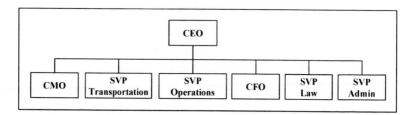

Exhibit V-4: Railroad Company's "Old" Functional Organizational Design

As a consequence, the company was focusing strongly on large national customers who provided more than eighty percent of revenues, revenues that were stagnant or even declining. The potential of growing revenues was developed by expanding small and emerging accounts and, therefore, the company decided to change its guiding organizational principle from functionally-oriented vertical to process-oriented horizontal. It established crosscutting processes that integrated marketing and sales, engineering, mechanical, and transportation on a regional basis. Eventually, the regions received Profit Center status and were used as the new guiding organizational principle. The idea was based on a key success factor: focused divisions are in charge of aggressively penetrating their regional markets. The regional divisions were enabled to act autonomously and to serve the local markets independently. The definition of five regional divisions created manageable zones with empowered teams. Teams are associated with a certain region and identify themselves within this region. As a result, tremendous entrepreneurial momentum across the company developed. As part of the divisional teams, each region received its own fully dedicated sales force, resulting in improved customer relationship management. Unutilized capacity was visible and could be proactively marketed and sold off. As an attempt to give the regional divisions even more autonomy, the firm decentralized some of the headquarters' functions such as finance and HR. As the regions obtained accountability for their local business, corporate also allocated the associated revenues and costs to the regions. Despite the fact that revenue and cost allocation in centrally managed network organizations can be quite painful and often a source for lengthy discussion and negotiations, the company set a simple but widely accepted model for allocation: revenues were assigned by ten percent to the originating location of a train and by ten percent to the receiving location. The regional rail network that was used to transport goods from point A to point B received the balance of the revenue on a pro-rated basis, factored by miles. Direct expenses can easily be assigned to distinct regions. Indirect costs are allocated in a similar way, as are the revenues. Even asset charges are allocated to the regions. Each region has its own fixed assets based on local requirements, which means locomotives or even rail cars are part of a region. Non-rolling assets such as track, yards, and terminals are part of each region, anyway. The case company has taken a very aggressive approach by charging assets at market value to the regions. This stimulates an even stronger desire by the regions to eliminate as many assets as possible. With assigned revenues, costs, and asset charges in place, the regional divisions are able to develop their own profit and loss statements and generate their own cash flow. It's obvious that the divisions automatically try to sign up profitable business first, reduce asset charges, and cut regional costs in order to generate profit. This is exactly the behavior the new structure intended. It turned the regions into independent entrepreneurs with interest in optimizing their local/regional business. Consequently, the operating scorecard was introduced as a performance measurement tool with particular emphasis on the region's profit and cash flow. Furthermore, performance is assessed on a team basis. The various operation functions and regional salespeople must work as a team to achieve their performance goals in order to be rewarded. Suboptimizing from a sales perspective in order to drive revenues without having costs and asset charges in mind will lead to unsatisfactory results on a regional level and vice versa.

In a business where the majority of revenues are still made with nationwide customers and where the Service Plan (as discussed above) is the key success factor to provide first-class service and operational best practices, not all accountabilities can be assigned to regions. As a balancing act, the company defined two central roles to strengthen the network: network marketing and network operations. Network marketing was set in place to exclusively focus on the national accounts. During the organizational redesign, some of the national customers had been assigned to the region where the majority of their customer group still remained centrally managed. In addition, network marketing coordinates all company-wide marketing activities and ensures pricing discipline. Network operations was established to keep the network balanced. This group develops and maintains the Service Plan and controls network services. They decide how to allocate and assign resources across the network. The network operations group is primarily staffed with highly skilled operations researchers who design overall-efficient network solutions. The efficient network design is locked into the Service Plan, and well-organized execution of this plan enables the company to operate with industry-leading service performance. Deviations from the Service Plan are not possible unless the network operations group decides upon a proposal from either a specific region or from the network marketing group in order to vary the overall configuration. However, as soon as alterations to the design are made, the Service Plan is updated and serves as the undisputed schedule for each train. Regions are only able to offer services within the boundaries of the Service Plan. The new overarching organizational design can be characterized as Regional/Functional Hybrid Organization with regions serving as guiding dimensions.

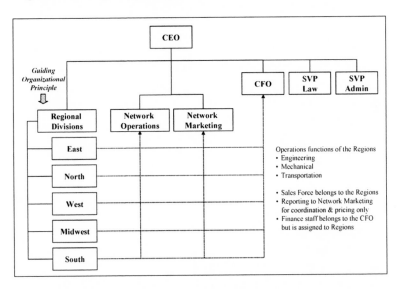

Exhibit V-5: North American Railroad Company's New Organizational Design

In 1999, the firm decided to create a new organizational structure. The new organizational design was developed, refined and detailed, confirmed through the senior management team and quickly implemented. Without time-consuming and complex change-management programs, the new model was literally set in place overnight. Of course, radical organizational changes are risky and challenging but can create a strong and sustained momentum when the management leaders are buying in very quickly. The company took three very important proactive measures to ensure the transition would be smooth and successful.

1. Selection of the right people for newly created leadership positions in the business model is extremely important. Delegating corporate responsibilities to regional divisions creates leadership needs that need to be filled by convincing, ambitious, and capable leadership candidates of the firm. Those who qualify for the new job will automatically surface while testing the new model. The urgent need for strong leadership will be perceived and attract the best leaders. As a result, the case company today has many regional leadership positions filled with managers and directors younger than 35. This is entirely new to the railroad industry.

2. The new approach has to be sold, sold, and sold. The advantages of the regional approach have to be explained and re-explained many times. The organization has to be convinced. The employees have to be converted to strong believers of the new model. As preachers, the company's senior executives must persuade every employee and turn them into a congregation of believers.

3. The composition of the Profit Center leader team was at least as important as the other two measures. In an organizational model that is based on a regional/functional hybrid principle with strong regions and corporate-provided essential services, both perspectives are equally important: regions and corporate. Selecting divisional leaders with strong capabilities to successfully drive autonomous business units but without substantial team player skills and the understanding of the big picture would have certainly

led to disaster. Regional heads need to be both regional entrepreneurs and corporate soldiers. The case company has succeeded in creating a well-balanced leadership team with the right chemistry who act as a corps and operate without regional silos.

The company's bold step to revolutionize the traditional railroad business model has made it an industry leader. Organizational effectiveness has been significantly improved and created an entirely new mindset for the firm. The most important new element of this mindset is the enhanced entrepreneurship. Through full profit and loss accountability in regions, the need of entrepreneurial behavior has been cascaded over the whole firm. Employees who were previously focused on granular, functional tasks are now much closer to the customer. They quickly understand how their action and behavior translates into revenue and cost effects and eventually impacts the bottom line of their respective region. The way in which the new structure was implemented, combined with its rigorous requirement of decentralized decision–making, has led to a quick decision culture. Business opportunities can be assessed from a region's perspective. Revenue and cost forecasts can be derived quickly, based on the standards provided. As a result, the region can immediately decide on the boundaries of the Service Plan and help to drive profits. Consequently, the new leaders have learned to react quickly. Moreover, there has been a new definition and interpretation of ownership that has emerged: a customer in the "old" railroad organization was referred from one department to another in search of a certain delivery. The operations department showed little or no interest for making customers happy – they only needed to run the railway. Marketing and sales were not the operations department's primary concern either. The case company's new regional approach has modified this mindset entirely:

everybody is obliged to serve the customer first. All operations, marketing, and other employees are aware of how important revenue and costs are for the region's profit; hence, it is in the interest of everyone to show ownership and responsibility to solve customers' requests. Strong regional focus and ownership have given the case company access to a new, emerging revenue source and profitable business – the region's small accounts.

The company has successfully applied both elements the Service Plan and Regional Profit Centers to achieve a shift in organizational values, which are the foundation for robust industry leadership.

25   Streamlining Corporate Functions to survive – The Telecommunication Supplier Case

In phases of severe economic downturns it is often not sufficient to cut operating costs to survive. Companies have to comb through their indirect cost categories and carefully screen administrative and general costs to identify all possible savings potentials to return above the water line. Even the headquarters' functions should not be excluded from this exercise. For the international telecommunications equipment supplier in this case, the challenge had to be mastered to stay in business after the economy, and especially the telecommunication business, faltered in 2000-2001. Its case points out how corporate functions can be significantly streamlined without negatively impacting the business.

The company, known for its strong foothold in the telecommunication technology market, offers services in mobility, optical, data and voice networking technologies; web-based enterprise solutions; communications software; professional network design and consulting services; and communications semiconductors and optoelectronics. The impressive growth path of the 1990s led to sales revenues of more than $25 billion in 2000. However, in 2001 the revenue alarmingly dropped by 25% below the $20 billion mark. Whereas the case company had lavishly showered its shareholders with an operating income of up to 15% in the past, the loss ratio in 2001 amounted to an unbelievable and disastrous −25%. To recover from this extremely weak financial performance, restructuring efforts had to include the SG&A side, and, in particular, the headquarters of the business as well.

The restructuring initiative that started in 2000 took place in two waves: phase one was launched in the fall of 2000 and was designed to bring the company back on track; but the further deterioration of market conditions forced them to execute a second phase of restructuring in 2001. As a result, costs of more than $2 billion were cut from the budget and headcount was reduced by 25,000 employees. One significant part of the restructuring plan dealt with the corporate headquarters' functions. Led by the definition of the critical priorities of the new corporate center, the new specific role of the center was determined.

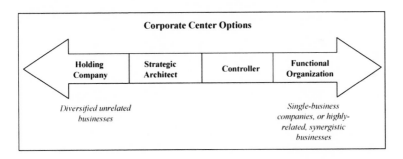

Exhibit V-6: Role of the Corporate Center

The framework shown above was used to visualize the general role a corporate center can potentially play. In relatively small companies or companies that focus mainly on one type of business, the corporate center is normally closely involved in the day-to-day transactional activities. The headquarters often performs finance and accounting, IT, HR, R and D, and general administrative tasks. Often the operative sales and marketing, distribution, and operations functions are centralized in the corporate center, too. Therefore, the size of the staff is usually quite large, especially as a percentage compared with decentralized headcount. The controller role already clearly differentiates between operational tasks and coordination activities. The corporate center mainly focuses on management reviews and is much less involved in the daily routine of the segment units. The units gain more autonomy; however, they are still closely controlled. As a result, the size of the corporate staff is still large. The corporate center that acts as a strategic architect provides the overall strategic direction. The center manages the corporate strategy and translates it into segment unit-specific strategic directions. It is more or less not involved in the business unit activities anymore despite the close strategic direction setting and control. All operational tasks take place under full responsibility of the units. The level of autonomy is, within the overall strategic direction, much stronger than in the controller model. Since the corporate center is involved in strategic guidance only, the size of the corporate staff is much smaller than in the two previous models. The holding company role goes even one step further. It abandons any involvement in strategy development and execution on the segment unit level. Its focus is mainly on reviewing corporate finances and allocating capital and funds. This type of headquarters requires only a limited staff size.

Based on this framework, the case company could identify its current corporate center role mostly as a controller role. Both strategically and operationally, the center had been closely involved in direction setting and reviewing. Although the segment units maintained substantial independence, the corporate center was very present on the unit level. In essence, both the corporate strategy and the segment strategy were not differentiated clearly so that pockets of redundancies on operational and strategic levels existed. Additionally, due to unclear performance measures, accountabilities to the center and the segment units were not clearly assigned. The consequence for the company was that it maintained a relatively large staff size on the corporate level that created significant interference with the daily activities of the units. The future state was clearly outlined to position the corporate center more closely aligned to the strategic architect model rather than the controller role.

Before the journey towards a new corporate center role started, an assessment of the current state was conducted to address and to detail improvement potentials. The assessment was conducted by comparing the company's expenses and staff size to industry and comparable-sized company benchmarks and best practices. The results indicated that there was clearly enough scope to streamline the center operations while converting its role to a strategic architect. For example, the IT and finance functions showed cost improvement potential of up to fifty percent. Other selected functions, such as real estate management, indicated potential improvement of up to eighty percent. In addition, the effectiveness of the functions had to be improved. The functions tended to operate in silos, and each function had no clear and consistent view of the function's overall role within the context of the overall corporate center strategy. Moreover, some cultural issues had to be resolved. Functions were based on a hierarchy with an "organization building" mentality. Since the number of direct reports was an important benchmark metric, one can understand that the functional organizations quickly became quite sizeable.

After identifying and understanding all of the assessment results, as well as defining the newly targeted role of the corporate center, the firm launched a rapid improvement program to reposition and reengineer its corporate center in the summer of 2001. Streamlining of corporate center operations carries the potential risk that certain activities are simply delegated to the segment units, where they are performed as "shadow activities." However, units might not be in a position to execute these activities with the same efficiency as centralized departments. Especially functions that need extensive expertise, like finance and accounting, IT, and HR, are often performed with less quality on a segment unit level. Moreover, additional administrative tasks potentially distract from core activities like generating maximum revenue growth and optimizing operational costs. Hence, the company first addressed that the focus of the segment units should remain market facing and that all administrative functions should be aligned accordingly. All general and administrative activities must support this end – ensuring services and service levels are rationalized to provide the appropriate added value and expertise as well as the appropriate service levels at the lowest cost possible. Some segment units may be large enough in scale to develop self-standing general and administrative functions – but this should only be realized where there is a clear business case to retain specialized-function personnel within the segment unit.

If borders between corporate activities and business units partly overlap, they get fuzzy, and clarification of roles and responsibilities is required. Corporate centers on a migration path from the functional role to the controller role, and, in particular, to the strategic architect role, reduce their involvement in segment unit activities step-by-step. It must be clearly defined who must step in and carry which responsibilities and decision rights. Basically, all cross-company processes, such as "order fulfillment" or "product management," must be redefined to ensure sufficient attention is guaranteed and expertise involved. The case company established clear roles and accountabilities between each corporate center function, the segment units and other "horizontal" organizational units (e.g., services, supply chain, etc.).

Some activities cannot be clearly assigned to either the corporate center or the segment units. The so-called transactional functions are the continuously recurring and repetitive activities that are considered to be non-core activities. Often, these functions include manual data entry, data collection, reconciliation, filing, generating data records, and so on. These transactional activities should neither be part of a corporate center, especially if the center evolves to a strategic architect role, nor should they be assigned to the segment units because they are not generating value and distract significantly from core business. However, somebody has to take care of processing orders, reconciling customer payments with receivables, updating employee files, and filing invoices. The company has migrated all these non-core activities to a scale-intensive "utility model" that is focused primarily on throughput and efficiency. Through the "utility model," neither the center nor the segments have to worry about them, and the service quality has been increased while costs are reduced through economies of scale.

The handling of the non-core activities has been realized in two different models. While the activities with low economies-of-scale impact have been considered for outsourcing, the non-core activities with high volume have been bundled in corporate-led, shared service centers.

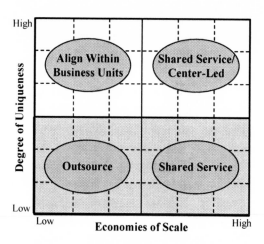

Exhibit V-7: Outsourcing vs. Shared Services

The outsourced services are delivered through a minimal number of geographically aligned vendors. The selected vendors have to prove that the service will be delivered with higher efficiency than if the company provided it internally, and with at least an equal or higher level of quality. The shared services are provided through an in-house organization. By aggregating services for multiple internal customers, substantial economies of scope can be yielded and overall costs reduced. Service level agreements ensure that the quality delivered by the shared service center meets the requirements of the segment units. Some services that are bundled in shared services require specific customization to segment needs, such as corporate control and reporting. Due to the complexity of these tasks and their strategic importance, these services are under direct control of the corporate center. Other activities that are very unique to the segment units, such as brand management, strategic planning, and market analysis, are too specific to gain significant economies of scope. For these areas, the corporate center provides support with its functional expertise and aligns its functions partly according to the segment needs.

In the strategic architect role, the corporate center must focus on value creation for the overall company. Through its close involvement in strategy definition on the segment level, the corporate center first identifies the potential to utilize synergies. It can guide segments and link them together to pursue selected strategic moves such as market entries, optimization of operations or logistic costs, and R and D efforts. The new corporate center has assumed this role and evolved into an important integrator and coordinator of different segment units. Hence, the new role truly focuses on value generation.

Eventually, the firm mastered its restructuring tasks in 2001. The redesign of the corporate center has played an important role in enabling the company to cope with the difficult economic conditions, returning it to its competitive position. Of course, the firm has mainly targeted substantial cost reductions with its restructuring, and has achieved most of the savings potential. Besides the cost cutting, it has also successfully managed to strengthen the organization. The new corporate center role and cooperation with the segment units have clearly enhanced the Organizational Effectiveness. The case company has gained sustainable advantages through its clearly positioned, streamlined, and well-integrated corporate center. The fact that the cost structure today approaches a world-class level is a nice, but vital, side effect.

26   Process acceleration and streamlining through a new "Sense of Urgency" – The Automotive Case

The bigger global corporations grow, the more they struggle with bureaucracy and lengthy and complex processes. Of course, it never happens on purpose but growth usually comes with additional products, product groups, business units and divisions. And as soon as business activities expand to new regions, countries, and continents, multiple corporate guidelines and policies are released and overlap with business units or local principles – and often these guidelines are even contrary. In addition, the bigger organizations grow, the more people are disconnected from the "real" business, meaning producing and selling the products. As a matter of fact, the large-scale businesses of today employ thousands and thousands of people dealing exclusively with administrative and supporting tasks. Their power base is built on factors such as information monopoly, hierarchy, and centralized decision rights. These factors often interfere with the interests of those who are closely attached to the products and customers. They suffer from slow-moving information flow, delayed decision processes, unclear bureaucracy, and lengthy processes. A lot of "waste" has piled up in process execution that blocks efficiency, lacks innovation, and hinders true value generation.

The case company here realized that it had suffered these symptoms. As the CEO phrased it at the end of the 1990s, the company was moving at automotive, not Internet speed. Moreover, the competitive nature of the automotive industry and the unending emergence of possibilities driven by technology were further aspects requiring faster organizational speed. Eventually, the results of an employee survey were sobering, too: employees confirmed that slowness and bureaucracy impeded business performance. All this added up to a convincing case to build internal capability for faster decision making. Thus, the CEO identified "moving with a sense of urgency" as a key cultural priority which laid the groundwork for the enterprisewide initiative, *Let's move!*

Initiated in late 1999, *Let's move!* is designed to increase organizational speed and sense of urgency by empowering employees to remove bureaucracy and other barriers to speed faced in their daily work. It provides an opportunity to look with fresh eyes at old problems, solve them and move on. It builds upon existing corporate initiatives and introduces coaching, problem-solving tools, and learning to accelerate the sense of urgency. *Let's move!* workshops provide a structured approach for stripping away bureaucracy from the organization, allowing employyees to concentrate on value-added work and to execute winning business decisions with speed, which leads to improved performance. It is a results-driven, enterprise-wide, change initiative designed to engage the "hearts and minds" of employees at all levels. The objective is to use *Let's move!* to deliver short-term business results while modeling, in the workshops, those new behaviors that will lead to sustained organizational transformation. The tangible results are, in essence, enhanced process performance through decreased costs, increased throughput, and improved quality. Employees clearly benefit as it is designed to engage and empower them – the people who do the work – to change the company. In workshops they are able to practice: candidly challenging the status quo, creating innovative solutions to the problems they identify, and courageously recommending those solutions to leaders. Workshops also "teach" leaders to be more decisive, more open, and more inclusive. In fact, *Let's move!* represents a "public stage" where business leaders can demonstrate and model these new behaviors in front of employees.

Additionally, employees trained as *Let's move!* Project Managers and Coaches, as well as business leaders, are inspiring other employees to do business differently by modeling behaviors such as global knowledge sharing, collaborative teamwork, and clear, frequent communication. The workshops address a broad spectrum of business problems with the common goal of achieving a greater sense of urgency. As a result, the case company is turning into a place where people can fearlessly challenge the way things have always been done in order to drive greater focus on the work that matters, creating a company that is both big and fast. Fast means, in this sense, accelerated processes and quicker decision making. Focus reinforces the customer focus and the importance of reducing non-value added activities. Fearlessly describes the empowerment of employees and a risk-taking mentality.

To be able to conduct these workshops across the entire corporation, two thousand (and still growing) employees throughout the organization have been trained in coaching and facilitation tools and techniques they need to run *Let's move!* workshops. Once certified (through a rigorous process, which involves increasing practice and responsibility in facilitative, consultative, and coaching skills in a workshop setting), these coaches facilitate the workshop sessions, provide insights on cultural issues, and counsel and coach workshop participants. To lead implementation of *Let's move!* at the local level, more than twenty business units have appointed a *Let's move!* project manager. These high-potential individuals are either full-time or part-time.

Additionally, a *Let's move!* website has been designed that serves as a dynamic reservoir of learning, where employees can obtain and contribute *Let's move!* information. The website achieves several objectives:

- Communicates the purpose of *Let's move!*
- Conveys the impact of *Let's move!* with an accessible, up-to-date, easy-to-search database of workshop decisions and their implementation status
- Creates a forum for sharing success stories
- Promotes knowledge sharing with a section devoted to collaborative approaches and shared issues
- Provides a powerful tool for coaches and project managers to download workshop tools, generate activity reports, monitor coach certification and share advice on what's working and what's not.

To further encourage employees to contribute to the initiative and to adopt the *Let's move!* behavior, so-called speeding tickets have been introduced rewarding the everyday *Let's move!* behavior: everyday fast decision making, focused effort, and fearless questioning of waste. Additionally, Speed Demons are issued by the CEO, to highlight exemplary results. They are a highly visible incentive for employees to get involved and to achieve results through *Let's move!*

Let's move! has led to multiple benefits for the company. Through mid-2002, approximately 3,000 workshops have taken place reaching almost 40,000 employees. Up to 15,000 recommendations developed by the workshops have been approved and are being implemented. Besides the quantitative workshop results, thousands of hours of non-value-adding work have been eliminated across the entire organization and there is a restrengthened focus on the core tasks. Even more important than these remarkable successes gained through the workshops are the substantial changes in the company's behavior. Today, employees are proactively challenging the way things get done. They always try to understand the rationale behind certain practices and focus on value contribution. The way the firm works has been significantly simplified. Processes are becoming streamlined and result-oriented. Thousands of unnecessary reports, meetings, and approvals have been eliminated. Customer focus and value generation are the guiding principles to design powerful processes. Furthermore, implementation is done quickly and concisely. The use of dedicated coaches, project managers and dedicated top-management support ensure that recommendations are implemented as rapidly as possible. This has positive motivation on those involved in developing the recommendation and illustrates the seriousness of *Let's move!* It is not another conceptual approach to improve process performance – it's real and truly changes the behavior of the company from top to bottom. Another behavioral aspect is that leaders learn to lead more visibly. The workshop approach enables them to jointly develop improvement recommendations with their subordinates. And leaders make decisions, on the spot, at the end of the workshop day.

The reputation that had followed the case company in the past of behaving like a slow and inefficient dinosaur due its size and the complexity of its operations has turned around. *Fortune* magazine gave the case company credit when it said, "It's finally looking good." The efforts of making the firm move faster and do better have succeeded: The firm's huge size has transformed from a dead weight into a lever. *Let's move!* has helped to reengineer operations and break bottlenecks. But the journey is not over yet: eventually the *Let's move!* behavior should be part of every activity and decision made by the company's people throughout the world without conducting formal *Let's move!* workshops. If this objective is accomplished, the sense of urgency will truly have become a cultural priority.

Effective organizations will always question the way things are done. Companies with a huge size, multiple organizational layers, and complex interplays of functions, business units, regions, and corporate activities are especially in latent peril that bureaucracy will eventually take over as the guiding organizational principle – even though it's not publicly admitted, factually these firms are often bureaucracy. Many big corporations today suffer from the symptoms discussed in the case above. Therefore, it is more or less a necessity to reinforce the value-added activities and to get rid of non-value-adding "waste." Standardized approaches such as Total Quality Management Programs or Six Sigma are a starting point, though. But to really succeed, a customized, company-spanning approach like the case company's *Let's move!* initiative is, in any case, more promising.

27   Mastering the Planning Challenge –
The International Construction Supplier Case

Planning is a challenge for most companies. Different markets and products, customer segments, production and logistical networks, and economic conditions have made reliable planning, especially for international companies, an almost insurmountable task. The case of this European-based international construction supplier will stress the challenges and demonstrate ways to overcome major roadblocks to effective planning.

The case company is well known for its innovative building material that combines the advantages of wood and concrete in one product: good thermal insulation, solid structure, easy to work with and handle – but without the disadvantages of combustibility and decay. For decades its building material has been in high demand, especially due to its environmentally friendly and energy-conserving attributes that meet all the requirements of the modern age.

The worldwide organization sells its products across all five continents, operates subsidiaries in fifteen European countries and maintains additional production facilities in Africa, the Middle East and Southeast Asia. Since the building materials industry considers transportation costs as a critical success factor, a widespread network of plants and partnerships to subcontract production is a necessity. Moreover, production facilities and their programs have to be tailored to the specific market requirements. On the sales side, the construction supplier industry faces quite heterogeneous market conditions: whereas construction markets in Slovenia and Croatia are still growing strong due to the demolition of the Yugoslavian war, markets in Germany or France are stagnant or even shrinking. Unpredictable events like the earthquakes in Turkey in 1999 or the flooding disaster in East Germany in summer 2002 lead to unforeseen peak demands. To create reliable plans in this type of business environment is truly a challenge but, nevertheless, the company has faced the challenge to develop a robust planning process to gain certain advantages: less effort, reduced timeframe, more reliable results, and reasonable performance targets.

Before the planning process was redesigned the company had established a lengthy and time-consuming process that ran through several iteration rounds and delivered imprecise results. Planning activities started as early as May when the Planning and Management Accounting department compiled, in a bottom-up approach, actual data, deviation analysis, and an outlook for the upcoming year. These inputs were used to develop a first estimate that was summarized in the first version of the plan at the end of June – more than six months before the planning period even started and forecasting year-end results that laid eighteen months ahead! Based on the planning results and the actual year-to-date data of June, the top management decided on the key performance targets for the next year and played back the first planning version to the operative units. They basically redid the May exercise with updated target figures and submitted the results to the Planning and Management department in early September, when the second-plan version was compiled, double-checked and presented to the senior management. As soon as management agreement was given, the operative units were in charge to develop detailed budgets. However, multiple reasons could still interfere with the current planning version: first, by detailing the plan data and converting them into yearly budgets, faulty assumptions used for the plan estimate surfaced and required correction. As a result the plan data as submitted were no longer valid because operational budgets grew too big. The root cause for wrong assumptions was often related to the seasonality of the construction business that usually peaks in summer and runs slowly in winter. As a consequence, positive outlooks in May (first version) and July/August (second version) can easily turn around if, for example, a rainy late summer and fall and unfavorable economic conditions lead to extended weak demand or vice versa. In fact, the detailed plans that were completed in late October were often useless due to unexpected business and market developments in August and September because the changed conditions had not been considered in the detailed plans. The second reason, however, turned out to be in most cases the more severe one: since detailing the plans was made by sales and operational units almost entirely in isolation, plan data were not coordinated and reconciled enough. Each country organization, sales unit, and plant was detailing its plan based on common goals but on its own assumptions. If a sales unit of a major country trimmed down its sales projections without ever letting the plants involved know about it, the overall profitability dropped below acceptable thresholds. As a result, when Planning and Management Accounting compiled the results of the detailed planning to the third plan version at end of October, often the initial targets agreed in early September were not hit and another iteration was required. Eventually, plan version four was completed and submitted for review by the Board of Directors in late November. If the directors were not satisfied with the outlook for the next year, then another iteration was usually launched and the fifth version was prepared by the end of December. Consequently, the official release of budget data often didn't happen until the planning year had already started. All in all, the Planning and Management Accounting department was busy doing planning from May until January of the following year without spending significant time on variance analysis of actual and plan data after the crucial summer peak season was over. Time to provide qualified decision–support, as expected and required, was reduced to the bare minimum; the analytical skills of the management accountants were wasted on transactional planning activities. Even worse, the operational units were significantly distracted by planning activities from May until January, too. Multiple iterations and plan revisions kept them busy with planning instead of execution activities.

In 1999 the case company embarked on a journey that led to a new planning philosophy and process. Having identified all the weaknesses mentioned above and all the risks associated with them, they set five basic planning principles in place that are now the guiding premises throughout the entire process:

1. **Planning is a top-down process.**
   To reduce time and effort of the planning process, strategic objectives and goals are defined first. They will be consistently cascaded throughout the entire

organization. All detailed plans should reflect the strategic goals.

2. **The planning process takes a maximum of three months.**

All planning activities have to be realized within a three-month time window to keep focus on the actual business. Analysis of actual versus plan deviations and execution are the most important tasks. Therefore, any planning activities outside this timeframe are abandoned.

3. **The planning process does not start earlier than September.**

To keep the summer months free from distracting planning activities, kick off of planning takes place not earlier than September. Furthermore, the delayed start of the process allows incorporation of actual planning figures as tracked over the summer peak.

4. **Objectives are ambitious but always in sync with strategic goals.**

The aggressive goals are reflected in planning targets:

- We grow faster than the market
- We are the cost leader of the industry
- We achieve profitable growth through innovation

Before the start of each planning season, detailed targets in terms of Return on Capital employed (ROCE) and Net Productive Assets (NPA) will be defined.

5. **Managers in charge have accepted the planning goals and commit themselves to achieve objectives.**

Managers provide all vital prerequisites to develop realistic first estimates. They support the top-down cascading process and are engaged in developing achievable subplans. They are committed to actively use variance analyses to close possible gaps between actual and to-be performance.

Based on this philosophy, the company has designed a process that consists of five major cornerstones, although the first cornerstone, the strategy meeting, is not considered to be part of the planning process. However, since this meeting that takes place sometime between May and July it sets the tone for the entire planning process.

1. The **strategy meeting** deals primarily with qualitative goals. New product innovations, market entries, and the overriding strategic course of the firm are major topics. Additionally, the competitive positioning will be critically assessed and action items addressed. With respect to planning objectives, growth potentials of product/market segments are scaled and new markets highlighted.

2. The **estimate** As preparation for the management meeting (step 3) an estimate will be compiled that contains the key market and financial figures. Based on current market conditions, the essential performance indicators are forecasted. The estimate already displays an assessment on volumes, prices ranges, sales revenues, major cost groups, operating profits, capital expenditures, and net operating assets. Accordingly, the ROCE forecast is part of the estimate, too. The estimate is prepared in the first two weeks of September.

3. The **management meeting**. The objective of this meeting is preparation of the planning and development of general assumptions. Major inputs for the meeting are the actual data, including variance analysis (ideally, at the time of the meeting, the months January through August exist as actual data), the estimates, and the actual market provision simulation model. Based on

estimates and actual data, this model creates an optimized distribution network including all worldwide plants. The management meeting decides on the essential planning objectives: ROCE, NPA, and operating profit. Moreover, the meeting decides already on the first cascading level and details the key planning targets for the regional divisions. Eventually, a decision on the most beneficial market provision model is made. The management meeting takes place in late September.

4. The **carousel meeting**. With all these determinants in place, the cascading process moves on with the first carousel meeting. It takes place on the divisional level and includes, besides the division head, the heads of sales and marketing and operations. The meeting itself is prepared and facilitated by Planning and Management Accounting. Further on, experts on distribution and market provision are present to continuously update and optimize the distribution model. The first set of iterations in this meeting deal with the target operating profit. Both sales and marketing and operations have to jointly agree on a way to realize the set target. It normally takes multiple iterations before an agreement has been made and the market provision model and asset requirements can be derived. During the iterations, alterations and refinements on product/market segment specific price ranges and sales volumes are tested, different market provision models are simulated and various capital investment assumptions are tried. As soon as agreement has been reached, details of the predefined target ROCE for the division have been realized. Due to its high complexity and lengthy negotiation processes, the carousel meeting is held in a two-day workshop, which ideally takes place for all divisions in parallel in early October.

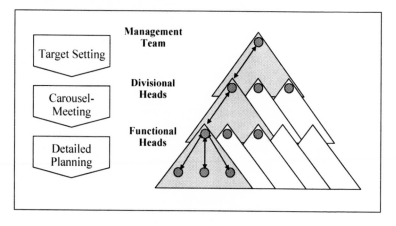

Exhibit V-8: Carousel Meeting – Overlaps

One major advantage of the carousel meeting approach is the relatively high level of acceptance and buy-in. Since the divisional heads have already been part of the decision-making process on how to cascade the ROCE target among the divisions, they accept their divisional ROCE target and will try to realize it with their division in any case. In the same way, their functional heads are parts of the decision-making process within the carousel meeting, too. By this the carousel meeting not only helps the company to streamline and shorten the entire process – it also significantly improves the quality of the planning outcome.

5. The **detailed planning**. Within this process, the targets – as defined by the carousel meeting – are cascaded to regions and product groups and allocated to months under consideration of seasonality. On the regional level, revenue targets for the sales force are defined. These revenues determine the sales volume, which automatically determines the production volume. The

production volume is eventually associated with certain costs of goods sold and investments, which lead to the region-specific detailing of the plan. Usually, detailed plans and budgets are ready as early as November, which still gives some room to incorporate smaller refinements or changes of assumptions. Because of the high-quality planning, major rework as required before reengineering the process does not take place anymore. As a result, planning is completed in early December and frees time and resources to focus on year-end activities.

The case company has gained significant benefits through the new planning approach. The process itself has been streamlined and is much less painful than before. Even more important, planning data have been integrated and are consistent today. Through elements like the carousel meeting, the level of acceptance has radically increased. Although the bottom-up philosophy has almost been abandoned, people identify themselves with planned data and objectives more strongly than before. They all have understood the importance of realistic and reliable plans and the necessity to operate against ambitious targets. The new planning process has enabled the company to survive the devastating economic downturn of the European construction industry in 2000/2001. The company's ability to forecast its future and to right-size its operations has become an essential competitive success factor. The new planning process has truly strengthened the Organizational Effectiveness.

28   Effective strategy execution through Integrated Strategic Measures
– The German Gearbox and Transmission Manufacturer Case

Strategy execution has been experienced as far more challenging than strategy development or strategic planning. Although the case company, a Germany-based automotive supplier, had developed a clear mission and goals, and had aligned their strategic capabilities accordingly, they were facing issues in strategy implementation. Furthermore, besides executing the strategy, it still had to be ensured that the strategy was, in fact, creating shareholder value. The case highlights how to utilize an effective performance management system as a key enabler to make strategy happen and to track closely value creation.

As one of the leading transmission manufacturers, the case company has been known for progress and quality for over 60 years. Outstanding engineering and the most modern technology have made the company brand an accepted term within the drive train division. Today, the company is the preferred supplier for almost all major auto firms around the globe: from high-end car manufacturers like Porsche, DaimlerChrysler, and BMW, to the midsize range with GM, Ford, PSA, RVI, VW, to the motorbike company Harley Davidson, all the way to the suppliers of heavy machinery engines such as Cummins and Caterpillar. With sales revenue of $1.8 billion in 2001 and more than 9,000 employees the corporate group, although still family-owned, has evolved to a major corporate player on the automotive landscape. Production sites are mainly located in Europe but also in the U.S., Japan, and India.

The firm has developed a vision that incorporates a well-reasoned stakeholder management approach. Based on the guiding principle, "We Do It Better," it addresses all key stakeholder groups: employees, suppliers, environment, family, stockholders, customers, company, and products. To stress the equal importance of each stakeholder group, each is called a "first violin" to the company. The strong stakeholder focus has led to an exceptionally strong Organizational Culture that nurtures Strategic Capabilities and lays ground for successful execution of strategic action. However, to combine vision with strategy and day-to-day activity, further detailing is required. And that was exactly the challenge when the company decided in 1999 to find ways to cascade and execute its strategic goals. Additionally, the firm had to cope with the challenging requirements of shareholder management in the automotive industry. To keep up with customers and potential partners like Ford, the company had to ensure that its strategic course would create shareholder value. Although family-owned, the company was scrutinized in detail by its customers and joint venture partners concerning reliability and sustainable value potentials of the overall strategic direction. So, the challenge involved both executing the strategy and demonstrating its positive financial impacts.

Before the development of a new strategy-driven performance measurement system, the company conducted an as-is assessment of its current state. The results displayed that the challenge was probably even bigger than expected. First of all, the financial performance of recent years had been continuously declining. Despite a straightforward and well-reasoned vision and strong market traction, profitability was falling below industry average. Additionally, a survey among the management team revealed that the firm pursued its actual strategic direction only half-heartedly. Merely one-third of the interviewees would value the company's compliance with strategic goals above average. Too little consensus among senior managers, lack of target breakdown, and inconsistent interpretation of goals were identified as major drawbacks.

With regard to performance metrics, the assessment uncovered that a wide set of different metrics were in use. However, just a few of them could be linked back to corporate goals. Basically, each function and production site had developed its own performance metrics and overpopulated the system. Hence, focus on the few important key measures had deteriorated.

The case company set a task force in place that first outlined the objectives of a new performance measurement system. The following five principles were subsequently developed:

1. The performance management system should be the platform to detail, discuss, and communicate the strategy across the entire organization.
2. Targets defined by the performance system should be consistently aligned with strategic goals and direction
3. The performance measurement system should enable ongoing progress control of strategy implementation.
4. The performance management system should enforce clear allocation of accountabilities, responsebilities, and decision-rights.
5. The performance measurement system should provide complete transparency of the operational business and surface critical issues immediately.

Based on this framework the overall vision was broken down to the underlying functional strategies. Through this exercise, gaps in existing functional strategies were identified and closed. Furthermore, the close conversion of corporate strategy to functional strategy could be tested and confirmed. Eventually, each functional strategy was detailed in terms of its subobjectives and potential performance measures that potentially could be utilized to monitor implementation progress.

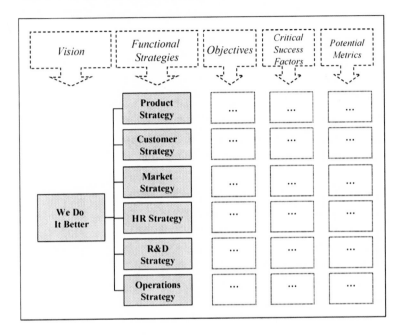

Exhibit V-9: The Strategy Tree

The detailed breakdown of the strategy tree served many needs. It provided information and experience with functional strategies and it highlighted possibilities. Eventually, compliance of functional strategies with overall strategic directions could be controlled. The functional fiefdom culture that partly existed was proactively addressed and eliminated. Through the clear understanding and, even more importantly, companywide agreement of functional objectives, the essential performance metrics were almost automatically derived. Useless performance metrics that had overloaded and distorted the reporting were identified and dropped from the repository. Last, but not least, the work around the strategy tree created an intense discussion of strategic goals and their subsequent functional subobjectives. The strategy formulation was sharper, better understood, and gained greater acceptance and buy-in than before.

Although major parts of the new performance measurement system were already being defined after the strategy tree analysis, the case company was only halfway done with its new approach. It still had to figure out how to link strategy and corresponding performance metrics to shareholder value creation. The first step in developing a shareholder value-focused approach was the selection of an appropriate top financial metric. Historically, the firm had operated with different metrics to measure profitability, growth, return on equity, and return on capital. But none of them had explicitly targeted shareholder value. Profitability measures such as net income before and after tax and before and after depreciation are useful. However, they neglect the capital invested in the business. Return on equity tells only part of true value generation because each company operates with equity and debts to achieve its operational performance. Return on capital comes close, but using just the straight accounting capital as shown on the balance sheet includes operating and non-operating assets. Thus, to really understand how its operational capacities were utilized to generate true value, the company decided to go with a return on capital employed (ROCE) approach. The capital employed in this regard is defined as total property, plant and equipment, plus current assets deducted by the non-interest-bearing liabilities. As a return metric, earnings before interest and tax (EBIT) were chosen to eliminate any distortion through the (especially in Germany) complex accounting and taxation policies. As leading financial performance metrics, ROCE and EBIT also can be benchmarked with the performance of other players in the automotive industry and can reveal useful insights into operational performance compared with peers.

While the ROCE is used to assess overall value generation, EBIT and capital employed are primarily monitored from a different angle: EBIT is controlled to understand the value contribution through increased profitability, and capital employed is monitored to highlight value contribution through improved asset utilization.

Having defined the strategic-driven performance metrics and the top financial performance measures to monitor shareholder value generation, the cornerstones of the new performance measurement system were in place. However, how should both be combined and interplay with each other? Or should the new performance measurement system be double-facetted with one part taking care of strategy while the other tracks value creation? The case company opted for an integrated system and interlocked both perspectives.

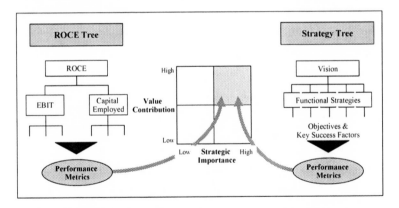

Exhibit V-10: Performance Indicator Selection

By using the framework as shown in the exhibit above, the case company was able to identify indicators that fulfilled both strategy focus and value orientation. To ensure a high quality of indicator selection and, at the same time, build acceptance and identification with the new system, the senior leadership team invited the entire management body to a two-day, off-site meeting. The objective of the meeting was to carefully screen the list of potential candidate measures and select the top-priority ones with regard to strategy and shareholder value impact. As a consequence, the number of indicators was substantially driven down, allowing the company to design a corporate scorecard with just a few performance metrics.

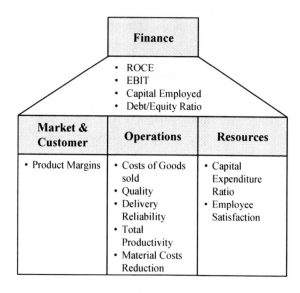

Exhibit V-11: Corporate Scorecard

Based on this scorecard the entire performance measurement system was cascaded through the organization. Each function developed its own integrated version of the scorecard that is closely integrated with the corporate model. Besides the purely down-cascaded performance metrics, function-specific measures according to the specific functional strategy were added. The company went even one step further and developed integrated scorecards on the cost center (shop floor) level, too. Like the functional scorecards, these were linked to the scorecards on the organizational level above and contained specific strategic and value-driven metrics for the respective cost center.

The firm has achieved significant advantages through its new performance measurement approach. Since the system is today an integral element of the planning process, performance targets are always closely aligned with strategic goals and value generation. The company has achieved transparency, broad understanding, and acceptance for its strategic course. The fiefdom mentality has been removed and replaced by a common strategic viewpoint. Eventually, each single employee has an idea of the link between his or her daily activity to the overall goals and value creation. Thus, the entire firm has strongly enhanced its entrepreneurial spirit and the sense of responsibility. Its financial performance today is outstanding and one of the major automotive giants has accepted the company as a trustworthy and well-managed joint venture partner. Its effective strategy execution with integrated strategic measures has surely contributed to this success.

Index

About the Author

Soeren Dressler is a Principal with A.T. Kearney's Global Technology and Transformation Practice and based in Chicago. He leads A.T. Kearney's Service Offering for Finance and Accounting and focuses his consulting work on Corporate Restructuring, Business Process Outsourcing, Shared Services and Offshoring.

Since the summer of 2002 he is Adjunct Professor of Strategy and Organization at Loyola University Chicago Graduate School of Business. He teaches the MBA capstone course "Organization and Strategy" and holds further teaching assignments at the DePaul University of Chicago Kellstadt Graduate School of Business where he co-teaches an Executive MBA course on Global Best Practices and Benchmarking.

Prior to his career with A.T. Kearney, he was with Arthur Andersen Business Consulting, and before joining the consulting industry, Soeren Dressler was with Daimler Benz InterServices.

Most of his academic career has taken place at the University of Technology, Dresden, Germany, where he has been teaching graduate level classes in Strategic Management, Organization Management, and Management Accounting.

Soeren Dressler holds a PhD in Organizational Design from the University of Technology, Dresden and a Diploma in Business from the Otto-Friedrich University, Bamberg, Germany.

Printed in the United States
66363LVS00002B/149